my **revision** notes

CW00495463

OCR AS/A Level

DESIGN & TECHNOLOGY

PRODUCT DESIGN

Simeon Arnold
Julia Morrison
Dave Sumpner

HODDER EDUCATION
AN HACHETTE UK COMPANY

Orders: please contact Hachette UK Distribution, Hely Hutchinson Centre, Milton Road, Didcot, Oxfordshire, OX11 7HH. Telephone: +44 (0)1235 827827. Email education@hachette.co.uk Lines are open from 9 a.m. to 5 p.m., Monday to Friday. You can also order through our website: www.hoddereducation.co.uk

ISBN: 978 1 5104 5896 3

First published in 2019 by
Hodder Education,
An Hachette UK Company
Carmelite House
50 Victoria Embankment
London EC4Y 0DZ

www.hoddereducation.co.uk

Impression number 10 9 8 7 6 5 4 3

Year 2023 2022 2021

Illustrations by Aptara Inc.

Typeset in India by Aptara Inc.

Printed in India

A catalogue record for this title is available from the British Library.

Get the most from this book

Everyone has to decide his or her own revision strategy, but it is essential to review your work, learn it and test your understanding. These Revision Notes will help you to do that in a planned way, topic by topic. Use this book as the cornerstone of your revision and don't hesitate to write in it – personalise your notes and check your progress by ticking off each section as you revise.

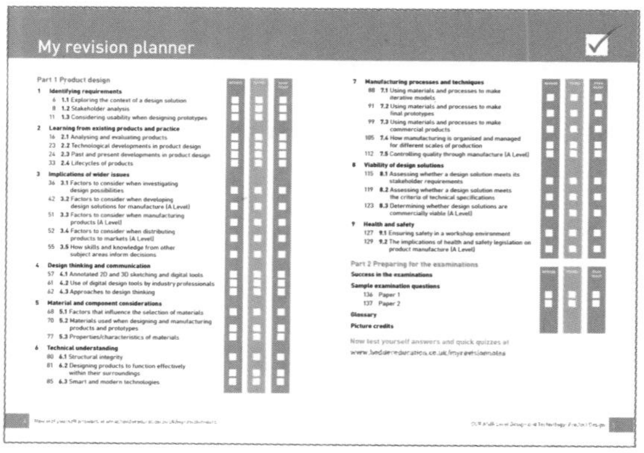

Tick to track your progress

Use the revision planner on pages 4 and 5 to plan your revision, topic by topic. Tick each box when you have:

- revised and understood a topic
- tested yourself
- practised exam questions and gone online to check your answers and complete the quick quizzes.

You can also keep track of your revision by ticking off each topic heading in the book. You may find it helpful to add your own notes as you work through each topic.

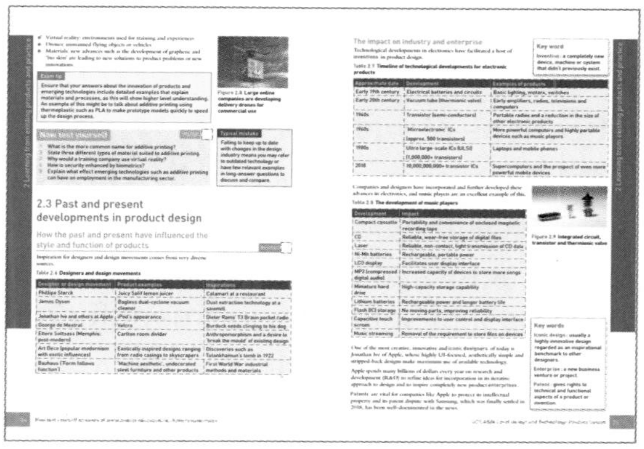

Features to help you succeed

Exam tips

Expert tips are given throughout the book to help you polish your exam technique in order to maximise your chances in the exam.

Typical mistakes

The authors identify the typical mistakes candidates make and explain how you can avoid them.

Now test yourself

These short, knowledge-based questions provide the first step in testing your learning. Answers are at **www.hoddereducation.co.uk/myrevisionnotes**

Definitions and key words

Clear, concise definitions of essential key terms are provided where they first appear.

Exam practice

Practice exam questions are provided at the end of each section. Use them to consolidate your revision and practise your exam skills.

Online

Go online to check your answers to the exam questions and try out the extra quick quizzes at: **www.hoddereducation.co.uk/myrevisionnotes**

My revision planner

Part 1 Product design

REVISED | TESTED | EXAM READY

Now test yourself answers and quick quizzes at www.hoddereducation.co.uk/myrevisionnotes

1 Identifying requirements

1.1 Exploring the context of a design solution

Environment and surroundings

REVISED

Products are designed to meet the requirements of the situation or place they are used in. The context or environment will have a direct influence on:

- the purpose of the product
- its features and functions
- the materials it is made from
- its cost
- the construction methods used
- the safety of the product
- its maintenance requirements.

An example is a ski helmet which must be designed to protect the user in the event of a crash and keep them warm but well-ventilated. The user is also likely to be wearing bulky clothing and goggles. The environment of use must be fully considered for the product to be successful.

Figure 1.1 A ski helmet in context of use

User requirements

REVISED

Product purchases are driven by humans' basic needs and their individual wants. As humans, our basic requirements are food, shelter, clothing and safety. Our 'wants' are products that make things easier and more comfortable, or provide enjoyment. These might include products such as mobile phones, magazines, pushbikes and computer games.

Understanding a user's requirements allows for the design of products that are fit for purpose and function. Other **stakeholders** will often influence the design of products for a primary user such as the Health and Safety Executive (HSE) or other regulatory bodies. Their aim is to ensure that products meet user requirements in terms of material choices and manufacturing technologies.

Figure 1.2 The four basic human needs

> **Key word**
>
> **Stakeholders**: the stakeholders of a product are all those come into contact with it, have some sort of interest or 'stake' in it, or are affected by it in some way.

Typical mistake

In discussion-style answers based on user needs, don't only focus on the user and ignore the wider context. Failing to address the external influences on designs from bodies such as the HSE often leads to simplistic answers which lack the range of points needed to meet the requirements of extended answer questions.

Economic and market considerations and product opportunities

REVISED

All stakeholders will have some influence on the marketing, economics or designing of a product and can be involved in or be a part of the product in different ways:

- In the designing, manufacturing, retailing and marketing processes
- In the repair, recycling and maintenance processes
- By suppling components or energy
- By working in the regulatory or standardisation bodies
- By working in government agencies.

To determine **user requirements**, it is important for a designer to investigate the context of use and observe how products are being used by people. Asking the questions who, why, what, where, when and how during the investigation will give them an understanding of:

- problems or difficulties
- opportunities for new products
- the merit of existing solutions
- users' interest in a new solution
- feedback from users and stakeholders.

Table 1.1 **Six questions to ask in a context of use investigation**

Where?	What is the environment, place or context of use? What implications does this environment have on the use of the product?
Who?	Who will use the product? What other stakeholders must be taken into account when designing the product?
Why?	Why is this product needed rather than other available options?
What?	What does the product need to do? What are the key criteria for its success?
When?	At what times of day and how often will the product be used?
How?	How will the product be used? How will the product be marketed?

Now test yourself

TESTED

1. State three factors which are influenced by a product's environment of use.
2. State four possible stakeholders of a product in your specialist area.
3. Outline the user requirements for a garden table within its context of use.
4. Outline the user requirements for a ski jacket within its context of use.
5. Outline the user requirements for a heavy-duty sack truck within its context of use.

Exam tip

When answering questions about user requirements, carefully outline the environment of use and consider how the product is used within it or is influenced by it. Aim to make references to specific interactions and body parts as this often leads to more complete answers with better examples.

1.2 Stakeholder analysis

Methods used for investigating stakeholder requirements

REVISED

User-centred design and stakeholder analysis

User-centred design (UCD) and stakeholder analysis allows designers to understand the needs and wants of the parties invested in a product and how different design solutions will impact them.

UCD may be used throughout the design process. It allows for a close collaborative working relationship between users and the designers of a product and helps to ensure that the product will meet users' expectations and preferences. UCD considers four key areas:

1. Understanding context of use
2. Requirements specification
3. Feedback on proposed design solutions
4. Evaluation by users on prototypes (normally through use)

Stakeholder analysis looks more broadly at the invested parties such as organisations, legislative bodies, manufacturers, retailers and other groups who will be affected by the product.

Typical mistake

Don't simply focus on the most obvious stakeholders such as users, manufacturers and retailers unless specifically asked to. You should aim to discuss issues surrounding a wide and varied range of stakeholders and show how the issues in the question impact on all of them.

SWOT analysis

SWOT analysis is a method used to examine the key factors associated with a product in order to maximise its opportunities and identify any problems or possible pitfalls. A product will be examined in terms of:

- **Strengths:** the advantages within the marketplace against competitors and of the product's USP.
- **Weaknesses:** problems within the proposed design in terms of its suitability, costs, sales or available resources.
- **Opportunities:** identifying new opportunities in the market due to changes in competition, technology, legislation or trends.
- **Threats:** understanding the competition or the possible adverse effects of consumer behaviour or legislation.

Focus groups

Focus groups are a key source of feedback in ensuring that products meet users' needs and wants.

- Focus groups are carefully selected to appropriately reflect the specific target market **demographic**.
- A discussion is led by a moderator to collect data regarding the group's views and experiences.
- Different activities are undertaken and the group's reactions are recorded.

Key words

Demographic: a particular sector of the population. This may relate to age, education level, spending power, geographical location etc.

Price point: the chosen price for a product to retail at.

Table 1.2 Different focus group activities and possible feedback

Activity	What may be learned
Direct questioning and discussions	Views on aesthetics, **price points**
Interaction with products	How easy the product is to use and how intuitively screens, interfaces and buttons are navigated

Activity	What may be learned
Suggestions for improvements	Common problems or aspects that are disliked
Audiovisual presentations	Consideration of marketing strategy and ways to engage users
Surveys of possible options for the product	Which designs or features are considered to be of most value

Qualitative observations

Qualitative observations allow stakeholders' reactions to a product to be recorded in terms of sight, smell, taste, touch or hearing. Interviews are often undertaken to allow for a full understanding of the products and how possible changes could be perceived.

Quantitative data involves the collection of numerical statistics such as sizes and weights.

Figure 1.3 As part of qualitative observations, users will be asked to try a number of similar products to determine which one is their favourite

Market research

Market research is undertaken in a variety of ways to allow designers and manufacturers to identify and understand potential areas for sales and profit through new or reimagined products. Research can identify:

- market trends
- demographic groups
- buying habits
- economic shifts
- competitors.

Market research will often involve:

- **Feasibility analysis:** will the product be possible and profitable?
- **Investigations:** which possible initial product concepts are suitable?
- **User trialling:** what do users think?
- **Small-scale launch of the product:** is there demand for the product and the manufacturing capability to meet it?

Designers will normally undertake a mixture of both primary and secondary research. Primary research comes from direct interaction or observation. Secondary research comes from existing books, documents or online resources.

Key word

Feasibility analysis: a consideration of how possible and realistic it is to proceed with a project.

Table 1.3 Market research methods

Primary research methods	Secondary research methods
• Questionnaires • Surveys • Interviews • Focus groups • Trials • Product analysis • Analysis of ergonomic data	• Magazines • Reference books • Social media • Guidance from government agencies • Available statistics, for example about large-scale or regional population trends • Style influences from other designers or art movements • Anthropometric data • Materials and manufacturing techniques

→

Exam tip

If you are asked to explain how data regarding a given product may be collected, don't simply say that it could be done in person or through questionnaires. Expand on the point by showing how the methods chosen would specifically engage a suitable target market and how the feedback could be collated to give clear guidance on the design of the product.

Primary research methods	Secondary research methods
Advantages	**Advantages**
• Up-to-date data • Data is specific to the design	• Cost-effective method of collecting data
Disadvantages	**Disadvantages**
• Expensive to conduct • Time consuming to arrange	• Research can be out of date • It may not be specific to the design

Forecasting technological and fashion trends

Fashion forecasting is used to compile an understanding of a wide range of influences from numerous sources closely related to the business such as materials, prints and colours. This allows designers and the fashion industry to determine what will be popular in the upcoming season.

Trend forecasting looks more broadly at global industry and allows companies to produce or buy a suitable number of products or garments. This ensures there are the right numbers in production or in stock to meet differing demand due to seasonal changes or fluctuations in buyer behaviour.

A broad range of technological approaches are taken to gather and interpret the data. Data collection may come from trends and patterns on social media or gathered from internet or television streaming statistics. This data is processed or compiled by computer software and compared against historical data to allow for accurate forecasting.

How enterprise can help drive the development of new product ideas (A Level)

REVISED

The term 'enterprise' in the design context is associated with **innovation** and those companies who are planning to capture new markets through new ideas or by approaching stakeholder needs from a new and exciting standpoint.

Entrepreneurship

Entrepreneurs are people who drive the designing, launching and running of a new business or service. They often take on the financial risks associated with the project with the hope of being successful and making profit.

Commercial partnerships

Commercial partnerships are formed between different businesses to allow for rapid growth or when there are mutually beneficial outcomes. Partnerships allow companies to share ideas and expertise and gain access to manufacturing, new technologies and new markets.

Venture capitalists and crowdfunding

Venture capitalists are stakeholders who invest in companies or new initiatives. The money they invest allows companies to expand or enables individuals to produce new ideas. Funding can be short- or long-term with the investors looking to make a healthy profit within this period.

The well-known television show *Dragon's Den* is a good example of the venture capitalist process.

Crowdfunding is another means of raising finance which is increasingly sought after by small start-up companies or individuals. Crowdfunding platforms such as Kickstarter or Crowdfunder allow companies to attract potential investors for ideas which have not secured investment from more mainstream sources. This is done by broadening the understanding of:

- the potential product or service
- the benefits of investing (this could be payback or a cheaper product)
- the minimal risk taken on by investors (other than losing their investment).

Now test yourself

TESTED

1 State three benefits of using user-centred design (UCD) throughout the design process.
2 State an appropriate focus group activity that may be undertaken by a market research company looking at a waterproof hiking jacket.
3 Explain the difference between qualitative and quantitative data.
4 State three methods for collecting primary research.
5 Explain why a national high-street clothing company may use forecasting to determine the stock levels needed when moving from spring into summer.

1.3 Considering usability when designing prototypes

User interaction

REVISED

For more on user interaction see also Section 4.3 (page 63).

The impact of a solution on a user's lifestyle

When developing products and/or systems, designers need to consider:

- how to meet the needs of a wide variety of users
- how to maximise the range of users who can access the product
- the ease of use and suitability of the product for consumers (**usability**)
- international standard usability guidance ISO 9241-11.

Usability factors include:

- **Effectiveness:** the ease of completing tasks with the product.
- **Efficiency:** how long it takes to complete the task using the product.
- **Satisfaction:** how enjoyable it is to use the product.
- **Simplicity:** often results in a product that is easier to use.

The ease of use and inclusivity of products

Inclusive design caters for the maximum possible range of consumers. It involves:

- taking into account factors such as age, gender, background, **culture**, size, weight and disabilities
- excluding as few people as possible
- removing barriers in order to promote equality and independence.

Key words

Usability of a product: how easily a product can be used, particularly with reference to understanding how it functions.

Inclusive design: designing products for ease of use by consumers with the maximum possible range of abilities, without the need for adaptations.

Culture: the social behaviour of different societies influenced by their customs and ideas.

Ergonomic considerations and anthropometric data

Ergonomics

Ergonomics relates to the interaction or 'fit' between people and their activities, products and environments. Good ergonomics can reduce stress, increase comfort and improve efficiency and accuracy.

Ergonomic 'fit', therefore, refers to both physical and psychological factors. Examples of ergonomic factors that can help to improve usability include:

- use of colour
- font design and size
- layout of controls
- user interface provided by software
- display screen clarity
- product weight
- consideration of sound and vibrations.

Additional benefits of good ergonomics include:

- improved worker productivity
- enjoyable user experiences leading to increased sales
- removing the frustration of difficult-to-use products.

Anthropometrics

Anthropometrics relates to the measurements of humans. Anthropometric data are provided in charts and tables and give a wide variety of measurements such as arm length, knee height and grip strength.

These measurements are usually grouped by factors such as age, gender and nationality. Designers need to consider whether to cater for the extremes or the 'average', and how adjustability can help.

Percentiles

The appropriate choice of **percentiles** from anthropometric data tables is very important. The tables normally include the 5th percentile, the 50th percentile (the average, most common measurement) and the 95th percentile.

- Using the range from the 5th to the 95th percentile disregards the extremes.
- Sometimes a wider range needs to be considered, such as in safety critical situations.
- Practicalities and budget restraints can result in limitations such as poor legroom in some football stadiums.

Key words

Ergonomics: the promotion of optimum design usability and efficiency through the study of how people interact with products and their working environment.

Anthropometrics: scientific measurements of the human body applied to the design and construction of products.

Percentile: a specific statistical percentage range, often used to define appropriate anthropometric data for design purposes.

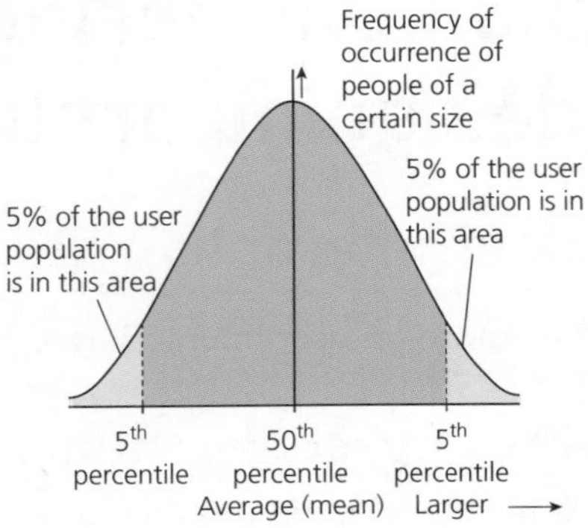

Figure 1.4 Percentiles

Exam tip

Don't be over-simplistic in your responses to questions on anthropometrics, for example by writing 'Products must be designed for the average size person' or 'Designers must use the 5th to 95th percentile'. Instead, write about the choice of data required for particular situations and make reference to male, female and child data, as well as to variations that may exist in overseas markets.

Aesthetic considerations

Visual impact is one of the most important aesthetic considerations, but all our senses, and even our emotions, are involved in aesthetic appreciation:

- Vision
- Hearing
- Smell
- Touch
- Taste

Designers must take care to balance aesthetic and practical considerations, particularly in the design of safety critical components such as car dashboard controls.

Intuitive designs function in the instinctive, conventional, standard or 'stereotype' way we expect and are therefore easier to use.

- Taps and valves usually turn anti-clockwise to increase output.
- Volume and speed controls usually turn clockwise to increase output.

- Car foot pedals are always in the same relative position.
- Standard colours are used for pelican crossing lights and danger warning signs.
- Logically designed and laid out controls and symbols make products easy to use.
- A fully intuitive design should require minimum training or instructions.

'**Affordance**' is a term used to describe the way that a product 'suggests' it should work, such as a door handle suggesting that it should be pulled, or the swiping movement required for a smartphone application.

Apple successfully incorporates affordance and simplicity in its designs for a range of intuitive products. Many Apple products were inspired by the minimalist designs produced by Dieter Rams for Braun (1956–78). Rams promoted sustainability in product design in the 1970s and formulated the now celebrated ten principles of good design.

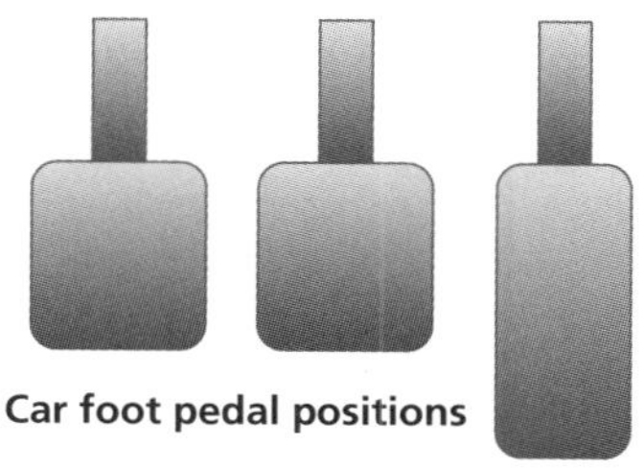

Car foot pedal positions

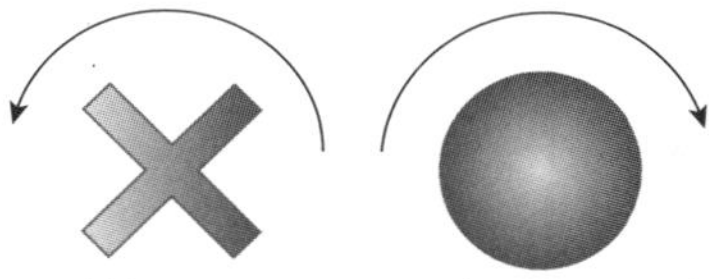

Turning direction for rotary controls

Figure 1.5 Intuitive, 'stereotype' operation of controls

Table 1.4 Dieter Rams' ten principles of good design

Good design:	Which means that Dieter Rams thinks that designers should:
is innovative	make appropriate use of modern materials, technologies and approaches
makes a product useful	address functionality to ensure that they solve the particular problem for the consumer's benefit
is aesthetic	create well-executed, beautiful products in accordance with 'Form follows function' principles
makes a product understandable	make products intuitive to use with no distracting elements that might cause confusion
is unobtrusive	ensure that designs are neutral and restrained, without superfluous decoration or detail
is honest	not deceive consumers – for example, by designing a table with a wood veneer pretending to be a solid timber product
has longevity	design products that will continue to be useful over time, like the 1960 Rams' 606 shelving system, which is still highly successful today even in our **throwaway society**
is thorough down to the last detail	consider every element of designs to ensure that they function well, such as by providing concave finger recesses in push buttons
is environmentally friendly	use sustainable materials and processes in the development and production of products
is as little design as possible	include only essential elements in a design, since superfluous features detract from the product's function

Key word

Throwaway society: the collective mind-set of consumers to dispose of products rather than repair them.

Shape, form and colour in aesthetics

Aesthetic appreciation involves shape, colour and form.

- **Shape**: refers to a two-dimensional arrangement of closed lines or area of colour, including circles, squares, triangles.
- **Form:** a three-dimensional manifestation of an article (geometric forms include cuboids, spheres and cones).

- **Colour:** contributes to the usability of a design and can stimulate an emotional and/or intuitive response such as:
  - red = stop, danger, heat, warning
  - green = go, environmentally friendly
  - blue = cold
  - yellow/black combination = danger warning.

Designers work closely with market researchers to discover current and predicted consumer preferences, in order to produce 'aesthetically pleasing' products to suit the tastes of appropriate target groups.

Ergonomic factors

REVISED

Anthropometric data

Anthropometric data are used to help define design parameters associated with the human body. For example, in relation to workstation seating, the Health and Safety Executive (HSE) gives specific guidance in its 'Seating at Work' HSG57 document which should be taken into consideration:

- Appropriate comfort level for the likely period of use
- Level of lower back support
- Level of support and comfort offered by the upholstery
- Shaping and padding of edges to avoid pressure points
- Adequacy of height, backrest and other adjustments
- Suitability of armrests for particular tasks (need for support and/or freedom of movement)
- Footrest provision, if appropriate
- Special user and/or task requirements.

Additional points for consideration in relation to the use of anthropometric data include the following:

- Car designers use full-scale mock-ups, along with crash test dummies.
- 3D virtual manikins are used in conjunction with various CAD (computer aided design) packages.
- Dynamic (moving) anthropometry needs to be used in many design situations to ensure that the data reflects what actually happens when products are being used. An example of this is when we reach across a table to pick something up.
- Data relating to strength are available for situations such as car footbrake design.

User comfort, layout of controls, software user interface

Ergonomics also provides data for designers on the way users interact with a product and their levels of comfort, for example:

- the range of temperatures that are comfortable to work in
- the appropriate noise and vibration levels for working in (although bear in mind the availability of appropriate personal protective equipment (PPE))
- the efficiency of communicating information, particularly a change of state such as aircraft fuel level.

User interface design, such as that used in smartphone, tablet and microwave displays, is particularly important. The user interface (UI) should be as simple as possible to reduce confusion and consideration should be given to the following factors:

Key word

User interface design or **user interface engineering**: a 'human-centred' design approach with a main focus on the effectiveness of the user interface for interaction with products, particularly electronic devices such as computers and appliances.

- The appropriate fonts and text sizes to use, depending on the viewing distance
- The clarity, combination and contrast level of task-appropriate colours
- How to make related elements similar in appearance, using the minimum number of different colours, along with simple shapes (which also helps people with colour blindness)
- How to avoid distracting reflections
- The appropriate use of flashing or colour changing to attract attention
- How to match display and controls to ease understanding and minimise confusion.

Developments in the design of software user interfaces include:

- the reduction/elimination of buttons and the introduction of 'soft keys' to match screen display
- the use of touch screens and voice recognition
- the avoidance of too many sub-menus
- the use of internal or back-lighting to suit the environment.

Figure 1.6 Soft keys on an ATM machine

Typical mistake

Don't concentrate only on anthropometrics when answering questions requiring an explanation of the term 'ergonomics'. Anthropometrics are an important element, but ergonomics also includes a wider range of product features such as the type of grip, tactile recognition of controls, use of symbols, or colour and sound.

Now test yourself

TESTED

1. Critically analyse the 'affordance' of two contrasting remote controls.
2. Explain the terms 'anthropometrics' and 'ergonomics'.
3. Explain how an 'intuitive' car dashboard/control design might be achieved and the resulting safety benefits.
4. Explain the term 'inclusivity' and who might benefit from its consideration in product design.
5. Explain how colour can contribute to the 'usability' of a design.

Exam practice

1. How might the design of a vacuum cleaner be improved by studying a range of ergonomic factors?
2. The designer of a new public transport bus wishes to make the design as 'inclusive' as possible. Explain **four** distinctly different inclusive features that might be incorporated in the design.
3. Produce a simple labelled drawing of the user interface for a domestic appliance (e.g. a washing machine, microwave, vacuum cleaner) and identify a range of desirable features.
4. Give **two** contrasting examples of designers relying on stereotype reactions to improve the safety of products or systems and explain how these reactions help.
5. Give an example of a product that contributes to a 'throwaway society' and explain how alternative designs and strategies are being developed to combat the problems it causes.
6. A new product is being designed to carry luggage and camping equipment around a festival site. Explain how the environment of use would impact on the design.
7. An entrepreneur is seeking investment for a new product idea. Discuss the possible available options and what risks or benefits they may bring.
8. State **three** ways in which a focus group might aid a designer to understand the user requirements of a new product concept.
9. A furniture manufacturing company has created a new seat. Explain how qualitative feedback could help the designers to meet user needs.
10. A technology company is designing a new phone interface to aid older users. How could information about the intended demographic help the designers to identify key criteria for the design?

ONLINE

2 Learning from existing products and practice

2.1 Analysing and evaluating products

Analysing and evaluating existing features and methods

REVISED

The context of the existing product and the context of future design decisions

It is important that any new product design will meet stakeholder requirements and result in a commercially viable and profitable product. Therefore, before designing takes place, research is undertaken into the context of use of a product and other existing designs. This research considers all the stages from initial concept through to marketing, and is a two-part process:

1. **Analysis**: involves the examination and investigation of a product.
2. **Evaluation**: assesses the suitability and value of a product.

Table 2.1 Analysis of existing products

Research type	Reason undertaken
Interviews/focus groups	Provides opinions on existing products
User surveys	Gives measurable data to determine facts or identify trends
Website forums	Provides opinions from interested stakeholders
Social media	Click rates and keyword trends can be analysed, although rumours can make this data unreliable
Used product analysis	Identifies reoccurring problems
Product recalls	Highlights the changes needed to existing and future designs
Customer service analysis	Records complaints which can be used to improve future services or products

Table 2.2 Evaluation of existing products

Factor	Evaluation
Ease of use	How easy is it to interact with the product and use it in its intended environment?
Performance	How well does the product perform or function?
Suitability of materials	Are the materials used in the product suitable? Can they be improved?
Suitability of construction	Are the construction methods used to meet the original specification suitable or can possible improvements be made?
Wider impact	What are the environmental impacts? What are the effects on the preservation of traditional skills and quality of life?
Value for money	What **price point** will generate revenue through numbers of sales and ensure profit?

Changing requirements

Meeting changing consumer requirements is vital to ensure there is a demand for the product. Research will track these changes and inform designers of new product needs and opportunities.

Product lifecycle

The natural lifecycle of a product determines demand and the need for new or improved products. You can read more about the product lifecycle in Section 2.4 (page 33).

Planned obsolescence

Planned obsolescence is a strategy that gives a product a limited life span and encourages consumers to purchase new products rather than look to repair them. This strategy can be seen as being:

- morally questionable
- leading to sustainability issues
- promoting a **throwaway society**.

See Section 3.1 (page 39) for more on planned obsolescence.

> **Key words**
>
> **Price point**: the chosen price for a product to retail at.
>
> **Planned obsolescence**: the process of designing a product to go out of fashion or no longer function after a specific time period.
>
> **Throwaway society**: the collective mind-set of consumers to dispose of products rather than repair them.

The multiple materials and components used

Materials and components are carefully selected to meet performance requirements for the intended product. Examining existing products will aim to identify whether the material:

- performed correctly during use
- became physically worn
- remained aesthetically pleasing
- continued to be the best choice given on-going technological and material developments.

Examining components will look at why certain components have been used and how successful they were in fulfilling their role. Standardised components are commonly used because they:

- allow low unit cost due to bulk purchase
- ensure ease of manufacturing due to fewer distinct parts
- reduce the need for the manufacture of specialist parts such as electronic components.

Figure 2.1 Disassembly of a camera shows the parts and allows an understanding of wear and which parts have met lifecycle requirements

Methods of construction and manufacture

Manufacturing is the process of transforming raw materials into final products. Factors which determine the methods and processes used include:

- materials used
- quantity required
- product function
- expected longevity of the product
- cost of each product
- time for production
- available equipment and tools.

Analysis of existing products allows designers to determine what processes and materials have been used and why they were chosen.

Product disassembly gives an understanding of the factors influencing:

- construction
- material choice
- function
- cost
- manufacturing processes and methodology.

Further analysis of a product can lead to an understanding of its manufacturing methodology, production scale and costs. These factors may be affected by:

- the type of product
- demand for the product
- available capital
- available premises
- available equipment and tools
- available labour skills.

How functionality is achieved

Performance and functionality are key to the success of any product. Analysing how well a product will perform is undertaken from the development stage onwards. Stakeholder feedback will be carefully scrutinised and, for more complex products, industrial tests may be undertaken. These may include an examination of how well the materials, components or manufacturing processes have performed. This examination may lead to guidance on:

- warranties
- replacement of parts
- care instructions
- maintenance instructions
- service advice.

Ease of use, including ergonomic and anthropometric considerations

Designers may evaluate ergonomics to understand a product's needs.

Table 2.3 Evaluation of ergonomics

Product needs	Evaluation
Height	What height does the product need to be to function?
Weight	What weight will the product be subjected to or need to be?
Hearing	What volume, pitch or audible qualities must the product have?
Sight	What size font, images or colours are to be used?
Temperature	What temperature will the product or user be exposed to?

Exam tip

Ensure that you understand the relationship between ergonomics and anthropometric data. Students often talk about the analysis of ergonomic issues without any discussion of human interaction with products or how anthropometric data have guided designers to certain decisions.

Anthropometric data are used to inform design decisions to ensure that a product meets its ergonomic requirements. Three principles determine choices:

1. What is the target market?
2. Which measurements are relevant to the product and target market?
3. Is the product being designed for the average or the extremes of the target market?

Adjustment

Adjustment uses anthropometric data to address the issue of inclusivity and determine the range of users that can use the product. The issues to consider here are:

- **Product adjustment:** can differing users adjust the product?
- **Ease of adjustment:** do users understand how to adjust the product to meet their needs?
- **Auto adjustment:** are standardised adjustments suitable for different users?

- **Material options:** has the suitability of different materials been tested for a wide range of users?
- **Data analysis:** analysing data may identify ways to address issues where the use of the product has resulted in injuries or accidents.
- **Specialist equipment and software:** ergonomic evaluation software can be used to assess human movement, strength and ability to perform tasks over a specified amount of time.

Percentiles are used to ensure a product can be used by the majority of the target market. Designers will normally aim to design products that fit users between the 5th and 95th percentiles. Above and below these numbers are considered to be extremes and can mean that the required design variance is expensive or impractical to achieve. For more on percentiles see Section 1.3 (page 12).

Typical mistake

Exam questions are often based around percentiles and the impact they have on design choices or the inclusivity of design solutions. Failing to fully grasp the cost implications and inherent difficulty of designing for the extremes of many groups may cause you to make unjustified statements about possible design opportunities that could never be viable for mass or batch production.

Inclusivity of products

Considering a target market's **user diversity** allows designers to analyse inclusive design and be mindful of design decisions that include or exclude sections of the population. Tests on existing products may consider how accessible product solutions are or what modifications could be made to improve inclusivity. Factors that may influence the design include:

- age
- gender
- weight
- height
- disabilities.

Environmental, social and economic implications can be considered by analysing existing products. The impact of the product can be assessed in terms of its effect on:

- energy use
- pollution
- climate change
- costs
- health
- social issues.

Moral and cultural issues may become apparent when analysis of a product shows that there has been disregard for:

- environmental issues
- waste
- working conditions
- traditions or faith.

Fitness for purpose

Examining products can help designers to understand if the design and manufacturing choices made can be improved to ensure the product is fit for purpose. They will often consider:

- functionality and usability
- material selection
- component selection
- methods of construction and manufacture
- ergonomic and anthropometric considerations.

Human factors will be analysed to ensure minimal risk to the user and to ensure the product can be operated comfortably and easily. Poor design may lead to discomfort or strain, slower work and possible errors.

Key word

Human factors: the study of how humans behave physically and psychologically in relation to a product.

The impact on user lifestyles

The aim of new product development is often to improve the user's lifestyle. Products that are intuitive to use or more efficient often benefit the primary user, making tasks quicker and easier.

Understanding the longer-term impacts of social and technological developments is also important and in itself will often lead to new products. Such developments include:

- Mass production which has led to products that are widely available and affordable
- Advertising and marketing which actively promotes products
- Awareness of environmental impacts such as waste and pollution
- Awareness of social impacts such as obesity and changing fashion trends.

Figure 2.2 Victorian architecture

The effect of trends, taste and/or style

Successful products are market-led, which means manufacturing products that are desirable to the target market. To remain desirable the product will likely follow the latest styles, trends and fashions.

Trend forecasting allows companies to predict current trends by analysing:

- media
- culture
- celebrities
- current styles and art movements.

Figure 2.3 Art Nouveau styling

In the past, distinctive art styles have had a noted impact on design, for example:

- Victorian – 1830s–1890
- Art Nouveau – 1890–1905
- Art Deco – 1925–1939
- Pop Art – 1960s.

Figure 2.4 Art Deco styling

Designers may choose to emulate designs from the past or follow modern trends. These trends are varied and have different influences. These could be:

- social issues such as ethical design
- company-driven design features and styling
- customisation.

Figure 2.5 Playful Pop Art

The effect of marketing and branding

Marketing and branding are used together as promotional tools and are often pivotal in the success of a product. Marketing is used to influence the target market into making them want or feel they 'need' a product.

When creating a new design, the manufacturers will aim to ensure it has a competitive edge. New markets, consumer demand, technology or materials may lead to new, innovative products.

A thoroughly considered marketing strategy will be used for most product launches. It will often aim to capture the target market's attention and promote sales through imaginative marketing options. The strategy will adapt over time to meet changing demand and trends.

Figure 2.6 Famous brands are easily recognised even when only a small portion of the branding can be seen

Branding on products is normally identified by a logo, name and 'tag line' such as Nike's 'Just do it'. Branding allows the products of a company to be easily identified by consumers and differentiates them from other available products. Brands that are fashionable can be sold at a premium price, so a positive brand image is fiercely protected.

The considerations of how to get a product to market

Good market research is vital to ensure products are designed and marketed successfully. Market research or **inbound marketing** will inform a manufacturer or designer about:

- trends within age groups
- current trends and fashion
- suitable price points
- competitors
- customer satisfaction
- suitable identification and branding.

Methods of market research are dealt with in more detail in Section 1.2 (page 9).

Outbound marketing utilises the **marketing mix** to promote a brand or new product. The marketing mix normally consists of the 4Ps:

- price
- product
- promotion
- place.

Key words

Inbound marketing: market research used to establish whether a gap in the market exists.

Outbound marketing: marketing that raises awareness and allows the customer to 'find' the product.

Marketing mix: the best blend of marketing methods used to engage the intended target market.

Table 2.4 The marketing mix

Product	Price
Key aspects: • The core product which is the benefit of the product to the customer. • The actual product which is the tangible, physical product. • The augmented product which is about customer service support and after-sales service. The quality of a product depends on factors such as its: • aesthetics • performance • maintenance, ease of servicing • durability • range of features • ease/effectiveness of use • brand name. The product has a unique selling point (USP) which appeals to customers.	The price of a product can depend on: • demand • costs • taxes • competition • its stage in the lifecycle. Methods of pricing include: • Penetration pricing – an artificially low price set to gain market share. • Price skimming – a high price set due to high demand for the product or it being a market leader. • Psychological pricing – charging £1.99 rather than £2. • Predatory pricing – undercutting competitors.
Promotion	**Place/Placement**
Promotion can be expensive but it creates awareness of the product by: • drawing attention to the product • creating interest • generating desire • inviting action. Methods of promotion include: • short-term promotions • exhibitions and trade fairs • publicity campaigns • personal selling/sales representatives • targeted advertising.	Placement refers to the distribution channel that allows the customer to purchase the product. There are four main channels of distribution from the manufacturer to the customer: • direct to the customer • via a retailer • via a wholesaler • via a wholesaler and a retailer. The functions of distribution channels may include: • contacting prospective buyers • matching the offer to the buyer's needs • negotiating price • negotiating terms for storing and transporting the products.

An **advertising strategy** must take into account the best way to target the intended users of the product. Considerations when selecting a medium will include:

- cost
- reach
- audience lifestyle
- level of impact.

Advertisements are controlled by the Advertising Standards Agency (ASA). It ensures that adverts are:

- legal
- decent
- honest
- truthful
- not misleading
- not offensive.

Table 2.5 Methods of advertising

Advertising medium	Advantages	Limitations	Cost issues
Television	Mass-market coverage, low cost per exposure, can generate a powerful emotive response	Fleeting exposure, scheduling dictates the likely viewers	Expensive
Radio	Local impact, high geographic selectivity, national radio for nationwide companies	Audio only, fairly low attention/impact on the listener	Relatively low cost for local radio
Newspapers and magazines	Local markets, national or geographic selected coverage, high believability, prestige	Very short life	High cost in national papers and prestigious magazines
Direct mail (post)	High audience selection, can be personalised	Often discarded as junk mail	Relatively high cost
Billboards	Flexibility, high repeat exposure, local targeting, electronic animated options are available	Little audience selectivity	Generally low cost, key sites can be expensive
Online (including email)	High selectivity, instant, can be impactful Pop-up advertising on websites, advertising within smartphone apps	Linked to spam and spyware 'Ad blocking' removes or blocks unwanted adverts	Relatively low cost
Social media	Caters to a large demographic, content sharing can have broad reach, encourages interaction and brand loyalty	Time consuming, little control over speculation, false or negative reviews	Low cost

Product launch

Prior to launch companies must ensure the product is ready for consumers. They will carefully check the following factors:

- Is all the research complete?
- Is all the testing complete?
- Is a competitor releasing a similar product at the same time?
- How will the new product compare to existing products to ensure it gains a market share and sales traction?

The timing of a product launch is essential. Releasing a product at the right time will lead to a greater awareness of the product and increased sales. Determining the right timing depends on whether, at launch time, the product is:

- offering unique features
- offering relevant features

- showing product superiority to the competition
- available to purchase.

Raising awareness of the product depends on effective communication tactics which may include the use of:

- press releases
- social media
- product testing by companies such as Which?

Now test yourself

TESTED

1. Explain the term 'penetration pricing'.
2. Explain the term 'price skimming'.
3. What years did the Art Deco period span?
4. Which advertising medium can be influenced by false reviews or biased opinion?
5. Justify which possible advertising medium(s) would be the most appropriate for a small-scale start-up company selling custom surfboards.

2.2 Technological developments in product design

New and emerging technologies

REVISED

New technologies allow manufacturers and designers to evolve their existing products to meet gaps in the market. Designers will use the **iterative design process** to develop innovate ideas, and in doing so may improve:

- aesthetics
- quality of use
- ease of use
- materials.

New manufacturing techniques such as **additive printing** allow scope for new innovations and construction techniques. Additive printing is offering new ways to manufacture goods at home or for bespoke products. 3D printing is now available in a wide variety of materials including:

- thermoplastics
- metals
- ceramics
- foodstuffs
- construction materials.

New materials and composites allow the construction of products in new ways, reducing the number of processes and materials required. This may lead to cheaper production or products with new qualities.

New and **emerging technologies** or materials may have wider impacts on people and society, such as impacts on:

- people's lifestyles
- the environment
- moral or ethical issues
- global or local economies.

Emerging technologies are evident in all areas of design including:

- Artificial intelligence (AI): intelligence shown by a machine or computer
- Biometrics: enables security and tracking via fingerprints, iris scans, voice recognition

Key words

Additive printing: a manufacturing process joining materials from 3D model data.

Emerging technologies: new technologies that are currently being developed.

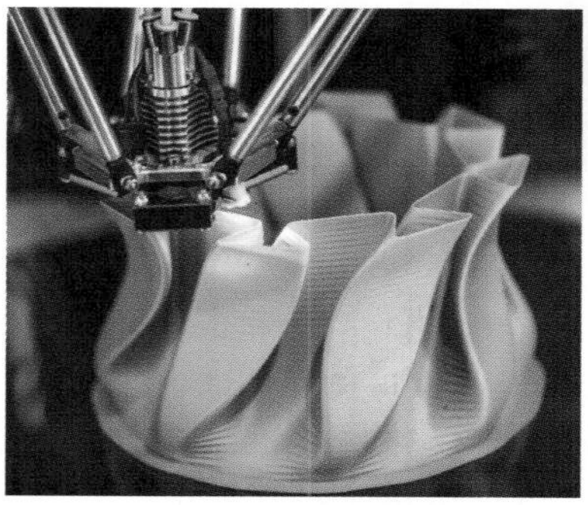

Figure 2.7 Additive printing of items at home is likely to become commonplace

- Virtual reality: environments used for training and experiences
- Drones: unmanned flying objects or vehicles
- Materials: new advances such as the development of graphene and 'bio skin' are leading to new solutions to product problems or new innovations.

Figure 2.8 Large online companies are developing delivery drones for commercial use

Exam tip

Ensure that your answers about the innovation of products and emerging technologies include detailed examples that explain materials and processes, as this will show higher level understanding. An example of this might be to talk about additive printing using thermoplastic such as PLA to make prototype models quickly to speed up the design process.

Now test yourself TESTED

1. What is the more common name for additive printing?
2. State three different types of material suited to additive printing.
3. Why would a training company use virtual reality?
4. How is security enhanced by biometrics?
5. Explain what effect emerging technologies such as additive printing can have on employment in the manufacturing sector.

Typical mistake

Failing to keep up to date with changes in the design industry means you may refer to outdated technology or have few relevant examples in long-answer questions to discuss and compare.

2.3 Past and present developments in product design

How the past and present have influenced the style and function of products

REVISED

Inspiration for designers and design movements comes from very diverse sources.

Table 2.6 Designers and design movements

Designer or design movement	Product examples	Inspirations
Phillipe Starck	Juicy Salif lemon juicer	Calamari at a restaurant
James Dyson	Bagless dual-cyclone vacuum cleaner	Dust extraction technology at a sawmill
Jonathan Ive and others at Apple	iPod's appearance	Dieter Rams' T3 Braun pocket radio
George de Mestral	Velcro	Burdock seeds clinging to his dog
Ettore Sottsass (Memphis: post-modern)	Carlton room divider	Anthropomorphism and a desire to 'break the mould' of existing design
Art Deco (popular modernism with exotic influences)	Exotically inspired designs ranging from radio casings to skyscrapers	Discoveries such as Tutankhamun's tomb in 1922
Bauhaus ('Form follows function')	'Machine aesthetic', undecorated steel furniture and other products	First World War industrial methods and materials

The impact on industry and enterprise

Technological developments in electronics have facilitated a host of **inventions** in product design.

> **Key word**
>
> **Invention**: a completely new device, machine or system that didn't previously exist.

Table 2.7 Timeline of technological developments for electronic products

Approximate date	Development	Examples of products
Early 19th century	Electrical batteries and circuits	Basic lighting, motors, switches
Early 20th century	Vacuum tube (thermionic valve)	Early amplifiers, radios, televisions and computers
1940s	Transistor (semi-conductors)	Portable radios and a reduction in the size of other electronic products
1960s	'Microelectronic' ICs (approx. 500 transistors)	More powerful computers and highly portable devices such as music players
1980s	Ultra large-scale ICs (ULSI) (1,000,000+ transistors)	Laptops and mobile phones
2018	10,000,000,000+ transistor ICs	Supercomputers and the prospect of even more powerful mobile devices

Companies and designers have incorporated and further developed these advances in electronics, and music players are an excellent example of this.

Figure 2.9 Integrated circuit, transistor and thermionic valve

Table 2.8 The development of music players

Development	Impact
Compact cassette	Portability and convenience of enclosed magnetic recording tape
CD	Reliable, wear-free storage of digital files
Laser	Reliable, non-contact, light transmission of CD data
Ni-Mh batteries	Rechargeable, portable power
LCD display	Facilitates user display interface
MP3 (compressed digital audio)	Increased capacity of devices to store more songs
Miniature hard drive	High-capacity storage capability
Lithium batteries	Rechargeable power and longer battery life
Flash (IC) storage	No moving parts, improving reliability
Capacitive touch screen	Improvements to user control and display interface
Music streaming	Removal of the requirement to store files on devices

One of the most creative, innovative and **iconic designers** of today is Jonathan Ive of Apple, whose highly UI-focused, aesthetically simple and stripped-back designs make maximum use of available technology.

Apple spends many billions of dollars every year on research and development (R&D) to refine ideas for incorporation in its iterative approach to design and to inspire completely new product **enterprises**.

Patents are vital for companies like Apple to protect its intellectual property and its patent dispute with Samsung, which was finally settled in 2018, has been well-documented in the news.

> **Key words**
>
> **Iconic design**: usually a highly innovative design regarded as an inspirational benchmark to other designers.
>
> **Enterprise**: a new business venture or project.
>
> **Patent**: gives rights to technical and functional aspects of a product or invention.

The impact on people in relation to lifestyle, culture and society

Lifestyle

Examining past and present products allows us to assess the impact that technological innovation has had on our lifestyles.

Table 2.9 Impact of technological innovation on lifestyles

Aspect of lifestyle	1920s examples	2018 examples
Travel/transport	Minority car ownership, heavy dependence on fossil fuels	Electric/hybrid vehicles, rapid transit systems
House cleaning and other domestic jobs	Basic, heavy, expensive vacuum cleaners Many tasks done manually	Highly efficient and robotic vacuum cleaners A massive range of electrical appliances
Office work	Manual notes and filing, typewriting, limited carbon copying and reliance on phones and mail	Computers/software (databases, spreadsheets, word processors), digital copying and printing, email and video-conferencing
Home entertainment	Board games, playing the piano, radio, reading	Vast array of television channels, music and video streaming, computer games, social media
Health and fitness	Walking, cycling and children playing outdoors	Exercise machines and gym facilities, fitness monitoring devices, lightweight specialised equipment and clothing

Culture and society

Developments in technology and product design have affected or been affected by:

- the rapid developments in national and international communication and transport
- the increasingly tolerant attitude towards people's alternative choices in fashion, body art, beliefs and lifestyles
- the growth in the multicultural nature of societies and the different demands and fashions that result
- the trend towards children 'playing' in a digital world rather than outdoors
- the ever-increasing influence of social media and digital recording technologies.

Figure 2.10 1920s office typewriter

Figure 2.11 Tablet and laptop being used in a modern office video conference

> **Key word**
>
> **Culture:** the social behaviour of different societies influenced by their customs and ideas.

Ethical considerations

Ethical considerations involved in the designing and making of products have prompted a variety of responses. These have been driven by issues such as:

- global material extraction, farming and manufacture
- the difficulties faced by communities in the developing world.

Table 2.10 Design responses to ethical issues

Issue	Designer/organisation	Response
Fair treatment for farmers and craft workers in developing countries	Fairtrade Foundation	Negotiated fair prices and secured sustainable work
Refugee housing	Ikea Foundation	Flat-pack 'better shelter' housing
Medical care	United Nations Population Fund (UNFPA)	'Hospitainers' and 'maternitainers' (adapted shipping containers)
Lack of radio batteries in parts of Africa	Trevor Bayliss	Wind-up radio requiring no batteries
Danger/expense of kerosene lamps in Kenya	GravityLight Foundation	'GravityLight' LED lighting
Poverty in developing countries	Practical Action	Appropriate, technological, 'open design' solutions that can be freely used where they are needed

Social footprint is the term used to describe the impact on society of issues such as the cultural and ethical ones referred to in this section.

Figure 2.12 Aerial ropeway to help transport workers and crops installed in Nepal by Practical Action

The impact on the environment

Ecological footprint is the term used to describe any impact on the environment and natural resources. The key issues that need to be addressed include:

- reducing our consumption of non-renewable resources
- reducing waste, pollution and energy use
- recognising the irreversible nature of environmental damage that is being done
- rewarding environmentally friendly strategies
- discouraging a throwaway society.

Key words

Social footprint: the impact on society of cultural and ethical issues.

Ecological footprint: the impact on the environment and natural resources.

Consideration of sustainability

Various strategies are being used by designers, companies, governments and consumers to promote sustainability and reduce the impact on the environment.

- Ikea is seeking to minimise its material and energy use with strategies such as:
  - using fully loaded, preferably electrically powered, vehicles for its distribution
  - producing lightweight, honeycomb structure products that use far less material
  - developing a method for constructing hollow table legs requiring minimal materials.
- Some companies are increasingly adopting returnable milk bottle deliveries.
- Old shipping containers are being used for community projects, offices and storage.

- Schoolchildren are using refillable water bottles rather than purchasing a new bottle each day.
- Websites such as Freecycle, and Freegle are encouraging the passing on of products.
- Car parts and components such as engines are being reconditioned, so that they can be reused, and thus extend their service life.
- Furniture is being upcycled from old pallets.
- Water butt systems are being installed rather than using mains water supply for garden watering.
- Differentiated bins and refuse collections are being used to facilitate easier sorting of waste for recycling.
- Legislative directives such as End of Life Vehicles (ELV) and Waste from Electrical and Electronic Equipment (WEEE) are being used to facilitate the ease of disassembly.
- A 'cradle-to-cradle' approach is being adopted which means that all materials in a product can be reused.
- Consumers are refusing to use products such as single-use water bottles and inefficient tungsten light bulbs.

Issues of sustainability are dealt with in more detail in Section 3.2 (page 48).

The influence of key historical movements and figures

REVISED

Historical design movements

This section noted earlier how designers are influenced by a variety of factors. Some of the major historical design movements that have influenced future developments are listed below.

These design movements and the designers involved with them continue to be influential in shaping aspects of current products, ranging from the materials that are used to their shape, form and colour.

Table 2.11 The Arts and Crafts movement

Arts and Crafts (1850–1900)	Key point: traditional crafts rather than machines
Influences	A reaction to the loss of traditional skills and overuse of ornamentation that was perceived to have resulted from the Industrial Revolution, as personified by the Great Exhibition of 1851
Inspirations	Medieval craft guilds, simplicity, natural forms and the beauty of timber
Features	• 'Honest', handmade, traditional methods such as pegged mortise and tenon joints • The beauty of materials such as the grain and figure of oak clearly displayed • The use of patterned, natural forms on tiles, wallpaper and textiles
Designers	William Morris, Charles Voysey, Richard Norman Shaw

Figure 2.13 Arts and Crafts oak dining table

Table 2.12 The Art Deco movement

Art Deco (1925–1939)	Key point: popular modernism with exotic influences
Influences and inspirations	• The end of the First World War, aspirational consumers, popularity of travel and growth of mass production • The discovery of Tutankhamun's tomb in 1922 • The Paris Exhibition of 1925 • A range of international styles such as Egyptian temples, Aztec motifs and African carvings
Features	• Ziggurat, stepped decorations and building styles such as New York skyscrapers • Sunburst motifs, often found as decorations and radio grille designs • Stylised, geometrical form of products, from jewellery to furniture, contrasting with Art Nouveau • Bold colours as well as black and chrome
Designers	Clarice Cliff, Eileen Gray, René Lalique, Walter Dorwin Teague

Table 2.13 Modernism: Bauhaus

Modernism: Bauhaus (1919–1933)	Key point: machine aesthetic approach to 'Form follows function'
Influences and inspirations	• Post-First World War idealism, abolition of censorship, Arts and Crafts' views on form and function • First World War industrial methods and materials • Geometrically pure forms, as also influenced Art Deco
Features	• Founded as an art school by Walter Gropius and eventually closed due to pressure from the Nazis • The course covered materials, form, metalwork, furniture design, architecture, graphics and more • Basic principle: 'Form follows function' (aesthetics are dictated by the way a product works), rejecting the liberal use of decoration such as the natural forms of Art Nouveau • Embraced mass production to create 'everyday products for everyday people' using modern materials such as tubular steel, contrasting with the Arts and Crafts movement's approach • Marcel Breuer's chairs typify its functional, ornament-free, 'machine aesthetic' approach • Its work was often criticised and the movement saw few of its designs being mass produced • Marcel Breuer's designs inspired Alvar Aalto and others to design similar bent plywood furniture
Designers	Walter Gropius, Marcel Breuer, Marianne Brandt, Mies Van Der Rohe

Table 2.14 Post-Modernism: Memphis

Post-Modernism: Memphis (1981–1988)	Key point: less is a bore
Influences and inspirations	• A Milan-based collective of designers rebelling against the functionality of Modernism • Art Deco and any other era, movement or design that interested them, from Pop Art to children's toys
Features	• Playful, bold, bright, colourful, sculptural designs that often overlooked functionality • Anthropomorphic (human like) and zoomorphic (animal like) features

→

Post-Modernism: Memphis (1981–1988)	Key point: less is a bore
	• Simplistic, abstract and often random juxtapositions of geometric forms, designed to shock • A range of non-traditional materials such as plastic laminate, neon tubes and printed glass
Designers	Ettore Sottsass, Michele De Lucchi, Martine Bedine

Designers and their work

Below are some of the designers that you need to be aware of, along with the key features to be found in their designs.

Figure 2.14 Furniture by Michele De Lucchi

Table 2.15 Phillipe Starck

Designer information	Product information
Phillipe Starck	**Juicy Salif Lemon Squeezer**
b. 1949	*1990*
French designer Post-modern ideas Designer for Alessi Challenges perceptions Many playful designs Thought provoking Experimental Modern materials Modern manufacture	Aluminium die-casting Inspired by eating calamari in a restaurant Sculptural aesthetics Leg angle stops juice running Space for a container Potentially unstable Oranges don't fit well Pip collection not perfect Costs approximately £50

Table 2.16 James Dyson

Designer information	Product information
James Dyson	**DC01 vacuum cleaner**
b. 1947	*1993*
British 'serial inventor' Technology innovator Designed the 'Ballbarrow' Many patent disputes Made thousands of prototypes Fans, hair dryers, hand dryers and other products	'Bagless' dual-cyclone concept inspired by sawdust extraction system No suction loss Colour scheme aids use 3D sculpted form based on flow of air Injection-moulded ABS Uses many integral fixings Clear PC bin 'shows off' dust

Table 2.17 Margaret Calvert

Designer information	Product information
Margaret Calvert	**'Men at work' road sign**
b. 1936	*1965*
Born in South Africa Graphic designer Joined Jock Kinneir in 1964 Developed 'Transport' and other fonts Updated road signage	Uses stylised pictogram Simple and clear communication of information Standardised sign system Arguably Modernist style Replaced old-fashioned signs with text

Figure 2.15 Road sign designed by Margaret Calvert

Table 2.18 Dieter Rams

Designer information	Product information
Dieter Rams	**Braun SK4 radio record player**
b. 1932	*1956*
Influential German designer Designed for Braun Post-Second World War context Developed ten principles of good design (Table 1.4) Believed in simple, honest, functional design Influenced Apple's Jonathan Ive	Innovative incorporation of thermoplastics and electronics Revolutionary at the time Highly functional No superfluous features Many iterations followed

Typical mistake

Remember that Dieter Rams wasn't a member of the Bauhaus school of design. His work follows the same 'Form follows function' principles, but the Bauhaus closed in 1933 and Dieter Rams was born in 1932. His work does, however, reflect his reaction to the needs of post-Second World War Germany, with some similarities to the way the First World War influenced the Bauhaus.

Table 2.19 Charles and Ray Eames

Designer information	Product information
Charles and Ray Eames	**Lounge Chair 670**
1907–1978, 1912–1988	*1956*
American husband and wife Creative design partnership Plywood moulded furniture Ideas evolved from designing laminated plywood leg splints Experimented with a wide range of materials	Luxury version of 1945 LCW (Lounge Chair Wood) Aimed for 'warm look' Combines industrial production with hand craftsmanship Moulded plywood shell Leather upholstery Rosewood veneer Comfortable Still on the market

Figure 2.16 Eames Lounge Chair and ottoman

Table 2.20 Marc Newson

Designer information	Product information
Marc Newson	**Lockheed Lounge**
b. 1963	*1986*
Australian designer Designs 'catwalk pieces' Challenges perceptions Prioritises form Uses rounded forms Some designs inspired by origami (paper folding) Collaborated with Jonathan Ive on the Apple Watch	Aircraft-style rivet construction Styled on a 'blob' of mercury Limited batch were hand made Statement piece rather than functional Needed only to be 'more comfortable than a bus stop' One sold for £2.4 million in 2015

Table 2.21 Marianne Brandt

Designer information	Product information
Marianne Brandt	**Tea Infuser MT49**
1893–1983	*1924 (designed)*
Former Bauhaus student Became head of the metalwork department in 1928 Employed simple forms that are still relevant to modern designs Developed a range of geometrically pure kitchenware Products were commercially successful	Typical Bauhaus design with simple, geometrical form Offset lid is functional in preventing drips Ebony handle positioned for ease of pouring One was sold for $361,000 in 2017

Exam tip

Study the work of the designers mentioned in this section and others that interest you to ensure that you are aware of a range of examples of:

- iconic designs
- designers' influences, methods and thinking
- enterprise
- how designing has changed over history.

Now test yourself

TESTED

1. Identify three different ways in which individuals and organisations have responded to the needs of societies and briefly state their impact.
2. Use notes and sketches to contrast the work of post-modern designers such as the Memphis group with that of the Bauhaus school.
3. Briefly outline four inventions and/or product innovations that have affected the way that clothes have been washed in domestic households over the last 100 years.
4. Explain why consumers are prepared to pay £50 for a Phillipe Starck Juicy Salif rather than buying a basic and probably more efficient juicer for less than £2.
5. Using two different examples of products, use notes and sketches to explain the diverse nature of the inspiration that led to their design.

Now test yourself answers at www.hoddereducation.co.uk/myrevisionnotes

2.4 Lifecycles of products

Initial demand, growth and decline

REVISED

A product's marketing **lifecycle** begins when it is first thought of and introduced to the market, and it continues until demand drops and the product is phased out.

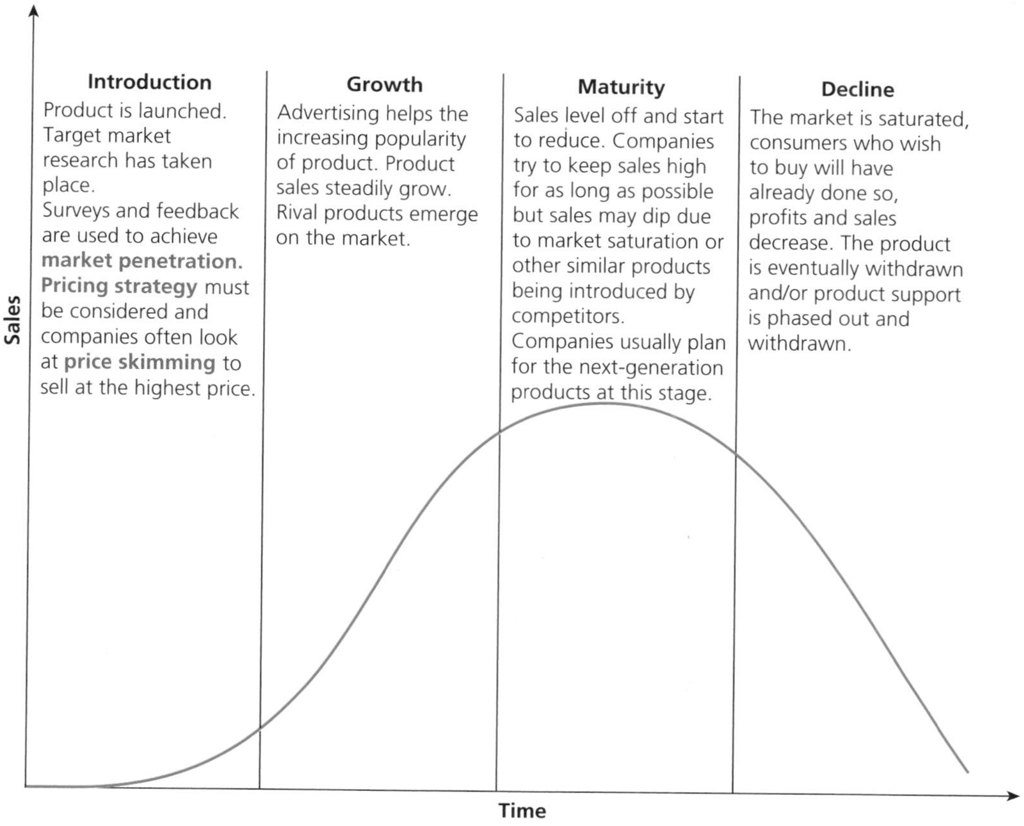

Figure 2.17 Product lifecycle

Key words

Product lifecycle: the marketing lifecycle from the introduction through to decline of a product.

Market penetration: increasing the market share of an existing product, or promoting a new product by using a variety of marketing and advertising strategies.

Pricing strategy: how companies price their products to take account of production, labour and advertising costs as well as incorporating a profit margin.

Price skimming: a company sets its prices high when launching a product to quickly recover initial expenditures associated with production and advertising. The aim is to achieve a profit quickly.

Exam tip

Make sure you know the stages in the product marketing lifecycle and are able to give specific examples of what happens at each stage. Try to become familiar with the marketing lifecycle of different products.

Creating demand and maintaining product popularity

REVISED

Staying ahead of competitors and maintaining or increasing profits is key to a company's success. Companies must therefore find methods to create more demand for their products and maintain the popularity of the product for longer. Product modifications usually occur in the maturity stage of the product lifecycle and companies use extension strategies to maintain sales. These include:

- Promotional offers such as price reductions to clear stock.
- Increasing usage, for example issuing software update with new features.
- Product redesign, for example with cars such as the Volkswagen Beetle, the Fiat 500 and the Toyota Corolla.
- New advertising campaigns aimed at a different target market.
- Change of branding or colours, for example the Apple iPod was initially only available in white and as the product developed, Apple slowly introduced new features such as coloured casings, colour text and video.
- Meeting consumer demand, for example increased battery life on mobile phones, larger memory in laptop computers.

Typical mistake

Don't confuse the product marketing lifecycle with the product lifecycle assessment (which is concerned with environmental issues). Read the question carefully to avoid this mistake.

New models of marketing and the influence of social media (A Level)

REVISED

Social media marketing (SMM) allows companies to ascertain the likes and dislikes of their target market, to track the success of advertising and to target specific potential consumers through their browsing history. For example, a social media pop-up for baby products might appear for people who browse baby furniture products, look at products in online baby stores or follow a local nursery or parent group.

The methods used by social media marketing fall into two categories:

- **Passive approach:** this is where individuals share reviews or recommendations for a product, which result in the product 'going viral' and is often seen in the introduction stage of a product's lifecycle. Companies use market analysers to track issues with products or identify the consumers' preferences, and these data are then used to improve the product or identify potential new features.
- **Active approach:** companies may use online forums to build rapport with the target market, or place specific adverts in specialist areas online, such as advertising motorcycle accessories on a motorcycling forum. Potential consumers can be encouraged to like, share or tag the company on a social media platform, for example by having a chance of winning the item in a competition. Many companies also use real people such as consumers with product blogs to review their products – if the product is well received this is great publicity but if it is not, it could damage the company reputation. Sports stars and celebrities are also used to endorse products. These people often have a large social media following with a worldwide reach.

Key word

Social media marketing (SMM): a form of internet marketing that utilises social networking websites as a marketing tool.

Now test yourself

TESTED

1. List the four stages of a product's marketing lifecycle.
2. Explain the meaning of the term 'market penetration'.
3. List two advertising strategies a company may employ during the launch of a new product.
4. What is social media marketing (SMM)?
5. State two common features which occur during the growth stage of a product's marketing lifecycle.

Exam practice

1. Use an appropriate product example to explain how design and technological innovation can impact on aspects of people's lifestyle.
2. Explain a wide range of factors relating to the 'ecological footprint' of a consumer product of your choice.
3. Use notes and diagrams to explain the inspirations and influences leading to a 20th century design movement of your choice.
4. Suggest **two** ways companies use social media marketing (SMM) to influence consumers.
5. Using a specific product example, explain the main stages of the product's lifecycle.
6. Give **two** examples of strategies companies use to extend product sales during the product lifecycle.
7. Explain what benefits using virtual reality could have for a company designing a fighter jet cockpit.
8. A board game manufacturer is releasing a new version of a popular table-top game. Outline a suitable marketing strategy and justify how this will reach the intended consumers.
9. To increase profits, many companies produce single-use items. Discuss the moral issues associated with a 'throwaway society'.
10. Explain what benefits a company designing an electrical appliance may gain though the disassembly of similar existing products.

ONLINE

3 Implications of wider issues

3.1 Factors to consider when investigating design possibilities

Social, ethical and environmental issues

REVISED

Consideration of lifecycle assessment (A Level)

Regulation, legislation and social pressures mean that there is greater demand for products which are more sustainable in all aspects, from sourcing of materials to disposal.

Lifecycle assessment (LCA) evaluates the impact of a product from cradle to grave. The LCA evaluates all the stages shown in Table 3.1 and allows designers to carefully consider the environmental implications.

Key word

Lifecycle assessment (LCA): analyses and evaluates the economic impact of a product through all the stages of a product's life, from the initial extraction of raw materials through to final disposal or recycling (not to be confused with the product lifecycle).

Table 3.1 Product lifecycle assessment

Stage	Considerations
Acquisition of raw materials	• Energy required to extract materials • Environmental impact of extraction • Possible deforestation and local issues
Transporting materials	• Distance travelled • Impact of possible disasters and spillages • Use of electric vehicles versus the generation of power
Processing materials	• Environmental impacts of processing • Energy requirements • Chemical or physical processing of materials
Manufacturing	• Energy required for processing • Impact of chemicals and other pollutants • Transportation of materials, parts and completed products during and after manufacture
Using the product	• Energy required during use • Reuse of components (like glass milk bottles) • Energy required to clean • Environmental impact of detergents and chemicals
Disposal or recycling	• Energy used in collection • Energy required to dispose of waste • Environmental impacts of landfill sites • Reduction in the need for raw materials versus the cost of recycling

Figure 3.1 Plastic disposal has become a global concern and threatens natural environments

Nearly all polymers can be recycled but infrastructure must be in place to allow this to happen. There has been a huge growth in the amount of recycling as consumers become more aware of environmental impacts but currently the creation of plastic waste far outstrips the levels of recycling.

Polymers can take hundreds of years to decompose and can be harmful to the environment, for example by polluting water and threatening sea life and birds.

Consider the lifecycle of a polymer bottle made from polyethylene terephthalate (PET):

- PET is produced from crude oil.
- Extraction of crude oil causes greenhouse gases and harms habitats.
- A refinery distils the crude oil.
- The oil is shipped to manufacturers to make polymer pellets.
- Bottle manufacturers produce 'preforms' from pellets.
- Preforms are manufactured into bottles using blow moulding.
- Bottles are cleaned, filled, capped, labelled and distributed.
- Consumer buys a bottle.
- Bottle is recycled or disposed of.
- Recycled bottles are shredded and reformed into pellets.

Figure 3.2 Shredded bottles can be reformed into pellets and then into new products

The source and origin of materials and the ecological and social footprint of materials

Natural materials come from plants and animals and include:

- wood
- metals
- cotton
- wool
- stone
- glass
- clay
- porcelain.

Synthetic materials are normally made from chemicals and include:

- polyester
- nylon
- Kevlar.

Our ecological footprint is the impact we have on the environment and on natural resources. Our social footprint refers to the impact we have on other people. Our **carbon footprint** is the amount of greenhouse gases caused directly and indirectly by human activity. Direct emissions come from burning fuels or domestic energy consumption. Indirect emissions come from the products we use.

Typical mistake

Don't only consider the lifecycle of a product during its use and disposal. Marks are lost if you don't take manufacture into account, or only think about the most obvious impacts such as emissions from production. Aspects such as energy, heat loss and waste materials are regularly overlooked.

Key word

Carbon footprint: the total amount of carbon dioxide released into the atmosphere as a result of the activities of an individual, a community or an organisation.

Table 3.2 Ecological and social issues for different materials

Material	Consequences of gathering the raw material	Material specific issues
Metal	• Mined from the Earth's crust • Mining can lead to destruction of the environment and large amounts of waste and unwanted rock • Energy use required for extraction is high • Carbon monoxide and carbon dioxide can be released during extraction	• Extraction of aluminium uses electrolysis which requires a large amount of energy • Silver is extracted using smelting and chemical leaching • Gold is found in rock that releases acid-generating sulphides
Timber	• Extracting timber without replacement causes deforestation, soil erosion, flooding, landslides and loss of habitat • 50% of hardwoods in Asia are endangered • Commercial production of softwoods is more sustainable due to speed of growth • The Forest Stewardship Council (FSC) ensures timber is harvested in a responsible manner	• Douglas fir is used for building, panelling and furniture • Bamboo growth is rapid and can be harvested every 5 years and requires no replanting • Man-made boards can be made from lower grade timber of waste wood

→

Material	Consequences of gathering the raw material	Material specific issues
Cotton	● Cotton is mainly produced in the USA, China, India, Brazil, Turkey and Pakistan ● Only 12% of cotton production is classed as sustainable ● Intensive farming uses large volumes of water and has a significant local social impact	Organisations aim to reduce the environmental impact of cotton production by: ● identifying risks in the supply chain ● enabling the tracing of cotton provenance ● training farmers in water management ● educating cotton-producing communities in fair working conditions and human rights
Leather	● Leather is sourced primarily from cows; cows have a significant impact on greenhouse gasses ● More than 50% of the raw material comes from China ● Tanning of leather produces toxins and causes pollution ● People for the Ethical Treatment of Animals (PETA) monitor animal welfare. ● Leather is widely traded	● Leather is durable, long-lasting and biodegradable ● The softest leather comes from new-born calves which raises ethical and moral concerns ● PETA promotes non-leather alternatives
Papers and boards	● Wood pulp is normally sourced from softwoods (spruce, pine, larch) or hardwoods (eucalyptus, birch, aspen) ● The social and environmental issues are the same as for wood ● The virgin pulp of 24 trees is needed to make 1 tonne of copier paper	● Recycling paper can reduce the need for virgin wood ● Recycled paper is normally less strong due to the breakdown of fibres ● Bleach and chemicals used in the processing to make white or coloured paper have environmental impacts
Polymers	● Main source of synthetic polymers is crude oil ● Extraction is specialised and expensive ● Natural polymers can be sourced from raw materials which include starch, cellulose, sugars ● Crude oil reserves are diminishing and will eventually need to be replaced by other sources	● Hydrocarbons can be sourced from methane, coal and biomass
Biopolymers	● Sourced from renewable feedstocks such as corn, potatoes, rice, palm and wood	Biopolymers fall into three categories: ● bio-based and biodegradable ● part bio-based and non-biodegradable ● fossil fuel-based and biodegradable Electroactive polymers are being developed

Exam tip

Make sure you know your materials and their properties. Too often students only know the details of a few materials. This means that they often refer to the same material repeatedly in their answers or choose materials which are inappropriate to the product identified in the question.

The depletion and effects of using natural sources of energy and raw materials

Using natural sources of energy and raw materials has its advantages but there are also impacts on the environment to consider.

Table 3.3 The advantages and impact of various energy sources

Method	Description	Advantages	Impact
Gas/coal/oil	Fuel is burnt to generate electricity	• Readily available • Gas-fired stations are very efficient	• Air pollution, including greenhouse gases • Limited resources • Non-renewable
Hydroelectric	Dam releases water to generate electricity	• Very low cost once dam built • No pollution • Quickly responds to demand	• High initial cost • Local impact on the environment
Wind	Blades catch wind to generate electricity	• No pollution • Can be sited in remote areas or offshore	• Unreliable • Some local visual and noise impacts • Can harm birds
Solar photovoltaic	Photovoltaic cells convert light to electricity	• Low cost after initial outlay • No pollution • Can be used at small or large scale	• Expensive initial cost • Unreliable • Storage system needed
Tidal barrage	Tide moves a barrage built across a river to generate electricity	• Low cost after initial outlay • No pollution • Predictable	• Very expensive initial cost • Can destroy local environment and habitats • Only generates power at set times
Wave	The motion of the waves generates electricity	• Low cost after initial outlay • No pollutants	• Unreliable • A hostile environment causes high maintenance • Low power output
Geothermal	Water is pumped through heated rocks, and the steam produced is used to generate electricity	• No pollutants or waste • Low cost for pumping • Small infrastructure required	• Few suitable locations • Possibility of gas emissions
Biomass	Fuel (wood, sugar cane) is burnt to generate electricity	• Fuel is easily sourced • Can use waste • Low cost	• Air pollutants • Needs large amounts of fuel • Can be seasonal depending on the fuel used

Planned obsolescence

Planned obsolescence aims to produce a product with a limited lifespan. This may be to do with changing fashion or simply designing parts which wear and need replacing. This type of design practice is morally questionable and leads to a 'throwaway society'.

Products are often simply thrown away when they break. Disposal of these products means that they:

- become landfill
- pollute the ground and atmosphere

> **Key word**
>
> **Planned obsolescence**: the process of designing a product to go out of fashion or no longer function after a specific time period.

- are shipped to low-wage economies and recycled – unused parts are often burnt.

To encourage sales and repeat purchases, designers have historically planned obsolescence in a number of products including:

- light bulbs
- refrigerators
- washing machines
- cars.

Fashion products are often subject to planned obsolescence as trends change quickly and with the seasons. This is known as **fast fashion**. In some cases, such as children's clothes, garments are changed so rapidly that high quality materials or a long life is not required.

> **Key word**
>
> **Fast fashion**: a term explaining a quick transition from catwalk to high-street stores to capture current trends.

Some products have a defined life – for example, single-use medical products must be disposed of to ensure safety for users. This type of planned obsolescence can benefit consumers. However, the traditional 'linear economy' of making, using and then disposing of a product raises concerns about our ecological, social and carbon footprints.

For example, repairing products is often expensive and difficult. For some products, the cost outweighs the price of a new product, but other products are hard to repair due to the way they have been designed. The 'circular economy' debate is based on the principle of minimising waste which would suggest that products should be designed to be cheaper and easier to repair.

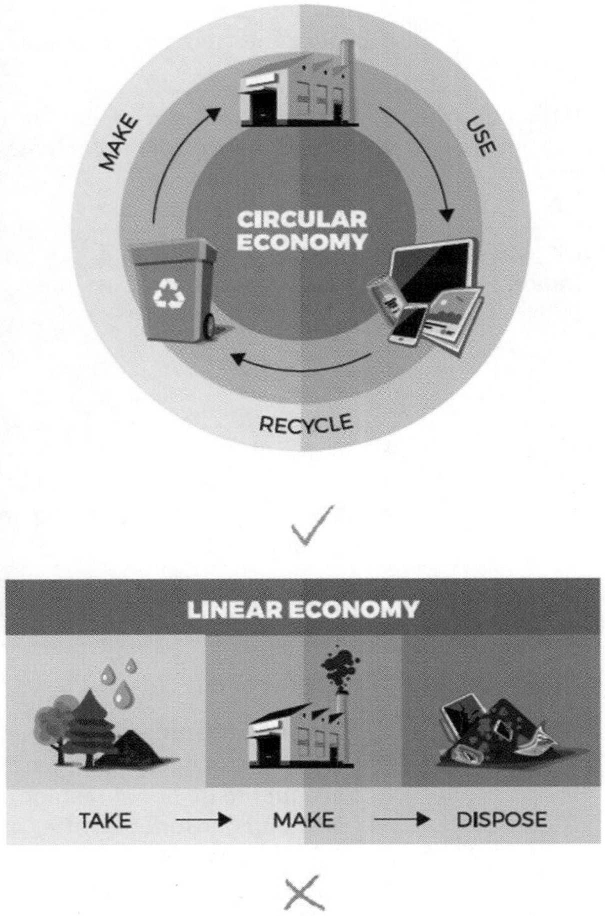

Figure 3.3 Circular vs linear economy

Buying trends

Consumers are rapidly changing the way in which they buy products due to technological advances and the new systems they offer.

Shoppers are influenced by a number of options and buying decisions. These may include:

- connectivity between devices
- subscription services instead of purchase
- renting products (including clothes)
- online purchasing
- customer reviews.

Social media and crowdfunding mean that products can be advertised and sold through many different channels, and consumers can have direct access to designers and are able to order bespoke products.

Table 3.4 Changes in buying trends due to new technology

Technology	Buying trend
Internet of Things	Linking automated systems together to allow integration of a variety of products and services
Virtual reality (VR)	VR is increasingly used as a marketing tool to allow consumers to wear or experience products before purchase
Robots	Drones, driverless delivery and automated warehouses are all being used to speed up processes and change the way shoppers buy products
Artificial intelligence (AI)	AI-powered shopping assistants and helpers are increasingly available to aid consumers to make buying decisions

Environmental incentives and directives

In 2016, the **Paris Agreement on Climate Change** set out targets to limit global temperature rises to no more than 2°C above pre-industrial levels. Concerns exist regarding the USA opting out and the likely weakening of regulation in the UK due to Brexit.

The **EU Renewable Energy Directive** requires the UK to generate 15 per cent of its energy from renewable sources by 2020. To meet this directive and various future goals, a number of initiatives are in place:

- The use of renewable resources has increased significantly and is undergoing rapid expansion. This includes wind, solar and biomass power.
- Increasing levels of biofuels will be used in vehicles with a possible ban on petrol and diesel by 2040.
- A switch to low-carbon energy sources will be required to meet the longer-term goal of an 80 per cent cut in carbon emissions on 1990 levels by 2050.
- Environmental initiatives to reduce unsustainable practices, including:
  - certificates of reliable forestry management through the Forest Stewardship Council (FSC) or the Programme for the Endorsement of Forest Certification (PEFC)
  - a target of a recycling 50 per cent of household waste by 2020
  - a target of recycling of 65 per cent of rubbish by 2030.
- Targets set by the Ambient Air Quality Control Directive to reduce harmful airborne pollutants through the use of clean air zones in cities.

International agreements also seek to protect the environment and include agreements on wildlife protection, climate change and air pollution. These are often less strictly enforced than UK or EU law.

Designers and manufacturers will take into consideration the targets set out in environmental directives in order to gain an environmental mark of compliance such as the European Ecolabel. This label signifies that the product or service is a better choice for the environment and demonstrates a designer's commitment to good standards.

Other environmental directives or regulations that impact designers include:

- Restriction of Hazardous Substances directive (RoHS) – concerns the reduced use of hazardous materials and chemicals.
- Waste Electrical and Electronic Equipment directive (WEEE) – concerns the reduction of electronic waste through free 'take back' schemes and approved disposal systems.
- Taxation on single-use bags and plastic packaging.

Now test yourself

TESTED

1 State four natural material types.
2 Outline the advantages and disadvantages of geothermal energy production.
3 State two products that have historically used planned obsolescence in their designs.
4 Explain why a local council may choose wind power generation over hydroelectric power, assuming there were suitable sites for both.
5 What is our 'social footprint'?

3.2 Factors to consider when developing design solutions for manufacture (A Level)

Responsibilities and principles of designing for manufacture

REVISED

Design decisions dictate around 70 per cent of the manufacturing costs. Design for Manufacture (DFM) aims to reduce the costs of production by:

- minimising the number of parts
- using standardised parts and materials
- standardising design features
- reducing the number of manufacturing processes
- creating modular parts or assemblies
- creating efficient joining methods
- minimising the reorientation of parts or assembly during manufacture.

Figure 3.4 The DFM process will aim to reduce waste at every stage – disposal of physical waste is an additional cost to the manufacturer

Planning for accuracy and efficiency through testing and prototyping

Accurate tolerances and finishes aid the ease of product manufacture and increase efficiency and viability of cost. Improved accuracy may be implemented by designing or using:

- multi-functional parts
- multi-use parts
- symmetrical parts
- standardised fittings.

Being aware of issues in relation to different scales of production

Reducing the total number of parts and processes reduces manufacturing costs. Fewer parts mean:

- less processing time
- reduced handling
- reduced difficulties in assembly.

Designers will aim to design products with fewer parts. Injection moulding or casting can allow the creation of complicated parts that require few additional components.

Modular designs can reduce the need for painting, polishing or machine finishing by simplifying the assembly process using:

- standardised parts
- a reduced number of part variations
- common parts across various components and products.

The use of fasteners is generally avoided due to the additional handling requirements and the time needed to fit them. Designers will aim to remove as many fasteners as possible by using:

- snap fits
- tabs
- parts made in a single moulding.

Designing for repair and maintenance

To maximise the opportunities for reuse, repair and maintenance, designers will consider how easily a product can be dismantled or accessed by:

- using threaded connections rather than permanent fixings like welds
- reducing coating and coverings
- identifying components by bar coding, e-tagging or stamping parts
- using multi-function parts that fulfil a number of functions such as conducting power, and structural support to reduce the total number of parts needed
- including access panels
- using standardised screws
- using modules that can be swapped if faulty.

Designing with consideration of product life

Manufacturers are increasingly aiming to reduce the environmental impact of their products. They may consider:

- reducing waste during manufacturing
- reducing the use of hazardous materials or processes
- reducing energy use during manufacturing
- reducing energy use when the product is being used
- increasing opportunities for maintenance
- using stronger materials to increase the product's lifespan
- using lighter materials to reduce weight and possible carbon dioxide emissions during use.

Manufacturers may also consider extending the lifespan of their products; however, in the long run, this may lead to reduced sales due to lower demand.

Typical mistake

Don't concentrate on the most obvious meaning of DFM – that the designer will produce a concept that is easy to manufacture. While this is true, the range of aspects that DFM considers and its on-going mandate to improve production efficiency should also be considered.

Figure 3.5 Using a range of parts or fittings slows production and increases the likelihood of errors

Figure 3.6 Stamped parts allow for identification at the disposal stage

Product lifecycles that extend useful product life

REVISED

Planning for and consideration of maintenance, repair, upgrades, remanufacture and recycling systems

New technologies, wear and reduced support often make older designs redundant or obsolete. The transition to new products can mean reduced sales if not managed correctly.

Compatibility

New technologies may bring about problems with system compatibility. Users may have invested money into a product range that may quickly become obsolete or unusable. Manufacturers' strategies for customer retention may include:

- new products that maintain some compatibility
- new products that are fully backwards compatible
- software upgrades to extend the life of the product or allow new functionality.

Maintenance

Mechanical wear may mean that there is a requirement for maintenance to avoid breakdowns. Users will possibly be affected by additional costs, inconvenience or the requirements to maintain a maintenance schedule. To retain consumers and create additional sales, manufacturers may provide:

- a planned service schedule
- replacement parts
- a warranty.

Product support and end of life

During product development, designers will plan a strategy for product support and end of life (EOL). Support during a product's life may be in the form of:

- guarantees or warranties
- the availability of spare parts
- software upgrades
- technical helpdesks.

A product may reach its EOL for a number of reasons and will normally mean that production of the product ceases and support is withdrawn. This may be due to:

- the release of a new product
- material, technological or manufacturing developments
- a decrease in demand
- planned obsolescence.

Environmental factors

REVISED

Sourcing and processing raw materials into a workable form

Raw materials need to be processed to become usable in manufacture. These processes often have environmental impacts.

Metals

Metal is mined from the ground in the form of ore and the raw metal is then extracted from the ore.

Table 3.5 The environmental impact of extracting metals

Metal	Process for extraction	Environmental impacts
Iron	Blast furnace used to remove oxides	• Heat • Energy use • Waste rock and materials • Greenhouse gases
Steel	Oxygen is blown into molten iron	• Heat • Energy use • Carbon dioxide • Carbon monoxide • Greenhouse gases
Copper	Smelting and purification through electrolysis	• Heat • Energy use • Waste rock and materials • Greenhouse gases
Silver	Smelting or chemical leaching	• Heat • Energy use • Sulphur dioxide • Acid rain
Gold	Limited processing required	• Waste rock • Sulphides from waste rock
Aluminium	Bauxite is mined and aluminium is extracted through numerous stages of electrolysis	• Large amounts of energy use • Waste rock

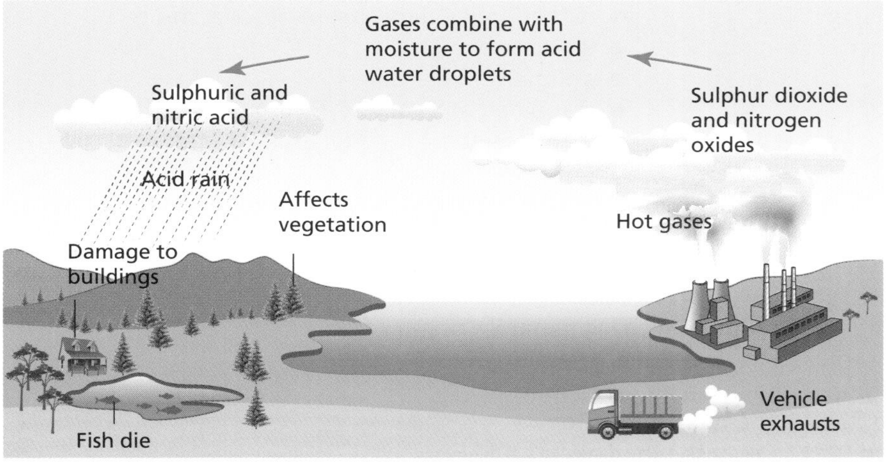

Figure 3.7 Various extraction, manufacturing and disposal methods result in acid rain

Wood

Wood processing to produce timber, paper and boards is completed at a sawmill. The process of 'conversion' means that trees are normally:

- debarked
- cut to size
- kiln-dried to reduce the moisture content (which uses significant amounts of energy).

Secondary processing may take place to convert larger pieces of timber into specific-sized boards or lengths. Often treatments will be used at this stage to make them heat- or rot-resistant.

Polymers and synthetics

Polymers and synthetics are produced from crude oil. During refining, large amounts of energy may be used during the 'cracking' process, which allows manufacturers to split the oil into monomers. Monomers can then be used to make polymer chains which make up polymers and synthetics.

The transportation of oil can result in spills which can have a very high impact on the environment. These spills often happen at sea and currents can spread the devastation across a vast area.

Natural fabrics

The farming and processing of natural fabrics often has a large impact on the environment.

Table 3.6 The environmental impact of farming and processing natural fabrics

Natural fabric	Farming and processing	Environmental impacts
Cotton	Large areas are planted and irrigated. The seed cotton is processed to separate the lint and seed.	• Pesticides • Intensive water use • Dust • Energy use
Wools	Wool fleece is washed to remove lanolin and grease.	• Water use • Greenhouse gases from herd farming
Silk	Labour-intensive process to harvest silk from cocoons using hot air, steam or boiling water.	• Energy use • Water use
Leather	Hides are processed using vegetable or chrome tanning.	• Greenhouse gases from herd farming • Land use • Intensive water use • Tanning can produce chromium (VI) which is carcinogenic

Exam tip

Be specific about the environmental impacts due to the use of materials. Students will often state that power will be used or that chemicals will be released into the environment. This generic response will not gain the marks required for the higher grades. Rather than simply stating, for example, that tanning hides may release toxins, you could look at outlining the two options for tanning (vegetable or chrome), and then look at the land, water and greenhouse gases that are created during the cattle-rearing and tanning processes.

The disposal of waste, surplus materials and components, by-products of production including pollution related to energy

Generating energy has a major impact on the atmosphere – over 80 tons of mercury and other toxic heavy metal pollutants are released into the atmosphere every year. Coal-, gas- and oil-fired systems also emit large amounts of carbon dioxide.

The Earth is surrounded by a layer of gases including carbon dioxide, methane and nitrogen oxide. This layer traps heat in the lower atmosphere. Greenhouse gases add to the thickness of this layer and are responsible for climate change and the warming of the planet.

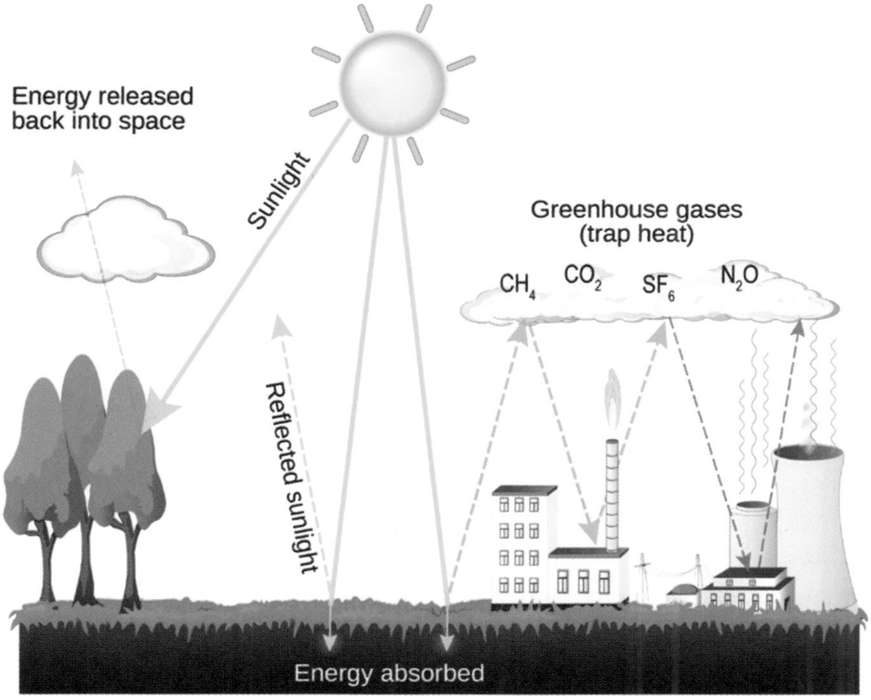

Figure 3.8 Greenhouse gases trap heat and create warming effects. This is known as the greenhouse effect

Governments require companies to reduce key pollutants through developing better technologies. These environmental regulations have been introduced to limit emissions of:

- sulphur dioxide
- nitrogen oxide
- polycyclic aromatic hydrocarbons.

Cost implications related to materials and process

Companies will often outsource manufacture to developing countries and low-wage economies as labour and premises costs make up a large part of a product's cost. While this is often beneficial financially, it can cause issues in quality control.

Companies need to monitor the quality of their manufactured products as faulty products could lead to:

- failures
- law suits
- returns
- product recalls.

Sustainability issues relating to industrial manufacture

REVISED

Fairtrade and the Ethical Trade Initiative

Fairtrade seeks to ensure that farmers:

- have safe working conditions
- have better working conditions
- receive fair pay for work completed
- have a stable income
- are not marginalised by larger companies.

Fairtrade also aims to promote sustainable production and good agricultural practices. Products that are often associated with or certified as Fairtrade include:

- bananas
- tea
- cocoa
- cotton
- rice.

The **Ethical Trade Initiative (ETI)** promotes respect for workers' rights across the globe. Its members are an alliance of companies, non-government organisations (NGOs) and trade unions. The ETI has set up a code of ethics to be upheld by its members. Its aims are to:

- aid disadvantaged workers by promoting sustainable and fair working practices
- raise awareness to reduce and ultimately stop forced labour and the production of non-ethical products.

Key word

Fairtrade: involves better prices, decent working conditions, local sustainability and fair terms of trade for farmers and workers in the developing world.

Economic issues and globalisation

Globalisation essentially means 'world trade'. It is now commonplace for products to be designed in one country, manufactured in another and assembled somewhere else. The development of large container ships means products can be transported easily and cheaply anywhere in the world.

Multinational companies work globally, looking to different countries to take advantage of:

- interest rates
- currency rates
- cheap labour
- cheap premises costs.

Globalisation can have benefits such as:

- access to products made or grown elsewhere
- access to a diversity of products
- availability of cheaper products
- job creation in developing countries.

However, because companies seek the cheapest option for production, the negative effects of globalisation can include:

- human rights violations
- forced labour
- child labour
- exposing domestic companies that have become inefficient or complacent.

Figure 3.9 Companies' drive for profit can lead to morally questionable production. Globalisation can lead to the use of child labour to reduce costs

Material sustainability and optimisation, availability, recycling and conservation schemes

Exploring the impact and use of eco-materials

Sustainable development is an idea that promotes development which does not deplete natural resources faster than they can be replaced or meets current needs without impacting on future generations. For examples of how sustainability works in practice, see Section 2.3 (pages 27–8).

Designers must consider the implications our decisions have on:

- the environment
- society
- the economy.

All decisions are interlinked:

- Making involves materials.
- Making materials into products requires energy and causes pollution or waste.
- Production of energy causes pollution.
- Pollution affects climate change.

To design more sustainable products, designers will often consider the 6Rs checklist (see Table 3.7). These principles will lead them to consider:

- How far must the chosen materials travel to be processed?
- Could the current materials be substituted for other materials or local alternatives?
- Can the chosen materials be recycled easily?
- Is it clear that the product can be recycled?
- Are the materials and packaging easy to separate?
- Can fewer materials be used to achieve a viable and usable product?

Table 3.7 The 6Rs

The 6Rs	Questions
Rethink	How can it do the job better? Is it energy efficient? Has it been designed for disassembly? Are the materials chosen environmentally friendly, could they be replaced?
Reuse	Which parts can I use again? Has the product got another valuable use without processing it?
Recycle	How easy is it to take apart? Are the materials recyclable? How can the parts be used again? How much energy is required to reprocess parts?
Repair	Which parts can be replaced or fixed? Which parts are going to fail? How easy is it to replace parts?
Reduce	Which parts are not needed? Do we need as much material? Can we simplify the product, remove parts?
Refuse	Is the product really necessary, do we need it? Is it going to last? Is it fair trade? Is it too unfashionable to be trendy and too costly to be stylish?

Design for Disassembly (DFD) is a strategy to aid EOL disposal or to lengthen the lifespan of a product. Designers using DFD may consider:

- using fewer parts
- using fewer fastenings
- standardising fastenings to aid disassembly
- using screws as they are quicker to disassemble than nuts and bolts
- avoiding glues and surface finishes
- adding built-in disassembly instructions.

Key word

Design for Disassembly (DFD): a strategy that considers the future need to disassemble a product for it to be repaired, refurbished or recycled.

Design optimisation is a process of identifying the best choices for:

- materials
- ease of manufacture
- ease of assembly
- quality
- size
- performance
- weight
- sustainability
- design features.

Figure 3.10 Cut layouts will be carefully planned to minimise waste

Optimisation software such as Altair or Dassault may be used. These systems and others allow engineers and designers to understand the quickest approach to manufacturing or modifying a design. Software aids the design process by reducing the need for prototyping and performance testing as these can be simulated. Optimisations that may be considered include:

- structural optimisation through algorithms
- size optimisation related to mass or structural elements
- topology optimisation of material layout.

Eco-materials are seen to have a positive environmental impact throughout the whole product lifecycle. Examples are shown in Table 3.8.

Key word

Eco-materials: often called environmentally friendly materials, those materials that enhance the environmental improvement throughout the whole lifecycle.

Table 3.8 Eco-friendly materials and their environmental impact

Eco-friendly material	Environmental impact
Papers and board	Easily recycled and can be repurposed as structural components or affordable furniture
Graphene	Electronic paper is currently the world's lightest and strongest material and potentially will be used in e-readers and electronic devices
Glass	Loses no material strength during recycling. Cleaning and reforming can use a lot of energy
Bamboo and cork	Fast-growing and rapidly regrown after harvesting. Can be used in a wide range of applications from flooring to clothing
Wood	Locally reclaimed wood is common. Due to the options for repurposing it has almost no environmental impact. New trees can be easily grown as trees are felled
Biopolymers	Bio-consumables made from natural products such as sugar cane and starch-based plant materials are available to replace petroleum-based products such as utensils, straws and coffee-cup lids
Fabrics	Hemp is fast-growing and requires few pesticides. It is suitable for clothing and furnishing applications. Soy is a by-product and can make a fabric similar to cashmere

Exploring how materials can be upcycled

'Upcycling' is a process of utilising an unwanted product and repurposing or improving it to meet new requirements or needs. This could be furniture which is cut, spliced and painted to produce a new product, or a T-shirt which is cut and made into a new garment.

Now test yourself

TESTED

1. State three gases making up the protective layer around the Earth.
2. What process is used to change crude oil into monomers?
3. What does DFM stand for and what is its purpose?
4. Why would symmetrical parts increase the efficiency of product manufacturing?
5. State three negative effects of globalisation.

3.3 Factors to consider when manufacturing products (A Level)

Optimum use of materials and components

REVISED

The cost of materials and/or components

Designers consider a number of different factors in the manufacture of most designs. These may be:

- the properties of the materials and the expected levels of performance
- the cost and availability of the materials
- the processing requirements to make the parts or product
- the environmental context of use
- the environmental impact of the part or product in use
- the environmental impact of the part during processing.

Designers must understand material properties to ensure the correct materials are chosen for a product. Decisions will be made according to:

- what the product or component must do
- environment of use
- maintenance requirements
- specific aesthetics
- the user
- cost
- product scale
- Design for Manufacture (DFM)
- what specific properties the materials must have
- sustainability issues.

Product requirements may include the following:

- reliability
- performance
- packaging including size and shape
- cost
- manufacturing and assembly
- regulatory directives
- intellectual property
- sustainability.

Material selection is often made according to cost. It is likely that material choices will be made by selecting the cheapest material which meets the core requirements of the product. This maximises the opportunity for profit and increases the product's viability.

Stock sizes and forms available

Materials are usually available in stock or standardised forms. Designers will aim to use standard size sheets, rolls, bars, tubes and sections that are often more readily available and cost less. Savings can be made by buying in bulk to reduce unit price and transportation costs.

Non-standard size parts will often require specialist manufacture or production and will cost significantly more. Designers will often avoid this to ensure the materials are easy to source and process, which increases the viability of the product.

Figure 3.11 Standard size stock will be readily available making it cheaper than bespoke sizes

Sustainable production

Design choices for materials can easily impact the environment and the product when in use. Sustainable choices will aim to:

- use less energy-intensive processing
- use fewer non-renewable resources
- use fewer resources overall (materials, energy, water)
- create less pollution
- reduce weight so that the impact of transportation is reduced
- make products lighter to be more user-friendly.

International guidelines such as ISO 50001 Energy Management are directed at reducing all aspects of energy use and emissions during production. To do so, sustainable production aims to use renewable energy sources. Examples include car plants using heat pumps to move and reuse heated gases to power machinery, or using locally generated solar energy with a view to have a net zero energy footprint.

Exam tip

Show a good range of material knowledge in your answers by selecting a variety of suitable materials and comparing them side by side. This shows a breadth of understanding and ensures that you are evidencing material selection according to design need.

Now test yourself TESTED

1 State five common requirements that designers will consider during the design of a product.
2 Why do designers tend to avoid items which are non-standard stock sizes or forms?
3 State four criteria that a designer will consider when selecting materials.

Typical mistake

Answers on questions regarding sustainability often consider only the environmental impact of the product and material selection. You should look at the whole product lifecycle and consider how the environmental impact can be reduced at other stages, for example at processing and disposal.

3.4 Factors to consider when distributing products to markets (A Level)

Effective and responsible distribution of products

REVISED

Cost-effective distribution

With few exceptions, products are sold to make a profit. Costs associated with distribution have a significant impact on the amount of profit a manufacturer will make.

There are normally three stages in distribution routes:

1 Manufacturer
2 Wholesaler
3 Retailer

To increase profit, manufacturers may use direct distribution and go straight to consumers. An example of this is the bicycle manufacturer Canyon who only sell online and deliver directly to customers. Direct distribution cuts costs significantly as the manufacturer can use its own salespeople and warehouses. However, for some products, users will want to try or use products prior to purchase and this must be considered as part of the business model.

Environmental issues and energy requirements

The environmental impact of packaging is regulated by the government and companies are obliged to:

- reduce their total amount of packaging
- reduce the packaging waste destined for landfill
- increase the amount of packaging suitable for recycling.

The environmental impact of product distribution may be achieved by:

- reducing energy use and costs by using a centralised distribution centre
- using less impactful transportation such as rail and water rather than road or air
- using fuel-efficient transport options
- using intelligent transport management systems
- using local suppliers
- outsourcing storage and distribution to specialist companies which will reduce the number of journeys made by delivering for numerous companies
- optimising packaging materials and design.

Lifecycle assessment (LCA) is used by many companies to assess all aspects of manufacture, distribution and use. This may highlight numerous possible changes to processes, packaging and distribution. Companies will often use just-in-time (JIT) production to reduce the impact of deliveries and distribution as part of their plans to reduce environmental impact.

Figure 3.12 Transportation avoiding roads is often highly energy efficient due to volume of product compared to the energy required to move it

Social media and mobile technology

Social media is increasingly used as a marketing tool and a distribution channel to sell directly to consumers. Social networks help brands gain exposure and reach by encouraging users to:

- share posts
- tweet
- 'like' products or brands.

Search engine optimisation (SEO) will draw new users to sites, and cookies give companies the technology to record the digital trace of unique users and allow them to track users' time and interactions on line.

Global production and delivery

Globalisation means that companies will often seek to reduce costs by outsourcing work to low-wage economies or developing countries. Transport systems must be managed to:

- plan logistics of shipments
- reduce the numbers of distribution journeys
- reduce miles travelled.

To streamline their distribution, companies use standardised pallet sizes to ensure a maximum loading potential for containers and other methods of distribution.

Reduction of road freight is being addressed by governments globally with a shift to rail and sea to reduce the environmental impacts from road congestion caused in part by individual delivery vehicles.

Figure 3.13 Container shipping is increasingly being used to move products around the globe. Complex logistical planning ensures vast container ships carry huge amounts of cargo efficiently and deliver to the correct destinations

Ethics in design practice and consumer rights

REVISED

Intellectual property

Intellectual property (IP) law can protect ideas and inventions. IP allows owners to control and prevent copying of:

- written materials
- artistic compositions
- musical compositions
- design ideas.

The various forms of IP law are discussed below.

Key words

Intellectual property: rights covering all types of intangible, non-physical products.

Registered design: give rights to appearance of a product.

Trademark: used by a company to identify and distinguish its products or brand.

Copyright: gives rights to creators of original ideas, information or intellectual works.

Design rights: give rights to the designer or creator of a design (does not cover 2D work).

Registered designs

To register a design, it must:

- be new or original
- be individual or have unique characteristics
- not resemble an existing design.

Registered design rights will protect copying of:

- the appearance of the design, including shape, pattern and decoration
- visual features, including lines, contours, colours and shape
- textures included in the design
- the design's materials.

Registered trademarks

Trademarks identify a product through branding, name, domain name, logo, song or symbol. They must be renewed every 10 years.

To register a trademark, it must be:

- unique and distinct
- fair and accurate
- morally acceptable.

Copyright

Copyrighted material can only be copied with the permission of the owner. This protection covers:

- artistic or musical compositions
- books or dramatic works
- original ideas
- intellectual works.

Copyright is automatic and registration is not required. Protection lasts for 70 years for most works, and for at least 25 years for photographs.

Copyright does not protect the ideas for a piece of work. Often several parts of IP law will be used to protect a design, so alongside copyright, the design may be registered to protect the idea during production and trademarked to protect its logo and branding.

Design rights and patents

Design rights can be bought, sold or licensed. They do not cover 2D design aspects such as patterns.

Design rights stay in force for 10 years after first marketing or 15 years after creation of the design. Design rights only give protection in the UK.

To obtain a **patent** an invention must:

- be new
- have an inventive aspect or non-obvious feature
- be capable of being made or used.

Obtaining patents can be a long and expensive process but they last 20 years and provide protection against the copying of technical or functional aspects of a product or item. This protection covers:

- how the product works
- how the product is made
- what materials it is made from.

Key word

Patent: gives rights to technical and functional aspects of a product or invention.

Typical mistake

Students often fail to learn the difference between the various IP laws and which type of product or material they apply to. Exam questions are usually specific about a single option and you will need more than an overview of IP to address the issues correctly.

Exam tip

Carefully consider a few products and determine which aspects of IP law will apply to them. Think about whether they have patents covering unique technical aspects, trademarks covering branding or other types of IP. You are more likely to attain higher marks if you have specific examples that you can easily expand upon to produce more complete answers.

Now test yourself

TESTED

1. State three criteria necessary to register a trademark.
2. If a company wishes to protect its logo, which IP law would best protect them?
3. What technology allows companies to track consumers on websites and search engines?
4. How does direct distribution benefit a manufacturer?
5. State four ways a company can reduce its environmental impact during distribution.

3.5 How skills and knowledge from other subject areas inform decisions

Incorporating knowledge from other experts and subjects

REVISED

Networking with specialists from a wide range of subject areas can lead to new solutions to product design problems. Specialists may include:

- **Stakeholders:** with various inputs as laid out throughout this revision guide.
- **Scientists:** with knowledge of technological developments in materials and manufacturing or with a better understanding of new theories.
- **Experts:** with knowledge of the human body, psychology, investigation and research, toxicology, ecology, ergonomics, social sciences and the cognitive process.

Primary and secondary research and interpreting technical data

REVISED

Design development is supported by technical data from a variety of sources. The chosen source or research methodology will be determined by the product being designed.

Table 3.9 Sources of technical data

Source of information	Type of data
Interview/discussion/questionnaire with user groups or first-hand investigations	Up-to-date feedback and first-hand evidence of problems and user needs
Analysing similar products	Identification of problems, features or context
Technical specification and size data sheets	Details of available components and parts, fixings and available sizes
Data from magazines, reference books or government agencies	Ergonomic and anthropometric data, historical trend data, material characteristics

While printed materials are available, online resources are widely used and are often more reliable as they can be kept up to date.

Table 3.10 Sources of online information

Source of information	Example	Website
Trade organisations	Timber Research and Development Association (TRADA)	www.trada.co.uk
	Society of Motor Manufacturers and Traders (SMMT)	www.smmt.co.uk
Website databases	Engineering Village	www.engineeringvillage.com
Educational websites	Granta Design	www.grantadesign.com
Multidiscipline databases	EBSCO	www.ebsco.com/academic-libraries
	ProQuest	www.proquest.com
Standards agencies	British Standards Online	www.bsigroup.com/en-GB/
Patent advice	Intellectual Property Office	www.gov.uk/government/organisations/intellectual-property-office

Now test yourself

TESTED

1. Why would a company seek to network with experts and specialists?
2. What sources of data would you use if you were seeking details of available part sizes?
3. How could analysing similar products aid the design of a new concept?

Exam practice

1. Explain how anthropometric data would aid the design of an adjustable office chair.
2. A company has created a new technology to recharge mobile devices without the use of trailing wires. What steps would be necessary to protect their concept using IP law?
3. A company operating around the globe wants to reduce the environmental impact of its deliveries. Explain **three** strategies it may use to meet this goal.
4. Explain how Design for Manufacture (DFM) will benefit a company producing and supplying parts to a multinational car manufacturer.
5. Explain how a UK-based furniture manufacturer for the domestic market can ensure the products it produces are sustainable.
6. Discuss the environmental impacts of leather production.
7. A company is producing a range of electronic products. Explain how it might benefit from using bought-in standardised parts.
8. State **three** steps a company may take to retain a customer as a product reaches its end of life.
9. Many products wear over time. How will a car manufacturer aim to ensure customer satisfaction and continued revenue from a product?
10. Discuss the issues of continued coal, oil and gas power generation and what barriers exist in moving to renewable sources such as wind and solar power.

ONLINE

4 Design thinking and communication

4.1 Annotated 2D and 3D sketching and digital tools

Sketching is an essential tool for communication between designers and stakeholders.

- It can be carried out with a range of graphical tools such as pencils, fine liners and biros.
- Even rough sketches with limited detail can play a role in recording and communicating ideas more effectively than words.
- The addition of annotation helps to communicate more information.
- Tablets and associated 'pens' facilitate digital sketches that can be incorporated into computer-aided design (CAD) work.
- CAD is often used to develop ideas, generate working drawings and to model prototypes.

Annotated sketching, digital tools and sketch modelling

REVISED

Various sketching and **modelling** methods can be used to communicate graphically in order to improve aspects of products such as:

- function, usability, construction, movement, stability, composition, strength
- aesthetic qualities
- manufacturing processes
- suitability of materials and components.

Key words

Modelling: preliminary stages of designing, using a range of 2D and 3D techniques to explore potential design iterations.

Perspective drawing: a 3D drawing method that adds realism by the use of receding size for more distant elements.

Isometric drawing: a pictorial drawing method showing horizontal lines sloping at 30° to horizontal.

Table 4.1 Sketching methods

Method	Application
Quick 2D or 3D sketches	• Used to explore design concepts • 2D sketches clearly show the layout of technical elements • 3D sketches show how ideas might look • Drawing software and tablet apps facilitate experimentation with visual variations
Perspective drawing	• Perspective drawing gives a more realistic impression of how designs might look • Three-point perspective is the most realistic, but two-point and single-point perspective are easier to draw and are more commonly used
Isometric drawing	• Facilitates the relatively easy generation of 3D drawings • Can be done freehand or more accurately with the use of a 30° setsquare or an isometric grid

→

Method	Application
Annotation	Adding annotation gives stakeholders and clients vital information such as: ● overall size ● features/mechanisms ● function ● structure ● ergonomics/safety ● materials/manufacture/cost
Storyboard or scenario sketches	● These show the context and anticipated user interaction involved ● They give an opportunity to explore the needs of the user, how and where the product will be used and other issues which will help to optimise the design in terms of functionality, materials, or manufacture
Sketch models	● Sketch modelling is a fast form of modelling used to convey the general idea of a design, rather than the details ● Easy-to-work materials such as foam, wire and card are used to make quick models to obtain feedback on aspects such as size, function and layout, which can be incorporated in the next iteration of the design
Mathematical modelling	● Simulation software facilitates the optimisation of designs and solution of problems by predicting the performance of designs and generating associated data, charts and graphs. These techniques are covered in Section 4.2 (page 61)
Generative design tools	● Such CAD software generates a wide range of alternative designs and optimum forms using a technique similar to biomimicry ● Constraints can be placed on the designs, which often take the form of structural elements with improved strength–weight ratio, aerodynamics or efficiency, that are often manufactured by 3D printing and other computer-aided manufacture (CAM) methods

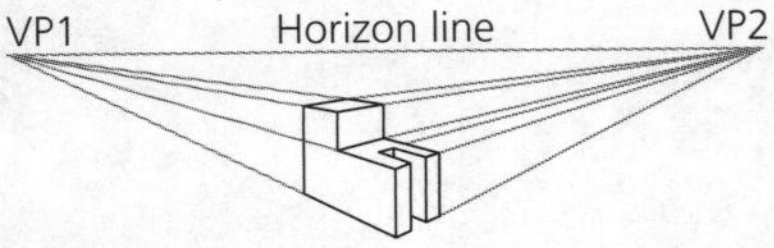

Figure 4.1 Two-point perspective

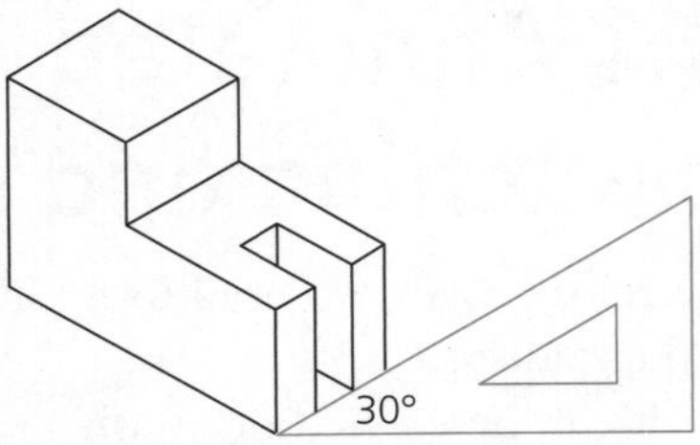

Figure 4.2 Isometric drawing

Key words

Sketch models: models made quickly using compliant materials in order to visualise ideas early on in the design process.

Mathematical modelling: the use of simulation software to model the effect of changes in designs prior to manufacture.

Generative design: the production of large numbers of alternative design possibilities using biomimicry-related techniques.

Methods used to communicate the construction of design solutions to third parties

REVISED

Working/technical drawings

All the information for the construction of a design solution are contained in **working drawings**.

- The conventions for standardised drawings are covered by British Standards in BS 8888.
- Orthographic projection (front and side elevations and plan) is normally used.
- Traditionally, working drawings are hand drawn using instruments, but are now often generated in CAD software.

Key word

Working drawings: detailed orthographic views supplemented by enough information to facilitate manufacture.

Working drawings will typically include the following elements:

- materials
- dimensions, often including **tolerances** (dimensional variation allowed)
- components
- assembly methods such as welding or nuts and bolts
- parts lists
- **exploded views** (when assembly needs to be shown)
- hidden detail/sections (to show parts that are not normally visible).

Typical mistake

You may not always obtain full marks for an example of an orthographic projection working drawing unless you align the views correctly. It also helps to include the appropriate symbol for first or third angle projection, a sample dimension and other features such as hidden detail.

Key words

Tolerance: the acceptable upper and lower limits of accuracy of a measurement.

Exploded view: a drawing, usually in isometric projection, showing the relative position of parts for assembly.

Digital visualisation

CAD software offers several advantages:

- Easy amendment of ideas (e.g. changing dimensions, modifying features such as 'shell' or altering line properties).
- Creation of complex shapes and forms (using tools such as extrude, revolve and deform).
- Transfer of files for rapid prototyping using files such as STL (stereolithography).
- Creation of assembly drawings (often in the form of 3D exploded views).
- Calculation of predicted stresses (using finite element analysis (FEA), see Section 4.2 (page 62)).
- A more rapid and consequently less expensive production process.
- Automatic generation of 2D and 3D exploded views and orthographic working drawings.

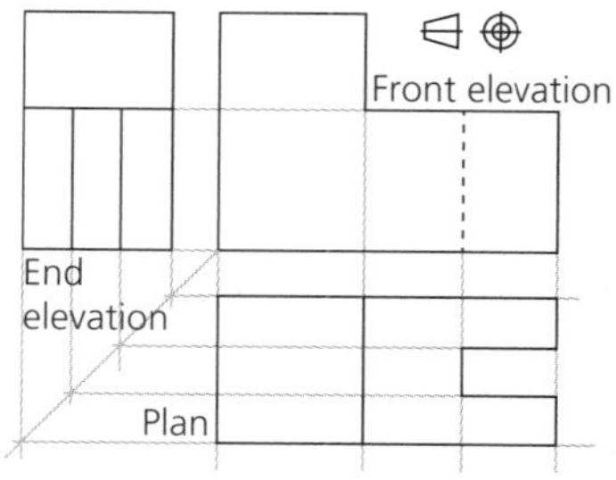

Figure 4.3 Example of orthographic projection with hidden detail

Schematic diagrams

Schematic diagrams communicate technical elements of a design and consist of connected symbols representing components that show how electrical, electronic, pneumatic and hydraulic circuits and systems will function.

Key word

Schematic diagrams: these show the layout of components such as an electronic circuit with transistors and resistors.

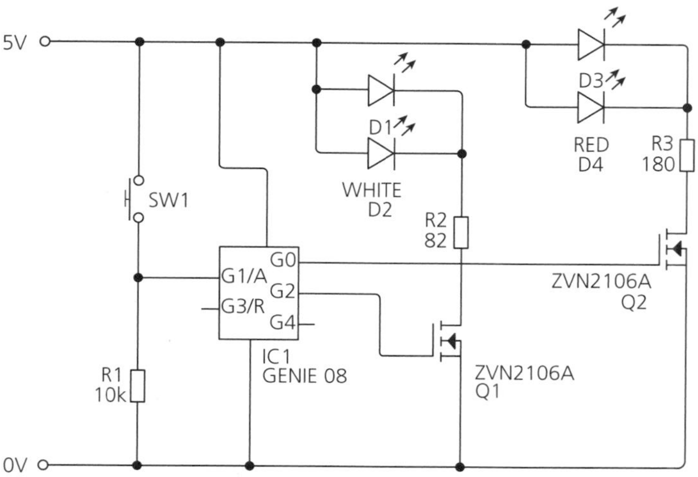

Figure 4.4 Schematic circuit diagrams

Flowcharts with associated symbols

Flowcharts are used to communicate the sequence of events that need to take place in processes such as manufacturing or quality control checks.

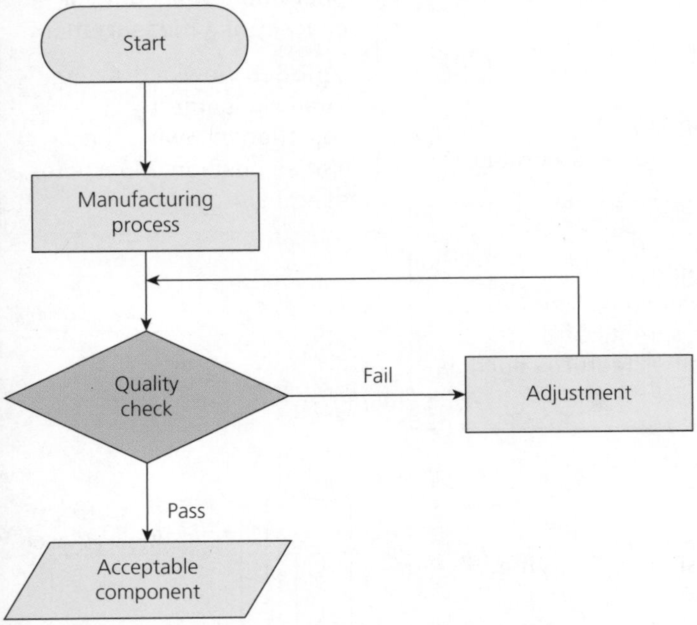

Figure 4.5 Quality control check flowchart

Key word

Flowchart: a diagrammatic representation of a process using standardised symbols.

Prototypes and models

More detailed models and prototypes can be made after freehand sketching has been used to generate ideas, or quick, sketch models have been done.

These detailed models and prototypes, made using more resistant materials and 3D printing, make it possible to check usability, function and aesthetics.

Exam tip

If you are asked to explain which type of communication technique is appropriate for particular situations, make sure that you give high priority to showing your understanding of the needs of the particular stakeholders involved. There is a massive contrast, for example, in the communication methods appropriate for a specialist manufacturer and a potential customer.

Now test yourself

TESTED

1. Which communication method would a designer use to communicate the details of a mould to an injection-moulding engineer? Why is this method appropriate?
2. If a designer in the early stages of generating ideas wished to obtain a quick idea of the proportions and layout of a particular design, which type of model might be appropriate?
3. Design a flowchart to show how you might carry out a simple workshop process such as cutting a slot in a piece of low-carbon steel and ensure that it has been done to the necessary standard.
4. Briefly explain two ways that BS 8888 specifies how details of technical products should be communicated.
5. Consider and give an estimate of the contrasting tolerance allowable in these situations:
   - building a wooden fence
   - manufacturing the mould to be used for injection moulding the cap for a drink bottle.

4.2 Use of digital design tools by industry professionals

How designers develop products using digital tools and online collaboration (A Level)

REVISED

Collaborative digital design software tools such as Onshape make use of web/**cloud-based** storage and networks. This facilitates:

- Stakeholder collaboration and input into the design process.
- Brainstorming and prototyping ideas.
- Development of ideas and concepts through computer, **tablet** and phone apps which facilitate real-time team (concurrent), collaborative designing, involving multiple designers and locations.
- Digital prototyping, including working models to accurately assess design iterations.
- **Project management** and communication essential for 'systems thinking' (see Section 4.3 (page 64)).

Typical mistake

Drawing a simplistic diagram of a computer and screen won't earn marks in questions relating to the use of digital design tools. A suitable diagram, however, showing the way that cloud computing can contribute to collaborative working, might be an appropriate way of showing your understanding of one of the important elements.

Key words

Cloud computing/storage: web-based hosting of computer files/applications for access in multiple locations.

Tablet: a mobile touchscreen computer. Note that graphics tablets are used mainly as input devices for design software.

Project management: the organisation of teamwork to satisfactorily achieve a particular objective.

How digital design software is used during design development

REVISED

Visual presentation, rendering and photo-quality imaging

Tablet-based sketching is used by designers for quickly generating and communicating ideas. 3D CAD design can then be used to render life-like images using a range of lighting, materials, backgrounds and effects.

Product simulation and scientific analysis

Computer-aided engineering (CAE) is the term used to cover a range of software tools used by designers and engineers to analyse and simulate the performance of their designs. At its simplest it might be used to calculate the centre of gravity of a component, but CAE provides a range of powerful professional tools.

Computational fluid dynamics

Computational fluid dynamics (CFD) is a 3D CAD simulation tool for fluid or gas flows in or around a product.

- Vehicle drag (wind resistance) can be tested in a simulated wind tunnel.
- Test results can then inform aerodynamic improvements.
- Marine craft designers use a simulated wave tank for similar purposes.
- Designers save time and money that is normally required for physical testing.

Key words

Computer-aided engineering (CAE): the simulation and analysis of product and component performance using computer software.

Computational fluid dynamics (CFD): 3D CAD simulation tool for fluid or gas flows in or around a product.

Finite element analysis (FEA)

Finite element analysis (FEA) is used to analyse stress in elements of a CAD design.

- It allows designers to simulate forces, vibrations or shock loads on products or components.
- Weak points are highlighted, usually using an easily identified colour-coded scale.
- Money and time can be saved as designs can be optimised by modifying and re-testing.
- Static and dynamic testing is useful for many products, such as bicycle frames and cars.

Key word

Finite element analysis (FEA): software which analyses the stress in elements of a CAD design.

Figure 4.6 Finite element analysis (FEA) being used to check the strength of a beam

Other digital software simulation tools include:

- Mould flow analysis (MFA) to optimise processes such as injection moulding and die casting.
- Electronic circuit or system testing, measurement and evaluation (e.g. Multisim Live).

Exam tip

Make sure you understand how CAE can help in determining the feasibility of designs. This might be, for example, showing your knowledge of how FEA is used to assess the extent to which a structural element can be reduced in size (to save weight and reduce cost) before its load bearing capacity is compromised.

Now test yourself TESTED

1. Practice drawing simple diagrams to illustrate how finite element analysis (FEA) and mould flow analysis (MFA) are used in typical design situations. You may need to research these techniques in more depth first.
2. Draw a simple diagram illustrating how designers, stakeholders and other elements involved in product design use the cloud to work and collaborate.
3. Explain the advantages of using a computer model and computational fluid dynamics (CFD) rather than a physical model in a wind tunnel.

4.3 Approaches to design thinking

Strategies, techniques and approaches to explore, create and evaluate design ideas

REVISED

Iterative designing

Iterative design involves repeatedly attempting to solve problems to work towards an optimum design, without worrying about unsuccessful attempts, but learning from them.

- In terms of the design process, this is the circular, or cyclic sequence of stages that are required to refine a design to suit the needs of users and stakeholders.

Key word

Iterative design: is a cyclic approach to creating optimum designs by incorporating feedback from on-going, evaluative testing processes.

- Designers as individuals or teams will move backwards and forwards through the process as required and will constantly evaluate what they are doing in order to improve their work.
- The cyclic nature of the iterative design process is apparent in Figure 4.7, which shows the impact of hypothetical issues affecting the development of a design for a power drill.

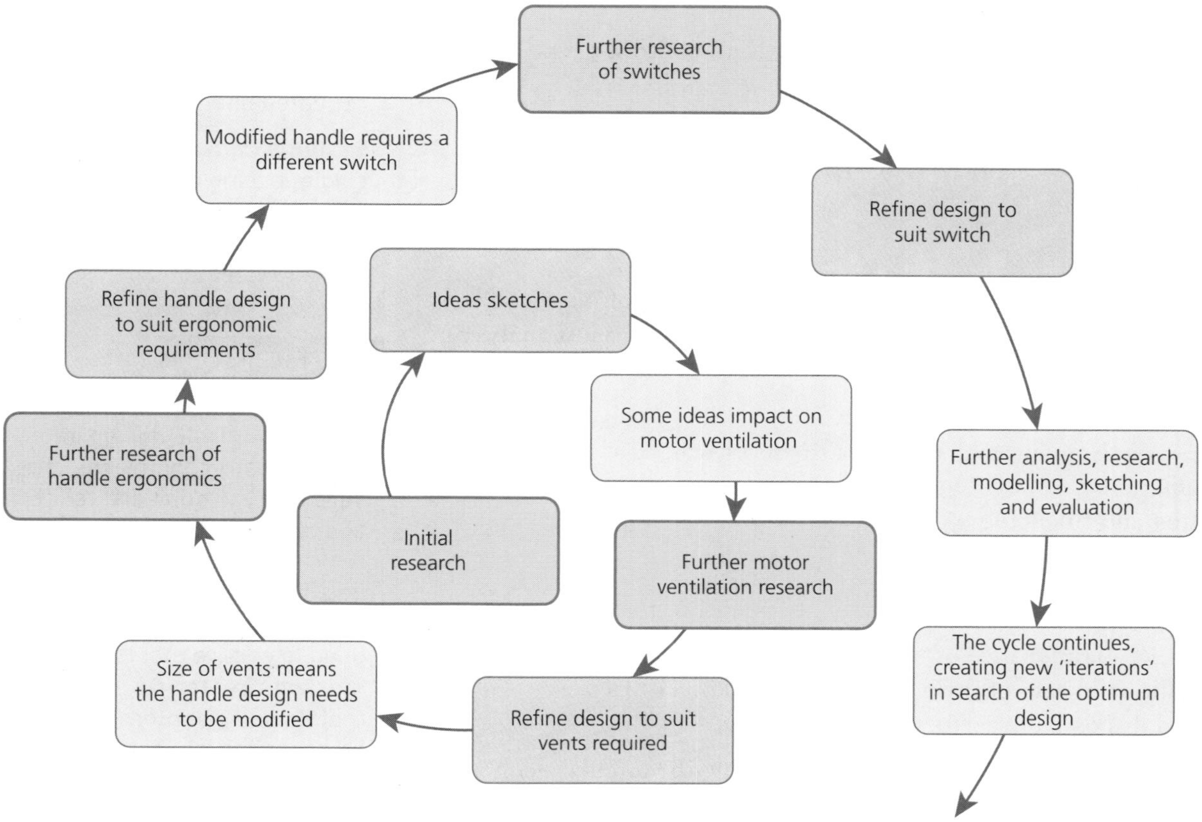

Figure 4.7 The cyclic nature of iterative design in the development of a power drill

User-centred design

User-centred design (UCD) aims to improve users' experience and the usability of products through:

- putting a major focus on the user interface
- prioritising the user interaction and relationship with the product
- ensuring that products are suitable for all users rather than users having to adapt to them.

Product designs which are compliant with the international usability standard ISO 13407 should:

- take full account of users, the task performed and the relevant environment
- involve users during design, development and evaluation
- result from an iterative design process
- be developed by a multi-skilled, multi-disciplinary team.

The methods used to achieve UCD standards:

- apply ergonomic principles for ease of use and comfort
- use anthropometric data to ensure a good 'fit'
- observe product interactions and use focus groups to identify problems
- have a **participatory design** process involving users and stakeholders.

Key word

Participatory design: a design process that requires the involvement of all stakeholders and users.

Circular economy

The circular economy is a cradle-to-cradle, rather than the traditional cradle-to-grave, approach to the product lifecycle. The circular economy:

- requires the continuous reuse of high-quality **biological** and **technical 'nutrients'**
- facilitates maintenance, repair and reconditioning to extend a product's life
- reduces reliance on sourcing new materials, in contrast to the linear economy's 'make, use, dispose' model.

For more on the implications of the circular and linear economy for designers, see Section 3.1 (page 40).

Key words

Biological nutrients: organic non-toxic materials that can safely re-enter ecosystems.

Technical nutrients: man-made materials (e.g. polymers and alloys) for repeated use.

Systems thinking: concentrating on component interactions and connections, and their role within the overall system.

Systems thinking

Systems thinking involves concentrating on the effects of interactions and connections between elements of a system rather than just analysing the component parts. It requires designers to look at the 'big picture' of the service provided by products.

Consider, for example, some aspects of the service associated with car ownership:

- choosing and financing
- driver/passenger experience
- pleasing aesthetics
- safety
- user/dealer maintenance
- availability and ease of fitting spare parts and accessories
- eventual disposal/replacement/upgrade options.

This example highlights the importance of UCD, the circular economy and the involvement of stakeholders in the overall system to provide a totally satisfying consumer experience.

Typical mistake

When explaining the role of cradle-to-cradle design in the circular economy, make sure that you don't just talk about biological nutrient recycling. You should also be able to explain how appropriate techniques are used to ensure that technical nutrients (materials such as metals and polymers) can be kept separate and free from contamination during dismantling procedures at the end of a product's life.

Collaboration

REVISED

Collaboration (working together) is an essential element of modern product design, since no individual designer can be an expert in all the areas involved. The benefits of collaboration for all designers include:

- Encouragement of creativity and innovation through the consideration of multiple perspectives.
- Avoidance of 'design fixation', where designers become blinkered to other possibilities.
- Group support to provide individuals with help when difficulties or errors occur.
- Solution of complex problems through the use of specialists.

Consider the areas of expertise needed for the commercial design of a rechargeable polymer torch:

- Electronics – switching and recharging circuitry.
- Battery technology – knowledge of the latest developments in rechargeable types.
- LED technology – appropriate energy consumption and light output/pattern.

Key word

Collaboration: working as a team, rather than individually, to achieve a goal.

- Injection moulding – mould design, taking account of integral fittings, clips and features such as ribs.
- Ergonomics – handle shape, grip and texture, switch positioning and user feedback.
- Materials – properties such as toughness, pigmentation, mouldability and potential for overmoulding.
- Aesthetics – issues such as appearance, feel and packaging.

A project co-ordinator is essential to facilitate communication between the specialists involved in a project. Several iterations would be required in order to develop the optimum design to the satisfaction of stakeholders and users, as we saw at the start of this section.

See Section 4.2 (page 61) for information on the use of digital collaboration tools by design teams.

Approaches to project management (A Level)

REVISED

Various project management tools are available to ensure that the requirements of all the stakeholders are met. Some tools are organisational, some are graphical/diagrammatic and most can be executed digitally.

Using such tools means concurrent (simultaneous/parallel) operations can be promoted and slippage (delays) avoided.

Gantt charts are a simple and effective way of laying out the schedule for a project, as seen in the example in Figure 4.8.

Key words

Gantt chart: a graphical method (bar chart) of showing the time allocation for organising the stages of a manufacturing process.

Critical path analysis (CPA): analysis of the stages in a project to ensure time-efficient completion.

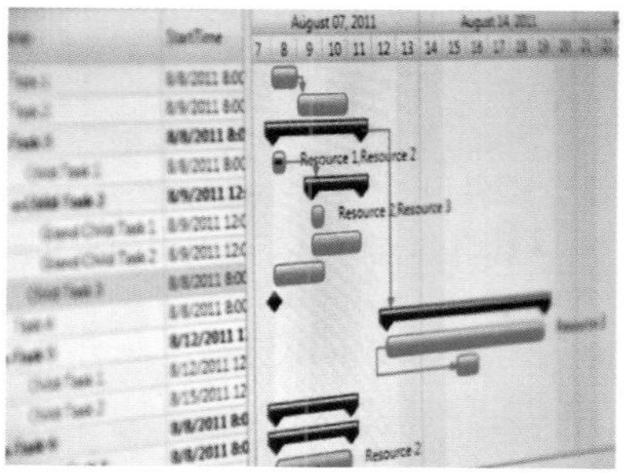

Figure 4.8 Gantt chart

Critical path analysis

Critical path analysis (CPA) is a project management method used to schedule efficient completion of all the stages in a project.

- A sequential order of tasks is established for a project or process.
- Unnecessary waiting time can be identified.
- Parallel processing opportunities can then be exploited for maximum efficiency.

Table 4.2 Simplified process for a single worker manufacturing the wooden sign shown in Figure 4.9

	Task	Time (minutes)	Depends on
A	Cut wood to size for routing	5	
B	Set up wood on router	5	A
C	Shape the sign on the router	15	B
D	Remove sign from router	5	C
E	Sand any rough edges	10	D
F	Cut steel for mounting plates	5	
G	Mark out screw holes in plates	5	F
H	Drill screw holes in plates	5	G
I	Screw plates to sign	5	H & E
	Total time	60	

Figure 4.9 Wood sign with mounting plates

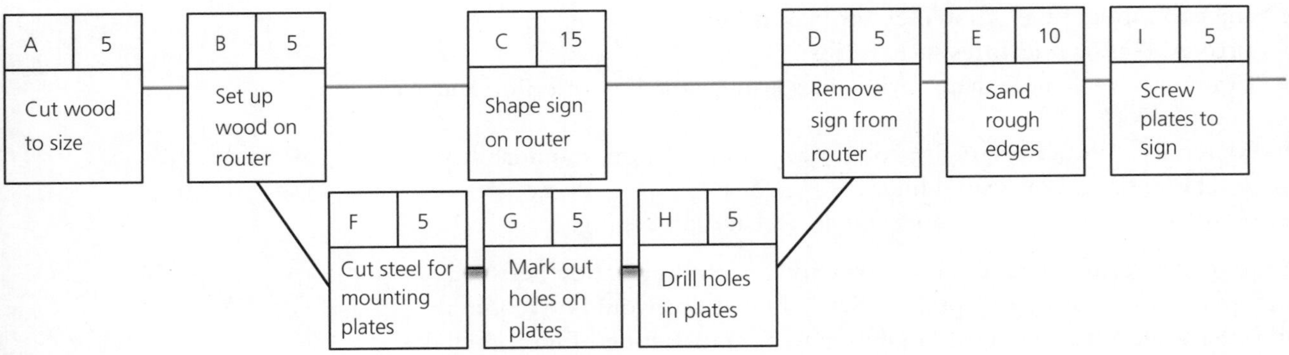

Figure 4.10 CPA for manufacturing the wood sign

The red line in Figure 4.10, indicating the minimum time (critical path), shows that optimum organisation of manufacture by a single person could achieve a reduction from 60 minutes to 45 minutes.

This is because parallel (simultaneous) processes can be undertaken during CNC machining.

In practice, commercial manufacture offers much more scope for parallel processing due to high levels of automation, the availability of multiple workers and the use of sub-assemblies.

Exam tip

Think about how you use parallel processing in the workshop, such as making progress with making other parts while you had components being made on a laser or CNC router. This will help to prepare you for any questions that might ask you to explain how critical path analysis (CPA) can make manufacture more efficient.

Scrum

The focus of **scrum** is the use of iterative design in a team context to reach goals in short timescale 'sprints'.

- Team goals are specified and individuals feed back progress at daily update meetings.
- Regular feedback meetings facilitate a quick response to issues that arise.

Six Sigma

Six Sigma is a system for process improvement to reduce defects to fewer than 3.4 in every million.

- The procedure monitors, assesses and improves each stage of design and manufacture.
- A key element is the training and utilisation of experts in each important area.
- Six Sigma certificates can be awarded to acknowledge and promote a company's achievements.

The five key stages of the Six Sigma approach are:

1. **Define** the issue requiring improvement (e.g. reduction of the **cycle time** for a process).
2. **Measure** the extent of the issue.
3. **Analyse** where the measured issues occur.
4. **Improve** by introducing rectification procedures.
5. **Control** the modified procedures through effective QA.

Key words

Scrum: this strategy makes use of workforce teams using iterative design methods to respond quickly to issues in product design and manufacture.

Six Sigma: this system aims to reduce manufacturing defects to the minimum possible level.

Cycle time: the time taken to complete a manufacturing process.

Now test yourself

TESTED

1 Draw a Gantt chart showing how you might organise a full day working in a workshop on a recent or current piece of practical work.
2 Make a list of the collaborators likely to work together on the design of a food processor and state briefly what their particular role would be.
3 Explain the term 'systems thinking' and discuss its potential for improving aspects of the design of a battery-powered lawnmower.
4 Draw a diagram in the style of Figure 4.7 to explain how iterative designing is used to improve an aspect of a consumer product of your choice.
5 Explain the benefits of adopting a cradle-to-cradle approach rather than a linear approach in order to achieve a 'circular economy'.

Exam practice

1 Suggest an appropriate non-digital communication method that would be used by designers for each of the following situations. Explain why it is used and draw an appropriate example:
   a Quick generation of initial ideas, along with information about possible design features.
   b Showing anticipated user interactions with a new product.
   c Giving a realistic impression of how a product design may look.
   d Communicating to a manufacturer the precise details of the position and size of a hole to be drilled in a rectangular piece of sheet aluminium.
2 Explain the advantages of using CAD software in the design of consumer products.
3 Draw a quality control flowchart to show how the accuracy of bending a piece of steel tubing to a particular angle in the workshop might be ensured.
4 Explain the term 'sketch model' and draw an annotated diagram of a sketch model of a simple design for a calculator suitable for young children, showing the materials used.
5 A car designer wishes to check the bending strength of the suspension component shown in Figure 4.11. Give the name of an appropriate digital design tool and use an annotated diagram to explain its application in this situation.

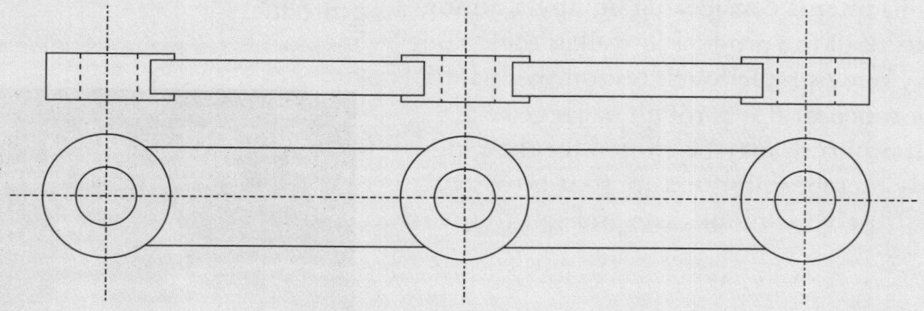

Figure 4.11 **Simplified working drawing of a suspension component with three mounting holes**

6 With reference to Figure 4.11:
   a What communication method has been used in this working drawing?
   b What additional information would be required on the drawing in order to make this part exactly as the designer intended?
   c If this part were to be made by pressure die-casting, which digital tool might be used to optimise its design for manufacture?
7 Explain, using a simple example, the purpose of critical path analysis (CPA).
8 a Explain the term 'user-centred design' (UCD).
   b How does the application of ergonomics and anthropometrics help to ensure that product designs are compliant with UCD standards?
9 Explain the importance of the cloud in facilitating digital methods of design collaboration.
10 Explain the meaning of the term 'tolerance' in relation to the quality of manufacture of two contrasting products.

ONLINE

5 Material and component considerations

5.1 Factors that influence the selection of materials

Selection of materials and components

REVISED

The success of a product is largely dependent on the correct choice of materials and components but when choosing the best material, a number of factors must be considered.

Exam tip

Ensure you are able to list the factors which affect the designer's choice of materials and components and can refer to specific examples.

Functional performance

Materials and components will be chosen by considering how the product has to function, for example a car headlight has to let light pass through so a transparent material would be chosen. **Functional performance** may also be quite specific such as a component needing to withstand a certain impact or load. The material for the component may be chosen by studying specific test data from a laboratory test.

Key words

Functional performance: how the product works or functions.

Aesthetics: aspects relating to the visual appeal of products.

Aesthetics

How a product looks is key to attracting a consumer. Materials and components will be chosen for their ability to take a shape, colour, texture and overall form. If a consumer is considering buying a dining table, they will consider the texture of the product as well as the colour and style. A consumer may carry out a simple touch test on the material to ascertain if it feels nice to the touch or if it is rough or jagged.
A hand-held product such as a toothbrush may be chosen for the range of colours to suit different family members, for texture so it is easy to grip when wet, and the overall shape which looks safe and soft to use in the mouth.

Figure 5.1 Transparent material for car headlights

Cost and availability

Material costs are an essential element of any product design and manufacture. It would not be economical to manufacture a product out of a material that costs more than the product could be sold for. The use of standard sizes of materials helps to keep costs down. Materials and components should be selected so that they are readily available and are of the correct quality for use. Components can be bought off the shelf (such as screws) which saves the manufacturer money as they do not have to manufacture components themselves (e.g. the manufacturer would not make screws if they could already buy them from a reputable source). A car manufacturer would buy LED bulbs for headlights from another supplier rather than make them themselves.

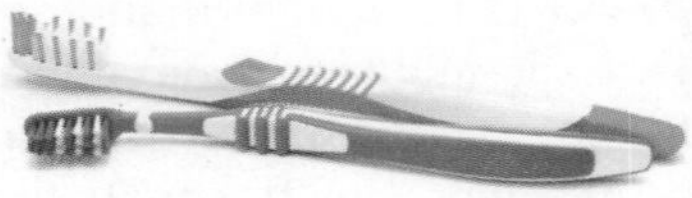

Figure 5.2 Toothbrushes

Properties and characteristics

Knowing the material properties is essential for creating successful products. Materials have:

- **Physical properties:** properties associated with the actual make-up or structure of the material such as density, magnetism, conductivity, corrosion resistance.
- **Mechanical properties:** properties associated with how the material reacts to an external force such as toughness, hardness, ductility, malleability, compressive strength. For example, a drill bit needs to be hard to resist abrasive wear when drilling holes.

Key words

Physical properties: properties associated with the actual make-up or structure of the material.

Mechanical properties: properties associated with how a product reacts to an external force.

Figure 5.3 Hard drill bit drilling into metal

Environmental considerations

The environmental impact of products is also a key factor in choosing materials and components. Designers are responsible for conserving resources and factors such the original source of the material (renewable, non-renewable or a cause of environmental scarring), the recyclability of the material as well the possible emissions during manufacture need to be considered.

The 6Rs are often used as a reminder for designers when considering material choice – rethink, reduce, reuse, repair, recycle, refuse. See Section 3.2 (page 48) for more on sustainable development.

Social, cultural and ethical factors

Designers have to think beyond the immediate product and also consider the impact the choice of material or component will have socially, culturally and ethically.

- **Social factors:** what are the working conditions for manufacturers, the impact on people's health of processing or emissions from manufacture?
- **Cultural factors**: does the product material choice and extraction impact on traditional methods or will it cause offence to a particular group of people?
- **Ethical factors:** how does the material choice impact on people's lives or the environment, such as deforestation or building roads (to access materials) that go through a community?

Typical mistake

Students often focus on only one or two factors affecting the designer's choice of materials and components. You are more likely to attain higher marks if you can discuss all the factors.

Now test yourself

TESTED

1. List the factors that influence the selection of materials for products.
2. What is 'functional performance'?
3. List three aspects of aesthetics.
4. List two environmental considerations for a designer when choosing materials and components.
5. State the two categories of material properties.

5.2 Materials used when designing and manufacturing products and prototypes

Products consist of multiple materials

REVISED

Timber

When choosing timber, the factors to consider include:

- aesthetics, such as grain pattern, colour
- physical properties, such as compression strength, hardness
- suitability for the location, such as indoor or outdoor use
- ease of machining
- commercial aspects such as cost, stock availability, consistency in quality, potential wastage in processing.

Timber is available in two classifications: **hardwoods** and **softwoods**.

Table 5.1 Properties of hardwoods and softwoods

Classification	Examples	Properties/ characteristics	Uses
Hardwoods	Oak	Hard, tough, attractive grain, good weather resistance, contains tannic acid which will corrode steel screws or fixings	Furniture, flooring, cladding, interior and exterior joinery
	Teak	Hard, tough, straight grain, natural oils resist moisture, acids and alkalis	Outdoor furniture, laboratory benches, traditional boat decks
	Beech	Hard, tough, close grained, available in steamed (white colour) and un-steamed (pink tinge)	Chairs, chopping boards, tools (e.g. mallets), kitchen ware, turned bowls
Softwoods	Pine (European Redwood)	Straight grain, knotty, can contain resinous knots	Construction work, roof beams and timber frame construction, interior joinery
	Spruce	Straight grain, resistant to splitting	Indoor furniture
	Douglas fir	Straight or slightly wavy grain, few knots, stable, good resistance to corrosion	Veneers, plywood construction, joinery and construction work

Key words

Hardwoods: timber from a broad leaf deciduous tree. Usually slow growing.

Softwoods: timber from coniferous trees. Generally, faster growing.

Typical mistake

Don't get your terminology mixed up, for example hardwoods and softwoods, and lose marks by naming an incorrect material or use. Know your materials.

Manufactured boards

Manufactured boards are categorised into two main groups:

- **laminated boards**, including plywoods
- **compressed boards**, including blockboard and MDF.

Man-made boards offer a number of useful advantages compared to natural timbers:

- They are available in large sheets – 1220 × 2440 mm.
- They are dimensionally stable – they do not shrink or expand, warp or twist as much as natural timbers.
- They have consistent properties and thickness across the whole board and between other boards.
- They can be available pre-finished using laminated plastic sheet (melamine), foil (PVC) or natural veneer surfaces.
- They have environmental benefits because they can be made from lower grade timbers and utilise the wastage associated with manufacturing natural timber.

Key words

Laminated boards: layers glued together in a well-organised structure with a synthetic resin that sets rapidly under heat and pressure.

Compressed boards: made from chips, strands or particles of timber glued together under a compressive force.

Table 5.2 Properties of manufactured boards

Examples	Properties/characteristics	Uses
Plywood	Thin layers of wood are placed and glued at 90 degrees to each other and compressed to form the board. Good strength in all directions, no grain weakness, always has an odd number of layers.	Structural work, desk tops, indoor furniture, floorboards
Flexible plywood	An odd number of layers glued together with the two outer layers made from open grained timber which allows the sheet to flex. Bent and glued around a former to achieve a solid shape.	Laminated furniture, curved panels
MDF	MDF is compressed wood fibres, although sometimes urea formaldehyde is added as an additional resin. It has two smooth faces, available in either standard grade or veneered with a layer of timber.	Model or mould-making, furniture items such as bookcases, cabinets and desks
Blockboard	Layers of strips of laminated timber which run perpendicular to the board surfaces.	Indoor furniture, shelving, table tops
Chipboard	Chips of timber compressed to form a board. Rather weak due to chipped structure, poor aesthetic value, usually veneered.	Flatpacked furniture where it is pre-finished with a surface veneer or coating, such kitchen cupboards or worktops

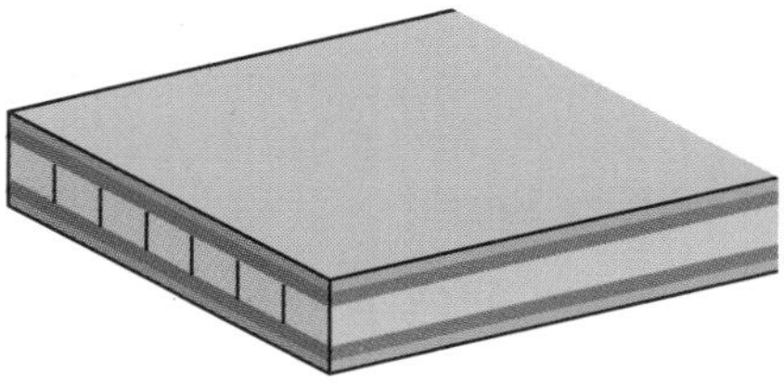

Figure 5.4 Blockboard

Figure 5.5 Chipboard with veneer

Metals

Metals have a variety of uses from construction to jewellery. There are two main classifications of metal: **ferrous** and **non-ferrous**.

Key words

Ferrous: metals that contain iron.

Non-ferrous: metals that do not contain iron.

Table 5.3 Properties of ferrous and non-ferrous metals

Classification	Examples	Properties/characteristics	Uses
Non-ferrous	Aluminium	Lightweight, ductile, malleable, corrosion resistant, electrical and thermal conductor, can be metal inert gas (MIG) and tungsten inert gas (TIG) heat welded Melting temperature 660°C	Drinks cans, aircraft bodies, bike frames, window frames, saucepans, cooking utensils, packaging, baking foil
	Copper	Ductile, malleable, tough, corrosion resistant, good electrical and thermal conductor, can be soldered and brazed Melting temperature 1,083°C	Electrical wire, printed electrical circuits, water pipes, hot water tanks, central heating pipes
Ferrous	Mild steel	Ductile, high tensile strength, tough, malleable, poor resistance to corrosion 0.15–0.30% carbon content Melting temperature 1,427°C	Nuts, bolts, washers, screws, car bodies, outer panels for white goods
	Stainless steel	Tough, hard, corrosion resistant 18% chrome, 8% nickel Melting temperature 1,510°C	Sinks, kitchenware, cutlery
	Cast iron	Hard outer skin but brittle core, good under compression 3.5% carbon Melting temperature 1,149°C	Disc brakes, machine parts, engine blocks

Metal alloys

A **metal alloy** is a material made by melting together two or more metals together with other elements. This creates a more useful material than the pure metal alone.

Table 5.4 Properties of metal alloys

Alloys	Properties/characteristics	Uses
Bronze	Tough, corrosion resistant, can be cast 90% copper, 10% tin Melting temperature 850–1000°C	Statues, coins, bearings
Brass	Corrosion resistant, good electrical and thermal conductor, low melting point, casts well 65% copper, 35% zinc Melting point of 930°C	Boat fittings, door furniture, cast valves and taps, ornaments
Tungsten	One of the toughest materials found in nature. It is very dense (about 1.7 times that of lead), resistant to corrosion, and has high tensile strength Melting point of 3422°C	High-speed cutting tools, tips for circular saw blades and masonry drill bits

Figure 5.6 Aluminium drink cans

Key word

Metal alloy: a metal made of two or more metals, or combining two or more elements, one of which must be a metal.

Figure 5.7 Bronze statue

Figure 5.8 Drill bits with tungsten carbide tips

Thermopolymers and thermosetting polymers

Thermopolymers can be re-melted back into a liquid and reused whereas **thermosetting polymers** remain in a permanent solid state once they have hardened.

Key words

Thermopolymers: deform whenever heated and can be remoulded many times. This makes them suitable for recycling.

Thermosetting polymers: once these polymers have been shaped and hardened, they cannot be reshaped or softened by heating.

Table 5.5 Properties of thermopolyers

Thermopolymer	Properties/characteristics	Uses
Low-density polyethylene (LDPE)	Very tough, good chemical resistance, weatherproof, available in translucent, low level of rigidity Safe working temperature 65°C	Squeezy detergent bottles, toys, carrier bags, bin liners, general packaging, food wrap film, food trays
High-density polyethylene (HDPE)	Available in translucent form, weatherproof, tough, good chemical resistance Safe working temperature 65°C	Chemical drums, jerry cans, toys, household and kitchenware, long-life carrier bags, buckets, bowls
Polypropylene (PP)	Available in translucent, good chemical resistance, tough, good fatigue resistance (hinge property) Safe working temperature 100°C	Rope, folders, folio cases, food containers, medical equipment
High-impact polystyrene (HIPS)	Hard, rigid, available in translucent, tough Safe working temperature 70°C	Yoghurt pots, refrigerator linings, single-use drink cups, toilet seats, instrument control knobs
Acrylonitrile butadiene styrene (ABS)	Tough, hard, available in opaque Safe working temperature 80°C	Telephone handsets, rigid luggage, domestic appliances (e.g. food mixers), handles, computer housings, remote control casings, calculator casings
Polyethylene terephthalate (PET)	Hard, translucent, good impact resistance Safe working temperature 65°C	Water bottles, fizzy drinks bottles, milk bottles, chocolate box liners
Rigid polyvinyl chloride (uPVC)	Rigid, opaque, tough, hard, good weathering resistance, good chemical resistance Safe working temperature 95°C	Window frames, external doors, guttering and downpipes for buildings, water service pipes, bank cards
Flexible polyvinyl chloride (PVC)	Available in translucent, tough, flexible, good weathering resistance, good chemical resistance Safe working temperature 95°C	Hose pipes, cable insulation, medical grade tubing, inflatable products, imitation leather, seat coverings

Figure 5.9 Polymer bank notes use polypropylene

Figure 5.10 PET bottles

Table 5.6 Properties of thermosetting polymers

Thermosetting polymer	Properties/characteristics	Uses
Urea formaldehyde (UF)	Hard, heat resistant, good electrical insulator, brittle Safe working temperature 80°C	Electrical fittings, adhesives
Polyester resin	Rigid, heat resistant, chemical resistant, brittle Safe working temperature 95°C	Castings, used in lay-up process for glass reinforced plastic (GRP) for boat hulls, car parts, chair seats
Epoxy resin	Rigid, clear, hard, tough, chemical resistant Safe working temperature 80–200°C	Adhesives, surface coatings, encapsulation of electrical components, cardiac pacemakers, aerospace applications

Natural and synthetic fibres and textile fabrics

Product designers may need to use textiles and fabrics in products, for example in cases or covers for equipment. A range of fibres with different properties are available:

- Cotton – absorbent and strong but has poor elasticity and a tendency to crease.
- Wool – a good insulator and water repellent but not very durable.
- Silk – good tensile strength, durable and light but hard to care for.
- Polyester – versatile and strong with good thermoplastic qualities.
- Nylon – strong and durable, with good elasticity and tear resistance.

Types of fabrics include:

- Woven – created by interleaving two sets of yarn. Different fabrics are created by using different types of weave.
- Non-woven – fabrics created from directly fibres which lack strength but are cheap to produce.
- Knitted fabrics – interlocking loops of yarn with good fluidity, elasticity and stretch.
- Blended textiles – textiles created from different types of fibre to combine the best properties of both.

Composite materials

A **composite** is a material comprised of two or more different materials, resulting in a material with enhanced properties.

- **Carbon fibre reinforced plastic (CFRP)** and **glass-reinforced plastic (GRP)** are two examples of composites.
- Both GRP and CFRP are made from fibres and the thermosetting polymer polyester resin. The resin is used in liquid form and sets when an activator is added.

Key words

Composite material: a material comprised of two or more different materials, resulting in a material with enhanced properties.

GRP: glass-reinforced plastic.

CFRP: carbon fibre reinforced plastic.

Table 5.7 Properties of composite materials

Name and composition	Properties	Uses
CFRP Carbon fibres mixed with polyester resin	Lightweight, corrosion resistant, tough, hard, good compressive strength, low thermal expansion	Sports equipment such as bicycle frames, tennis racquets, fishing rods, racing car bodies and parts, helmets, prosthetics
GRP Glass fibres mixed with polyester resin	Lightweight, corrosion resistant, tough, hard, low thermal expansion, good compressive strength	Boat hulls, pond liners, kayak shells, sports car bodies and parts, locomotive train cabs

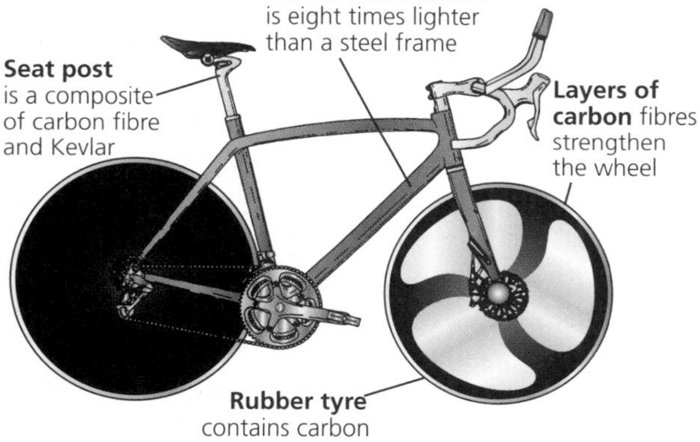

Figure 5.11 CFRP racing bicycle

Modern materials

Modern materials are developed to perform specific functions, through the invention of new or improved processes and they will continue to evolve as technology advances. They are not naturally occurring materials.

Key word

Modern materials: materials that are developed through the invention of new or improved processes.

Table 5.8 Features of modern materials

Name	Features	Uses
E-textiles (electronic textiles)	Also known as smart clothing or smart textiles. They incorporate conductive fibres directly into the textile itself to produce clothing or textile items.	Textiles with smart colour displays, heating elements, the ability to use kinetic energy to produce heat, for example in hats and gloves. Garments can monitor the wearer's heart rate, fabric keypads can control smartphones.

➜

Name	Features	Uses
Super alloys	Significantly enhanced characteristics such as mechanical strength, high temperature performance, resistance to corrosion or wear resistance.	For use in extreme applications, such as turbine blades and components in jet/rocket engines, ships and submarines. Also used in chemical processing such as energy plants and power stations, nuclear reactors and in the oil and gas industries.
Graphene	Currently the world's thinnest (one atom thick) and strongest material, consisting of carbon atoms arranged in a hexagonal lattice. Harder than diamond, extremely lightweight, 300 times stronger than steel, excellent conductor of electricity and heat, 97% transparent, excellent elasticity (extends to 120% of its original length).	Ink-based smart security tags, tennis rackets, skis, cycle helmets, low temperature li-Ion batteries, flexible and foldable phones and tablets. Still in development are products such as membranes to purify water, and biomedical products such as drug delivery in the body, sensors for early disease diagnosis, smart contact lenses.
Bioplastics	Bioplastics are made from plant-based sources, such as vegetable oil or corn starch.	Disposable items such as packaging, plates, cutlery, straws, bags, trays for fruit and vegetables, egg cartons, soft drinks bottles, milk bottles. Non-disposable items such as mobile phone casings, carpet fibres, insulation, car interiors.
Nanomaterials	Made by altering a material's properties by changing the individual atoms in the material (at the nanoscale). Results in a greater relative surface area which gives rise to altered properties such as improved strength-to-weight ratio, elasticity, conductivity, optical performance.	Aerogel for foam insulation in buildings, clothing, refrigeration. Tennis racquet cores and aeronautical applications such as aeroplane bodies.

Exam tip

Make sure you know the specific names, uses and features for modern materials.

Figure 5.12 Super alloy turbine blades

Smart materials

Smart materials react to their environment and their properties change according to different inputs. An example is thermochromic pigment used in a strip thermometer where the colour changes in response to temperature change.

The properties and uses of smart materials are discussed in detail in Section 6.3 (page 85).

Figure 5.13 Graphene structure

Key word

Smart material: material whose physical properties change in response to an input or change in the environment, such as electricity, pressure, temperature or light.

Typical mistake

Modern materials are not smart materials! Don't confuse the two.

Now test yourself

TESTED

1 List three advantages man-made boards offer over natural timber.
2 Suggest a reason why aluminium is one of the easiest and most commonly recycled metals.
3 Explain the meaning of the term 'composite material'.
4 Explain the meaning of the term 'smart material'.
5 Explain the meaning of the term 'modern material'.

5.3 Properties/characteristics of materials

The suitability of materials for use

REVISED

Understanding the properties and characteristics of a material is essential for selecting the correct material for the product. Different materials work in different ways and selecting the best material will be a compromise between factors such as aesthetics, cost, volume of manufacture and manufacture method. The final choice is mostly influenced by the product function and the material's properties.

Exam tip

You will be expected to use technical language in your answers to questions about material properties. Ensure that you know the definitions of each property.

Table 5.10 Properties/characteristics of materials

Property/characteristic	Meaning	Application or consideration
Compressive strength	The ability to withstand being crushed or shortened by pushing forces (compression).	A seat surface when people sit on it, a multi-storey car park.
Tensile strength	The ability to resist stretching or pulling forces (tension).	Ropes and cables, for example climbing ropes, cables on suspension bridges.
Stiffness	The ability to resist forces that may bend the material.	The deck of a bridge or a shelf between two supports.
Hardness	The ability to resist abrasive wear such as scratching, surface indentation or cutting.	Drill bits or scribers so they can do their job without failure.
Durability	The ability to withstand wear, damage and weathering.	So that products can last a long time such as kitchen utensils or outdoor play equipment.
Impact resistance	The ability to absorb impact force without fracture.	A drink bottle so it doesn't smash when dropped, a mallet.

→

Property/characteristic	Meaning	Application or consideration
Plasticity	The ability to be permanently deformed (shaped) and retain the deformed shape.	Similar to ductile and malleable materials. A brittle material, such as glass for windows cannot be plastically deformed.
Elasticity	The ability to be deformed and then return to the original shape when the force is removed.	Elasticated cuffs in wetsuits, stress relief balls.
Malleability	The ability to withstand deformation by compression without cracking. Malleability increases with a rise in temperature.	How well a metal may deform when heated and hammered into a shape.
Ductility	The ability to be drawn out under tension, reducing the cross-sectional area without cracking, for example stretching a material into a wire.	Stretching wires into cables for elevators, electrical wiring.
Density	The mass of the material in a standard volume of space.	Can impact on considerations for portable products.
Strength-to-weight ratio	Comparing the weight of the structure to the amount of weight it can support without failure.	Sports items such as track cycles, aerospace and motorsport products which require good strength-to-weight ratios for fuel and performance efficiency.
Flammability	How a material burns once ignited and the degree of difficulty required to cause combustion.	Soft furnishings such as sofas, cushions, kitchen worktops.
Biodegradable	The ability of a material to break down naturally and decompose by the action of microorganisms.	Single-use products such as plastic bags, packaging as well as longer-life products such as white goods and electrical items.
Electrical conductivity	Electrical conductor: allows the flow of electrical current through the material. A good conductor gives very little resistance to the flow of charge. Electrical insulator: does not allow the flow of electricity through the material.	Electrical items, circuitry, protective products such as plug casings.
Thermal conductivity	Thermal conductor: allows the transfer of heat energy through the material. A material with high thermal conductivity allows the transfer of heat to occur quickly across the material. Thermal insulator: prevents the transfer of heat through the material.	Thermal conductors for products such as cooking pans, insulating for pan handles, home insulation.
Corrosion/degradation resistance	The ability of the material to withstand environmental attack and decay.	Outdoor structures such as marine products, outdoor furniture or street furniture.

Making decisions about the suitability of materials

REVISED

The final design and choices about materials depend on the product function as well as the material's properties, costs and available form. Using standard sizes and stock forms of materials as well as standard (potentially pre-made) components will help to reduce costs and potentially decrease manufacture time.

When selecting materials, designers must consider:

- **Product function and end user needs and wants:** for example, does the product need to be outdoors, have electrical conductivity, have high-quality aesthetics, durability? What is the budget set by the end user or client?
- **Material availability and form:** such as standard sizes of tubing, thicknesses of timber stock form, polymers in powder, liquid, sheet or resin. Standard pre-made components and their sizes should be investigated and used as well.
- **Method of manufacture:** this will depend on production volume as well as the manufacturing methods available for use with the chosen material. What method will be most economical in terms of time, cost, material waste and speed of production?

Typical mistake

Don't just refer to 'strength' in an answer; identify specific types of strength such as compressive or tensile strength and give examples of how this may influence a material choice.

Now test yourself

TESTED

1 Explain why a workshop drill bit needs to be made from a hard material.
2 Explain the meaning of the term 'density'.
3 What type of thermal property is required for the handle of a cooking pan?
4 Give one reason why a Formula 1 racing car needs good strength-to-weight ratio?
5 Name a product which requires good tensile strength.

Exam practice

1 Give **one** example of a tough material and describe a product where its toughness is desirable.
2 Explain why a manufacturer may select a manufactured board rather than natural timber for product manufacture.
3 Give **two** reasons why PET is suitable for a single-use water bottle.
4 Social, cultural and environmental factors must be considered by designers. Explain the meaning of the terms 'social', 'cultural' and 'environmental'.
5 Explain the meaning of the term 'smart material'.
6 Give an example of a product which uses smart materials and discuss the advantages the use of this smart material brings to the product.
7 State the meaning of the term 'strength-to-weight ratio'.
8 Give an example of a product which requires a good strength-to-weight ratio and explain why this property is required.
9 Explain the difference between physical and mechanical material properties.
10 State **two** advantages the modern material super alloys give to a specific product of your choice.

ONLINE

6 Technical understanding

6.1 Structural integrity

Reinforcing or stiffening to fulfil the structural integrity of a product

REVISED

When designing products, the designer must not only consider the intended function, but also other forces or **stresses** the product may be subjected to during use.

For example, a standard dining chair may have four legs and may be designed for the user to sit using all four legs for stability. However, the user may decide to swing back on two legs of the chair and although this is not the intended use, the designer must consider how the chair will withstand this without product failure.

Well-designed products make efficient and appropriate use of materials to fulfil the function and provide **structural integrity**. Structural integrity can be achieved by:

- Analysing the product to ascertain weak sections or points.
- **Reinforcing** parts of the product, for example polymer remote control casings are usually designed with extra material at the corners so the polymer does not thin and become likely to fail if the remote control is dropped.
- Including **sacrificial parts** which are designed to fail in order to protect a larger section of function of the product. For example, in an electrical product, the fuse is designed to fail in order to protect the rest of the product.

Key words

Stresses: a range of factors that may cause a material, or product to fail.

Structural integrity: the ability of a product or system to hold together when under load.

Reinforcing: adding to, or altering the form of, a material or component to strengthen it or reduce its chances of wear.

Sacrificial parts: weaker parts of a product designed to fail first in order to protect more significant parts.

Processes used to ensure the structural integrity of a product

REVISED

Example of processes used to ensure structural integrity include:

- **Triangulation:** rectangular frames are often used in products such as tables but a rectangle is naturally unstable. If the table frame was loaded at one corner it could easily deform. One way to avoid this is to use triangulation to provide stability. This can be added as a cross-member or by smaller triangular sections at the corners of the frame, thus distributing the load and providing a stable structure.
- **Material reinforcement:** this can be done either through the addition of material at weak points in a mould or as an external addition which can also ensure structural integrity, for example adding corner protectors.
- **Material stiffening:** adding folds, ribs or webs to a product during the manufacturing process can increase its rigidity.

Key words

Triangulation: adding cross-members to increase the rigidity of a framework.

Stiffening: reducing flexibility in materials or structures.

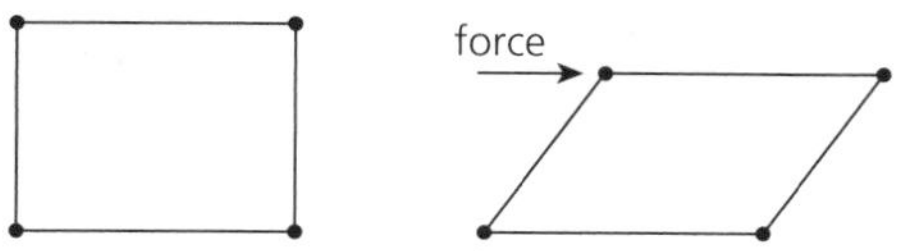

Figure 6.1 A rectangular frame is naturally unstable

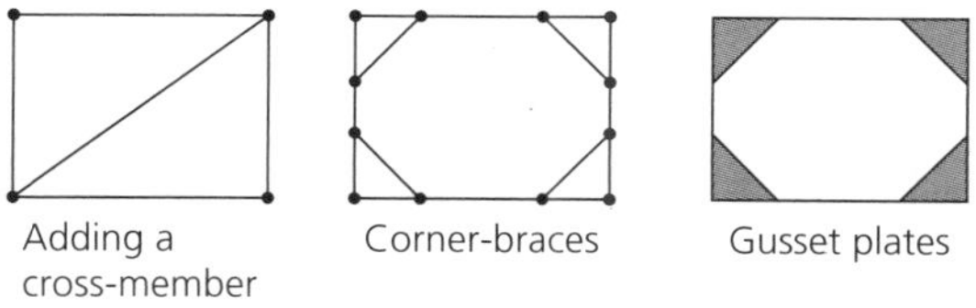

Figure 6.2 Methods of triangulating a framework to increase its rigidity

Figure 6.3 Corner protector screwed on to a speaker case

Figure 6.4 Ribs moulded in to the base of a monitor to increase rigidity

Exam tip

Make sure you are able to describe, using notes and sketches, how structural integrity is achieved in the design of a product.

Now test yourself

TESTED

1. What does 'structural integrity' mean?
2. Describe how a rectangular frame could be made to withstand stresses.
3. What is a 'sacrificial part'?
4. What are the range of factors that may cause a material, or product to fail called?
5. Give an example of a sacrificial part used in a standard three-pin plug to protect a television in the event of a power surge.

Typical mistake

Don't just state that adding material thickness will provide structural integrity. Considering other methods such as support at weak areas only, or triangulation, will earn more marks.

6.2 Designing products to function effectively within their surroundings

Surface finishes and coatings to enhance the appearance of products

REVISED

Surface finishes are used because they:

- prevent the material from absorbing moisture
- protect against decay, corrosion or wear
- ease maintenance through dusting or washing
- enhance the appearance of the final product.

Finishing timber

Timbers are sanded using glasspaper or wire wool to create a smooth surface before a finish is applied. A smooth, dust-free surface creates the perfect base for a finish to be applied.

Table 6.1 Methods of wood finishing

Wood finish	Method of application	How they enhance appearance or prevent decay
Polyurethane varnish Acrylic varnish	Available in gloss, satin and matt, clear or colours. Apply a thin coat with a brush in the direction of the grain. Several thin coats can be applied, rubbing down between coats with fine-grade glasspaper.	● Provides a hard, tough, heatproof, waterproof finish. ● Clear finish allows the grain of the wood to be seen through the finish.
Water-based paints	Available in gloss, satin, matt and metallic effects. Applied with a brush, roller or spray. Wood knots should be treated with knotting solution to prevent the resin oozing out and spoiling the finish. The surface should then be primed and an undercoat applied before the paint finish.	● Paint provides both protection and colour. It can be applied for both indoor and outdoor use, and is predominantly used for softwoods. ● Paint makes surfaces more aesthetically pleasing, tougher, harder and resistant to moisture.
Wax	Available in clear and coloured waxes for indoor products. Applied with a brush or a stockinet cloth then, once, dry buff with a clean lint-free cloth.	● Can be buffed to provide a high-gloss finish. ● Increases the surface hardness and toughness. ● Clear finish allows the grain of the wood to be seen through the finish.
Danish oil	Available in clear and colour tints. Apply with a lint-free cloth, rub the oil into the surface of the wood in the direction of the grain. Leave the wood to absorb the oil for 5 minutes then rub away the excess oil with a clean cloth. Lightly sand or rub with wire wool to open up the grain between coats.	● Maintains the natural appearance of the timber, soaks into the wood and enhances the grain. ● Not a very hardwearing finish but regular application and subsequent coats build up a matt, water-resistant finish.
Teak oil	Available in clear tint. Apply with a lint-free cloth, rub the oil into the surface of the wood in the direction of the grain. Leave the wood to absorb the oil for 5 minutes then rub away the excess oil with a clean cloth. Used for naturally oily woods.	● Primarily used for outdoor wood products to improve weather resistance and resistance to fungal and insect attack. ● Aesthetically pleasing as grain is enhanced.
Preservatives (pressure treating)	Wood is placed in a pressure vessel containing a solution consisting of copper sulphate and other preserving salts. Vacuum and pressure are controlled to force the preservative deep into the fibres of the wood and then the wood is steam dried.	● Helps protect wood for up to 50 years from rot, insect and fungal attack and weathering. ● Suitable for products such as decking, overhead cable poles, harbour or bridge construction.

Finishing metals

Metal surfaces need to be degreased and cleaned before painting or applying a coating.

- Most metals (except steels) have an oxide layer which provides some barrier against environmental effects.

- Some non-ferrous metals and alloys look aesthetically pleasing, for example aluminium is a bright silvery colour, and as such requires no finish to enhance its aesthetics.
- Steels (but not stainless steel) have an oxide layer which is porous, allowing moisture to penetrate the metal, leading to rust.

Key words

Electroplating: involves the coating of an object with a thin layer of metal by using electricity.

Galvanising: a process in which steel is coated with zinc.

Table 6.2 Methods of metal finishing

Metal finish	Method of application	Purpose
Cellulose and acrylic paints	Paints are primarily used on low-cost metals such as steel. The surface of the metal is cleaned and degreased, which ensures that the primer coat has a sound surface to 'key' (or grip) to. Paints can be applied by brush or spray.	• Provide colour and a textured finish. • Provide a barrier against corrosion. • Specialist paints provide texture or special graphic effects such as pearlescence.
Electroplating and **galvanising**	Metals for electroplating include silver, gold, zinc, copper and tin. The product and donor material are placed in a container with an electrolyte solution. As the direct current is applied, the product attracts the donor metal and the product is electroplated. Electroplating with zinc is specifically called galvanising.	• Provides a protective layer, a more hardwearing finish and enhanced aesthetics.
Polymer dip coating	The metal product is heated to approximately 230°C. The hot product is then dipped into a tank of fine polymer powder, which has air blowing through it (fluidisation bath) to provide an even coating on the product. The retained heat from the product melts the polymer powder over the product, which is then air cooled to allow the coating to set evenly.	• Used on products such as wire coat hangers, kitchen dish drainers, coat hooks, dishwasher racks and outdoor play equipment frames. • Provides colour and a protective barrier against corrosion.
Metal dip coating	Metals are coated by dipping the product into a tank of molten plating metal (the donor metal). The metals must be clean and degreased. Tin plating: pass sheets of steel through a tank of molten tin at approximately 320°C. Zinc plating (galvanising): dipping steel into molten zinc at approximately 460°C.	• Provides a barrier against corrosion. • Tin plating: often used to provide a non-corrosive coating to food cans. • Zinc plating: used for many industrial and agricultural applications such as beams, gates and animal pens. Also as the first protective layer in car bodies made from low-carbon steel.
Powder coating	The product to be coated is statically charged (negative). Thermoset polymer resin (positively charged) is then sprayed through an airgun. The use of charge results in a strong attraction between the powder and the product. The product is then baked in an oven; the heat melts the powder over the product to give an even coating.	• Protection from corrosion and aesthetic appeal, more hardwearing than paint. • Used on washing machine bodies, dishwasher bodies and refrigerator bodies, metal gates, fencing and railings.

→

Metal finish	Method of application	Purpose
Sealants	The sealant is applied with a cloth or machine pad to produce a film that is then allowed to cure for up to 15 minutes. It is then buffed with a cloth to a shine.	● Tough polymer-based sealant coatings to protect polished surfaces from decay and tarnishing. Often used in the automotive industry against the effects of weathering, road salts and insect attack.
Anodising	The electric current passes through the sulphuric acid electrolyte solution from the part to be treated to a negative cathode. As the current flows from the part to be treated (positive anode) to the negative cathode, the aluminium oxide layer builds up on the treated part, producing the anodised finish. Anodised products can then be finished with a clear lacquer or varnish to seal the finish and provide further protection against surface scratches.	● Commonly used for aluminium products to enhance the natural oxide layer, resulting in increased hardness and toughness. ● Can also provide colour. ● Used in the outer casings of torches, external hard drive covers and casings for mobile phones or digital music players.

Key word

Anodising: coating (usually aluminium) with a protective oxidised layer by electrolysis.

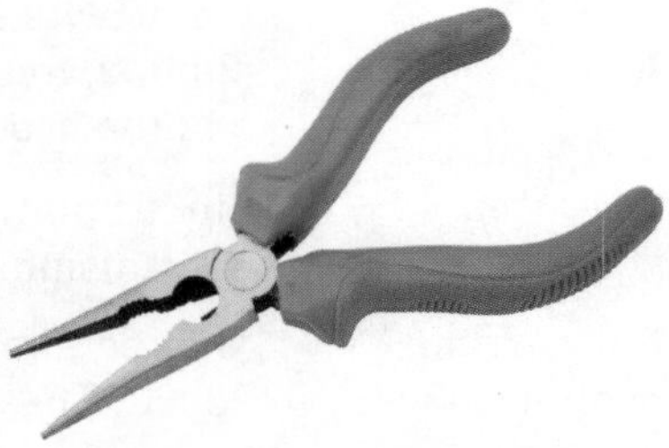

Figure 6.5 Pliers with plastic-coated handles

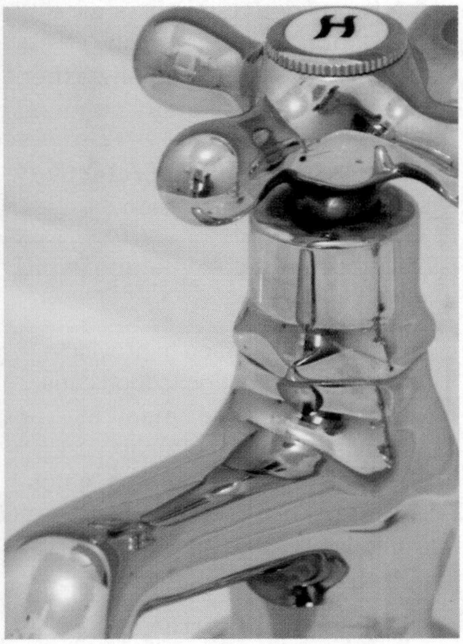

Figure 6.6 Chrome-plated bathroom tap

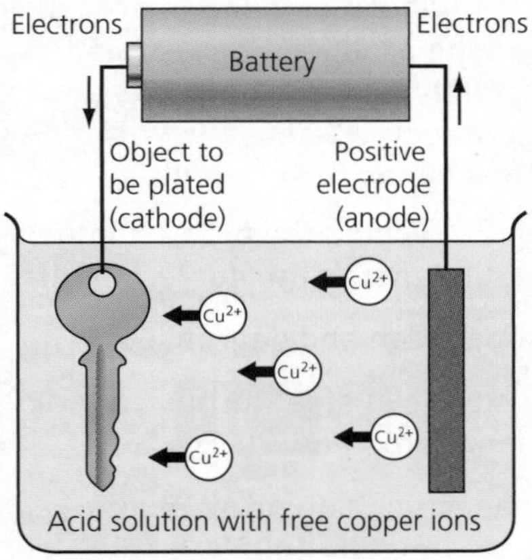

Figure 6.7 Positively charged copper ions are free in the solution, but are being attracted by the negatively charged key metal plate

Exam tip

Make sure you know the specific names of finishes, the method of application, and what products the finish is used on and why.

Now test yourself

TESTED

1. Name two types of paint for metals.
2. What metal is used in galvanising?
3. Name the coating suitable for dishwasher bodies.
4. List two reasons why a finish is used on a metal product.
5. Name the metal which is suitable for an anodised finish.

Typical mistake

Don't refer to paint as 'paint'; be specific with the type of paint, for example acrylic paint.

6.3 Smart and modern technologies

Smart materials

REVISED

The use of smart materials has led to many advances in the design and function of products which have also helped improve user experiences.

Table 6.3 Classification of smart materials

Feature	Name	How does it work?	Product use
Colour changing	Thermochromic pigment	Changes colour in response to temperature change. Thermochromic pigment can be integrated into a number of materials such as paint, polymers and textiles. The colour change can provide an indication of 'too hot', 'too cold' or 'temperature OK'.	Room thermometers, medical thermometers for children, bath water thermometers, colour change mugs and kettles, food packaging to indicate food is hot to eat or cool for drinks, baby feeding spoons, battery charge indicator strips
	Photochromic pigment	Changes colour with light intensity. Photochromic pigment can be integrated into a number of materials such as paint, polymers and textiles.	Welding goggles, reactive spectacle lenses, security markers that show up under UV light
	Electrochromic material	Changes colour when a voltage is applied.	Liquid crystal displays (LCD), smart goggles and motorcycle helmets, self-darkening rear-view mirrors in cars, window glass with different tint settings for privacy screens
Shape shifting	Shape memory alloys (SMAs), e.g. nitinol	Changes shape in response to a change in temperature or electrical input, for example nitinol wire in dental braces changes length in response to a change in temperature. Some SMAs have two programmed temperatures, high and low, which can be used for applications such as automatic greenhouse windows.	Dental braces, self-closing windows, aeroplane wing flaps, shape-shifting aircraft wings that mimic bird flight, bioengineering such as stents, bone plates and screws
	Shape memory polymers (SMPs), e.g. polymorph, coolmorph	Changes shape in response to a change in temperature, light, stress or magnetism. Have improved elasticity, low density and high chemical resistance.	Moulds, furniture or toys that can be re-shaped, specialised adjustable containers, packaging and sensors
Motion control	Motion control gels	Uses the **viscosity** of the liquid to control the speed of the object passing through it. Some liquids increase viscosity when the liquid is stressed. The faster the object moves through the liquid, the more viscous the material becomes, hence controlling the speed.	Soft-closing drawers, doors and toilet seats, adjustable suspension in vehicles, earthquake-dampening systems, motion control gels in bearing systems

➜

Feature	Name	How does it work?	Product use
Self-cleaning	**Hydrophobic** materials	Highly water repellent so dirt cannot stick to them. When water moves across the surface, it takes all the dirt particles along with it.	Self-cleaning windows, stain protector products for textiles, wall paint
	Oleophobic	Highly oil resistant, which helps in the removal of fingerprints on surfaces.	Mobile phone screens, tablet screens, ATM screens
Self-healing	Self-healing polymers	Damage is healed by the material, for example some polymers re-form molecules at edges if there is a cut or puncture.	Graphics cutting mats, chopping boards
	Self-healing concrete	Limestone-producing bacteria capsules are included in the concrete mix. Water from a crack releases the bacteria and heals the crack.	Concrete paving, carpark decks, building structures, outdoor seating

Key words

Shape-shifting materials: materials that change their shape in response to a physical stimulus such as an electric voltage or current, a change in temperature or the presence of a magnetic field.

Viscosity: (of a liquid) a measure of its resistance to an object moving through it.

Hydrophobic: highly water repellent.

Oleophobic: highly oil resistant.

Typical mistake

Don't refer to smart materials in generic terms, such as 'colour changing material'. Give specific examples such as thermochromic or photochromic pigment.

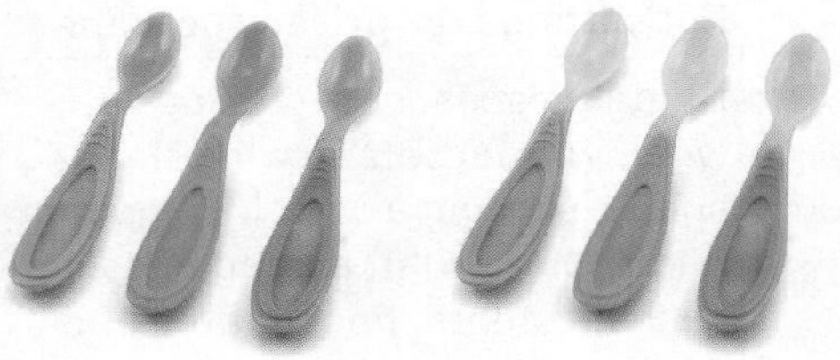

Figure 6.8 Colour-changing baby feeding spoons

Figure 6.9 Car rear-view mirror automatically darkens in the presence of dazzling headlights

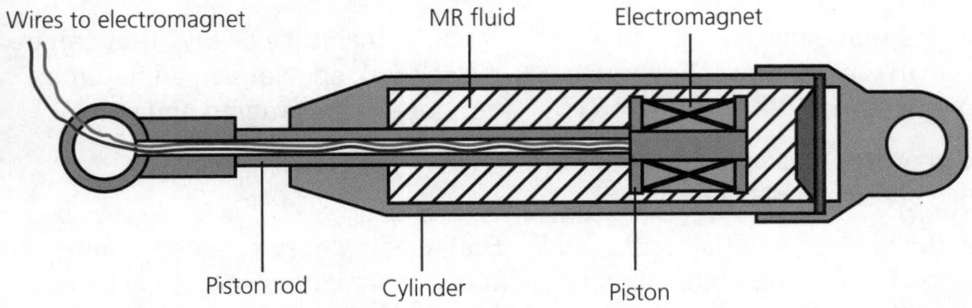

Figure 6.10 MR fluid damper – when the electromagnet is switched on, the viscosity of the magnetorheological (MR) fluid increases, making it 'thicker' which provides a greater resistance to the piston as it moves in the cylinder. Therefore, the damper can be made harder or softer under electronic control

Exam tip

Make sure you are able to give specific examples of colour changing, shape shifting and self-healing materials, and know how they work and the products they are used in.

Modern technologies

REVISED

Programmable devices such as **microcontrollers** can be embedded into a product to improve or enhance product functionality.

A car uses many microcontrollers to talk to sensors (such as parking distance sensors) and then display that information to the driver in the form of a visual display and/or noise. Microcontrollers also allow the development of features such as automatic braking systems when a hazard appears in the path of the vehicle. The microcontroller is programmed and coded to 'react', thus improving product function and user experience.

Microcontrollers are used in many products from GPS and satellite navigation systems, to mobile phones which can be used to track the speed and distance a person moves in a day. They are also used in many wearable technologies such as smart watches or jewellery which track activity and health markers (such as heart rate).

Key word

Microcontroller: an electronic device that can be programmed to carry out specific tasks.

Now test yourself

TESTED

1 What smart material is incorporated into reactive welding goggles?
2 Give a specific application for an electrochromic material.
3 What is meant by the term 'shape-shifting material'?
4 If a material is hydrophobic, what does this mean?
5 Name a product which uses the viscosity of liquid to improve product function.

Exam practice

1 Using a specific product example, explain where and why sacrificial parts have been used in the product's manufacture.
2 State **three** reasons why a surface finish is used on a material.
3 With reference to a specific product, explain why anodising is an appropriate finish.
4 Explain the meaning of the term 'hydrophobic'.
5 Give an example of a product which uses a hydrophobic material.
6 Give **two** examples of smart materials and identify a practical application for each one.
7 With reference to a specific example of a product, explain how the use of programmable technology has enhanced its operation.
8 Explain how the properties of self-healing concrete benefit the wear resistance of an outdoor bench made of concrete.
9 Explain how triangulation can help with structural integrity.
10 Give a specific example of a product which uses a shape-shifting material.

ONLINE

7 Manufacturing processes and techniques

7.1 Using materials and processes to make iterative models

3D iterative models

REVISED

Models augment drawings as an on-going method of communicating, visualising and testing ideas to optimise product designs and facilitate better understanding for all stakeholders.

Modelling

Models can be made from a range of materials and components to create block models and working **prototypes** to communicate and test ideas, moving parts and structural integrity. Modelling:

- avoids potentially expensive production problems occuring later in production
- saves time
- reduces the potential for mistakes.

Key word

Prototype: a functioning or non-functioning pre-production design evaluation model.

Various scales of models can be used, depending on the nature of the product. Several iterations are often required, which may dictate the modelling method to be used.

Initial quick 2D and 3D sketch models are useful in the early stages of designing:

- There is no need to consider finish at this stage.
- They facilitate checks on function and proportion.
- They provide an early visualisation of ideas.
- They are understandable to clients.

Later in the process, more detailed models may be required for:

- an exploration of aesthetics
- the development of technical elements
- a consideration of moulded, cast and vacuum formed parts.

Types of models

Block models:

- are shaped blocks without working/moving parts
- show the appearance of the design
- are realistic, with a high standard of finish used.

Working models:

- are used to test mechanisms, components, circuits
- range from simple models to highly complex and sophisticated ones
- go through iterations, and elements used in later iterations will be incorporated into the final product.

Modelling materials and related processes

Two categories of processes are used:

- **Additive** (e.g. 3D printing or assembling pieces of card)
- **Subtractive** (e.g. machining or carving).

Manual methods of modelling can involve assembling a number of pieces/parts to form the final product and applying an appropriate finish, which can be time consuming. However, models made of simple materials are often quick and effective, for example James Dyson's early card models of design iterations for the DC01 vacuum cleaner.

The model-making process can be made simpler using CAD/CAM programs:

- Parts are relatively easy to produce from highly accurate design files.
- The files can be sent to 3D printers to make models or prototypes.

See page 90 for more on digital methods of modelling such as 3D printing.

Key words

Additive manufacture: involves joining or building up material such as the creation of models in a FDM 3D printer.

Subtractive manufacture: methods, such as machining or carving, which involve material removal.

Table 7.1 Examples of basic modelling methods and materials

Modelling methods and tools	Materials	Points to note
Cutting with hand tools such as a craft knife, scalpel, junior hacksaw Use of adhesives, including glue-gun and solvent cement	• Foam board • Cardboard (several types) • Corriflute board • Balsa • Styrofoam • High impact polystyrene (HIPS)	• Quick and easy 'sketch' modelling • Sophisticated equipment unnecessary • Clips/fasteners can be used • Some thin sheet materials can also be bent easily around formers
Hand-forming pliable materials Use of simple moulds	• Clay • Plasticine • Polymorph • Hard wax	• Clay is often used to model car forms • Polymorph can be machined, facilitates re-forming by heating, is strong enough for mechanical parts
Testing circuits with breadboards or electronics kits	• Components • Copper wire • Clip-together kit elements	• Components and kit elements fit together without soldering, allowing for quick testing of circuit designs
Wire cutting, bending and joining (using adhesive tape, epoxy resin or soldering) to create frameworks of varying complexity	• Metal wire	• Copper and brass wire solder easily • Aluminium wire is easy to manipulate
Thermoforming, including vacuum forming and dome blowing	• Sheet polymers such as HIPS and acrylic	• Facilitates more complex 3D forms, but a suitable former is required
Computer numerical control (CNC) laser cutting and engraving	• Card • Plywood • Polymer sheet (not PVC)	• Very effective for flat panel sections with complex profiles, as well as mechanism linkages
Textiles and equipment, including fabric, sewing machine, scissors	• Calico • Rip-stop nylon	• Used for modelling upholstery and other fabric elements of designs

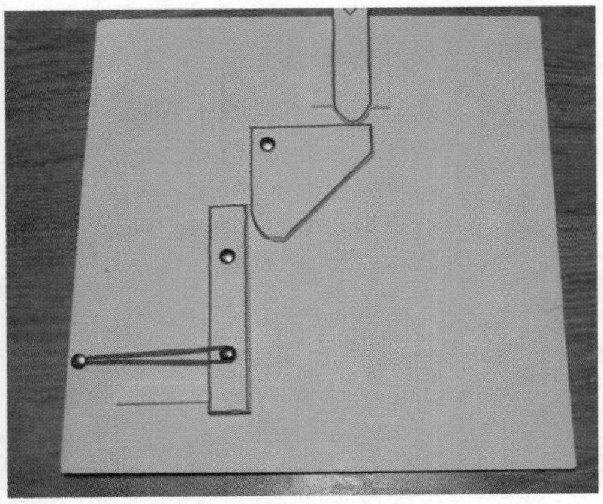

Figure 7.1 A simple linkage mechanism modelled in card

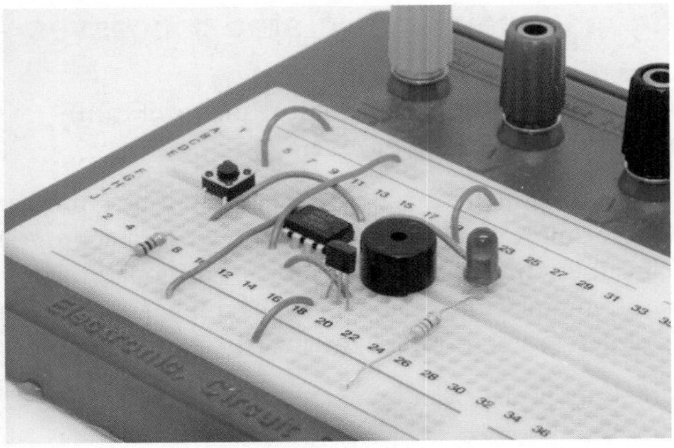

Figure 7.2 Using a breadboard to model an electronic circuit

Modelling ideas using digital methods

REVISED

Rapid prototyping

Realistic 3D models can be made using **rapid prototyping** technologies such as 3D printing. 3D printing is an additive manufacturing process which builds parts layer by layer. The advantages are:

- Innovative, complex designs can be produced quickly, speeding up production times.
- Iterative design is facilitated due to low cost of producing numerous models in 3D CAD packages and linked 3D printers.
- Parts can be printed in various colours and textures, although some parts may require hand-finishing.

Key word

Rapid prototyping: the use of machines such as 3D printers to produce realistic 3D models from CAD files.

Rapid prototyping technologies include:

- Fused deposition modelling (FDM) which builds up layers of polymer such as ABS to create parts.
- The use of 3D body scanning data for creating of footwear and specialist clothing prototypes.
- Stereolithography (SLA) which uses a UV laser to solidify layers of photopolymer (light sensitive resin) and is useful for applications such as pottery modelling.
- Multi-jet modelling (MJM) which facilitates a very high-quality finish.
- Selective laser sintering (SLS) which uses a laser to fuse powdered materials into solid models.

CNC routers and milling machines are more likely to be used for relatively simple model parts, but they don't generally have the capabilities of 3D printers for manufacturing complex models.

Figure 7.3 FDM 3D printing machine in action

Digital simulation

Digital simulation offers many advantages over conventional modelling techniques, including:

- Time and cost savings due to the use of existing CAD models rather than making physical models.
- Virtual reality makes it possible for stakeholders to assess real design proposals at an earlier stage.
- 360° viewing capability reduces the likelihood of errors.
- Rapid modifications and reappraisal can take place within an iterative design process.

See Section 4.2 (page 61) for details of digital product simulation and scientific analysis.

Exam tip

When asked to explain the use of models in the iterative design process, try to include a diverse range of techniques, such as basic sketch models using compliant materials, circuit breadboarding, 3D printing and digital simulation.

Typical mistake

Don't confuse the terms 'rapid prototype' and 'quick prototype'. The term 'rapid prototype' has become synonymous with models made using computer-based technology such as 3D printers, but 'quick prototype' is more likely to refer to 'sketch modelling' with foam, card, wire and other similar materials.

Now test yourself

TESTED

1 What is the difference between additive and subtractive manufacture?
2 Explain the importance of modelling in the iterative design process.
3 Name and give reasons for using a suitable computer-controlled machine for making 2D model parts in card.
4 How does a FDM 3D printer create models?
5 Name three advantages of modelling by digital simulation.

7.2 Using materials and processes to make final prototypes

Joining methods

REVISED

When manufacturing a final prototype, the choice of tooling will be less than in industry but in order to create a functioning prototype, knowledge of tooling and processes is essential. Selecting the most appropriate tool for the material and knowing how to join materials for the proposed design is key to success.

Joining timber

A variety of traditional timber joints are shown in Figures 7.4–7.7.

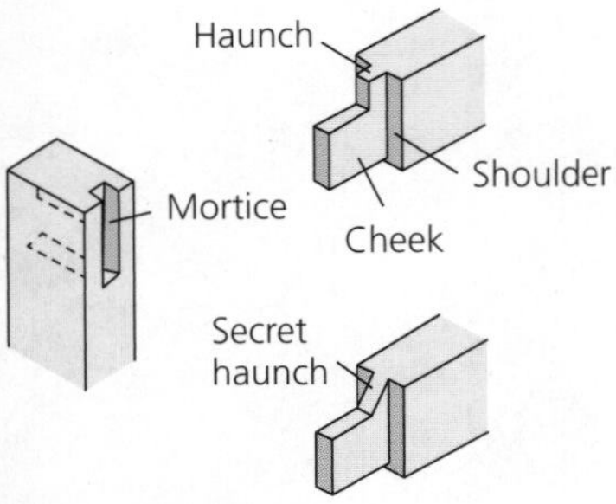

Mortice and tenon joint

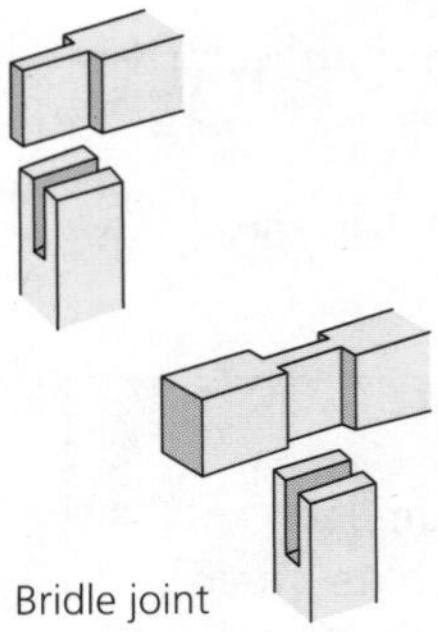

Bridle joint

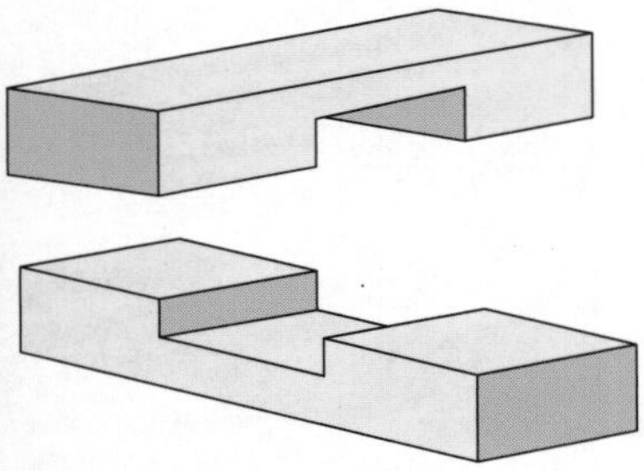

Halving joint

Figure 7.4 Timber joints

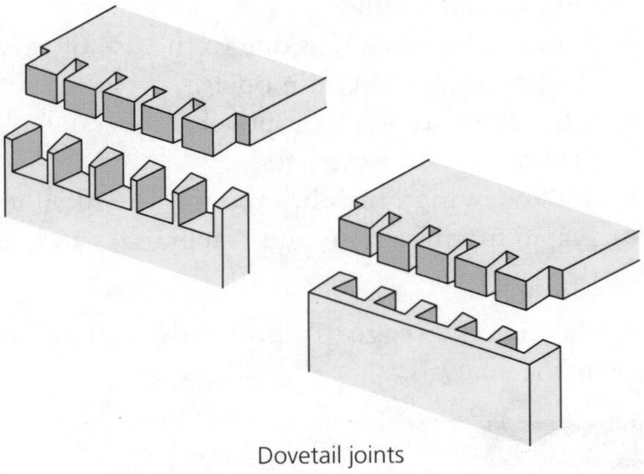

Dovetail joints

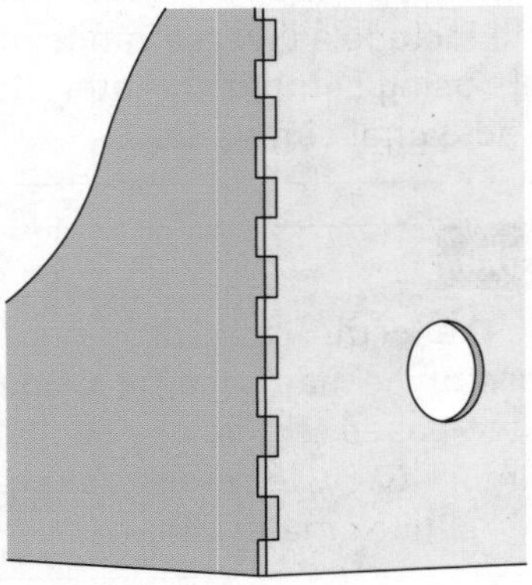

Finger/comb joint

Figure 7.5 Dovetail joint and finger joint

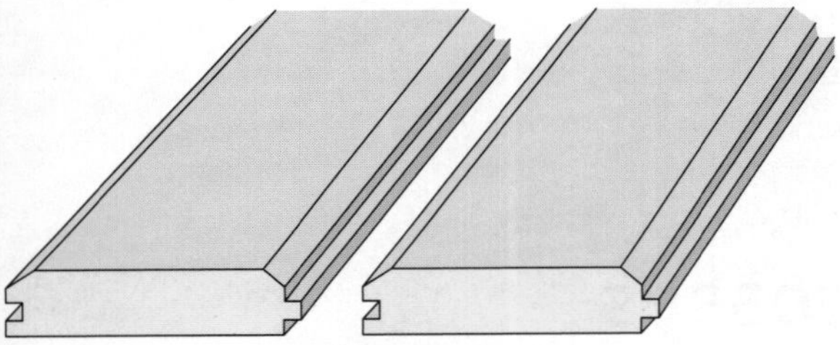

Tongue and groove

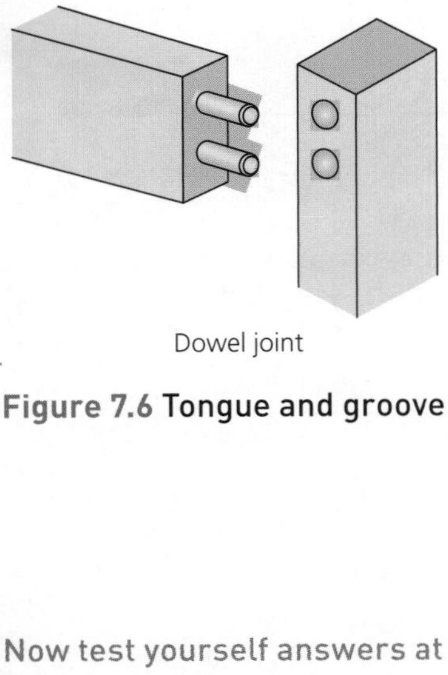

Dowel joint

Figure 7.6 Tongue and groove joint and dowel joint

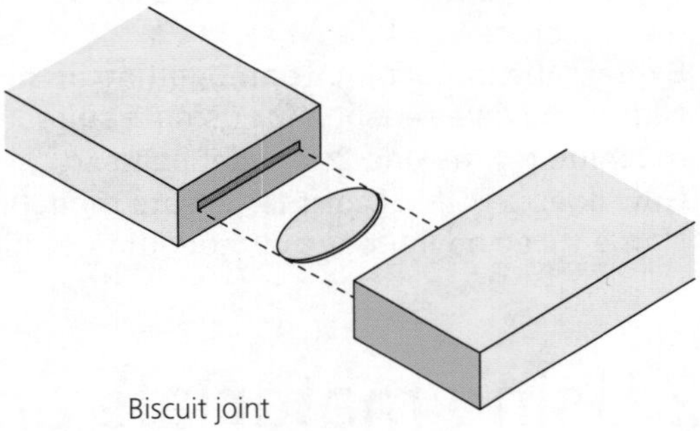

Biscuit joint

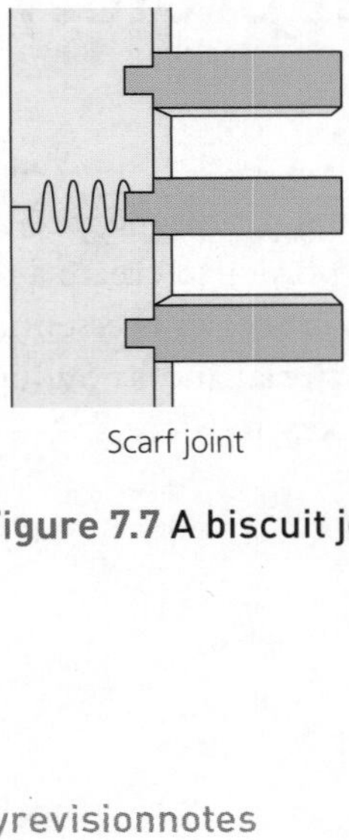

Scarf joint

Figure 7.7 A biscuit joint and a scarf joint

Joining metal

Methods of joining metal include:

- **Riveting:** usually associated with joining flat sheet metal together. Two pieces of metal are overlapped and drilled, a rivet passes through the holes and the end of the rivet shaft is then hammered over to join the sheets. Pop riveting is used where the underside of the join is inaccessible.
- **Soldering:** joins two or more metal components together by melting and flowing a metal filler material into the joint. Commonly used for soldering electrical connections and printed circuit boards.
- **Brazing:** involves a higher temperature than soldering. Uses a brass filler rod and is carried out using either oxy-acetylene or a gas and compressed air brazing hearth, to join dissimilar metals such as mild steel sheet to aluminium and copper.
- **Welding:** involves joining metals (and polymers by using ultrasonic welding) via heat. Types of welding include:
  - Friction welding where a rapidly rotating component is pressed against a stationary component.
  - Gas welding which uses a mixture of oxygen and acetylene.
  - Electricity is used in arc-welding (MMA), metal-inert gas (MIG) and tungsten-inert-gas (TIG) welding and spot welding.
  - Ultrasonic energy (sound waves) is used in the welding of polymers.

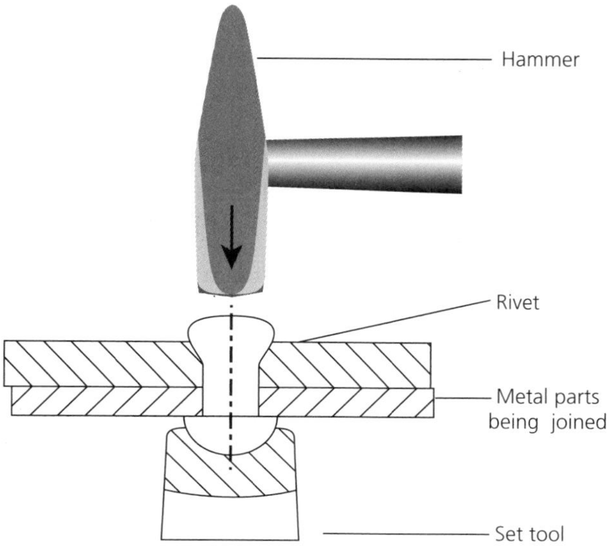

Figure 7.8 Stages in riveting

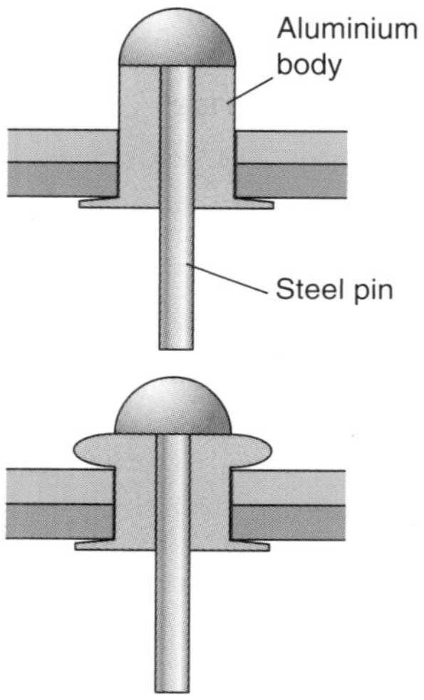

Figure 7.9 Stages in pop riveting

Temporary joining methods

Temporary fasteners are used where a permanent joining method is not required, or in situations where either a product needs to be able to be disassembled or repaired.

There are generally three types of fasteners used for metals. Some can also be used for polymers and timbers:

- **Self-tapping screws:** used for joining thin sheet metal and can also be used on polymers. A pilot hole is drilled and as the screw is screwed in, it cuts its own thread, to hold the metal in place.
- **Machine screws:** a type of bolt where the thread is on the entire length of the shaft. They are used to join thicker pieces of metal. The top part to be joined will have a clearance hole; the bolt goes through and is screwed into a threaded hole in the bottom part. Machine screws are often tightened with a spanner or allen key.
- **Nuts and bolts:** bolts are similar to machine screws, but instead of being inserted into a threaded hole, they go all the way through both pieces of metal and a nut is tightened on to the end of the bolt to keep the pieces together. The same principle can be used to join sections of timber together or differing materials such as polymer sheet to metal sections.

Adhesives

Different types of adhesives are used to stick different materials together.

Polyvinyl acetate (PVA):

- Used to bond most woods and wood-based materials together.
- Can be used to bond wood joints together for furniture and other wooden products.

Contact adhesive:

- Used for bonding large areas such as sheet material of the same or different materials.
- The two surfaces areas to be joined are coated in contact adhesive and left for approximately 10 minutes, or until the adhesive feels 'tacky'. On contact with the other surface, adhesion is instant.

Solvent cement:

- The most common is a clear liquid called dichloromethane which is used to join polymers such as acrylic, ABS and PVC.
- It softens the surface of the polymers to be joined, allowing them to fuse together.

Epoxy resin:

- Comes in two parts, resin and hardener, and is used to join different materials together, for example timber to metal, metal to polymer, polymer to timber.
- Equal amounts of resin and hardener are mixed to form the adhesive which then takes a time to fully set.

Due to the rise in the popularity of flat-pack furniture, a range of mechanical joining systems have been made which allow the user to assemble furniture without the need for highly skilled labour or tooling. These joining systems are called **knock-down (KD) fittings** and allow products to be assembled and disassembled many times, without weakening the joint.

Key word

Knock-down (KD) fittings: allow products to be assembled and disassembled many times, without weakening the joint.

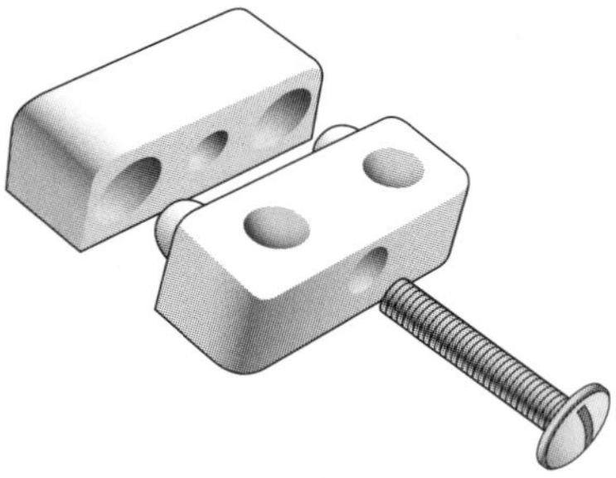

Corner blocks

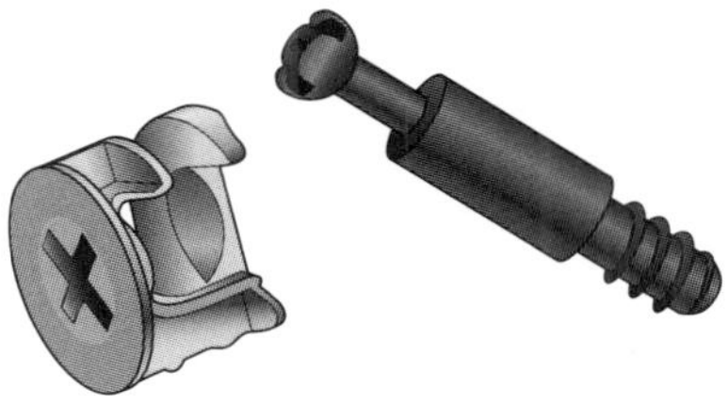

CAM lock fittings

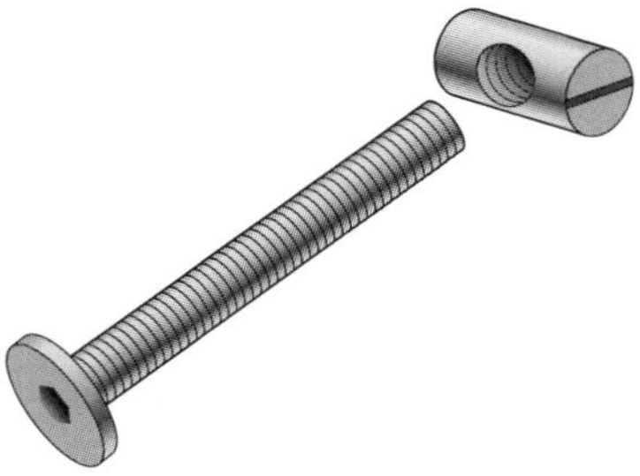

Barrel and screw

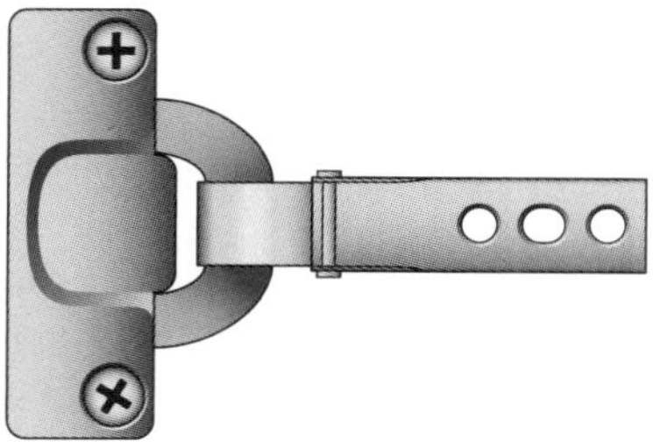

Cabinet hinges

Figure 7.10 Commonly used KD fittings

Processes, tools and machinery

REVISED

Wasting techniques

Wasting is a subtraction process whereby material is cut away or removed to leave the desired shape.

Table 7.2 Wasting techniques

Wasting process	Material	Tool or machinery
Drilling	Timber, metal, polymer	• Hand-held electric drill • Pillar drill
Sawing	Timber	• Back saws – tenon saw, dovetail saw • Frame saws – coping saw, piercing saw • Hand saws – cross cut, pane, rip • Bandsaw • Scroll saw • Jig saw
	Metal	• Hacksaw • Power hacksaw • Jig saw
	Polymer	• Coping saw • Bandsaw • Scroll saw • Jig saw
Turning	Timber	• Wood lathe
	Metal	• Centre lathe
Milling	Metal	• Milling machine
Filing	Metal, polymer	• Files

→

Wasting process	Material	Tool or machinery
Abrading	Timber, metal, polymer	• Disc sander • Belt sander
	Timber	• Glasspaper
	Metal	• Grinder

Moulding methods

Polymers can be moulded for prototypes by using thermoforming or vacuum forming. Both methods use thermoplastic sheet – the sheet is heated and formed over a mould (usually made from MDF). Thermoforming uses a second mould pressed over the top of the sheet to give extra detail to the product.

Casting of metals

Metal shapes which are hard to achieve by standard wasting processes may be made by casting processes where molten metal is cast into a **mould**.

- **Lost wax casting:** wax patterns are cast from a master mould, repeatable quality process. Used for intricate shapes that are difficult to mould with other cast processes and gives a high quality and finish.
- **Sand casting:** a labour-intensive process – moulds are made then set into a sand box, sand is packed around the mould, the moulds are removed to make a cavity into which molten metal is poured. The surface finish is not high quality.
- **Low temperature casting:** usually done with pewter for jewellery or decorative items. Can be used with simple MDF moulds.
- **Resin casting:** used for polymers to create small figures or 3D objects. The resin is mixed with a hardening agent, poured into a mould where it hardens to form the shape. The mould is usually flexible silicon rubber.

Key words

Mould: a hollow shape used to pour material into, like a jelly mould.

Sand casting: a metal-casting process that uses sand as the mould material.

Low temperature casting: used for metals such as pewter which melt at low temperatures and can be poured into a variety of mould material.

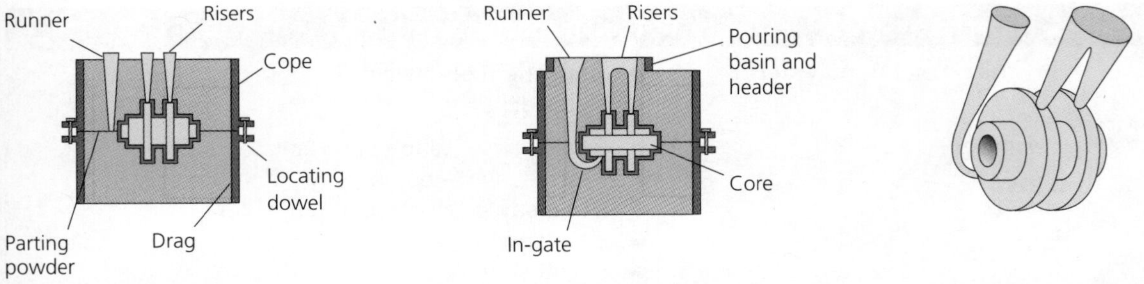

(a) The ramming operation of the drag and cope is completed.

(b) The completed mould ready for pouring.

(c) Casting retrieved from the mould and ready for finishing.

Figure 7.11 The sand casting process

Forming and lamination

Forming and laminating are processes used to change the shape of timber or manufactured boards such as flexible plywood.

- Laminating bonds materials together to make sections such as curves.
- Wood veneers or thin manufactured boards such as 3 mm plywood can be glued together, bent over a **former** and clamped. When dry, they form a thicker board in the shape of the former.
- Laminating can be done by using male and female formers or by using a vacuum press system.

Key word

Former: used to make sure that parts are formed or bent to the same shape.

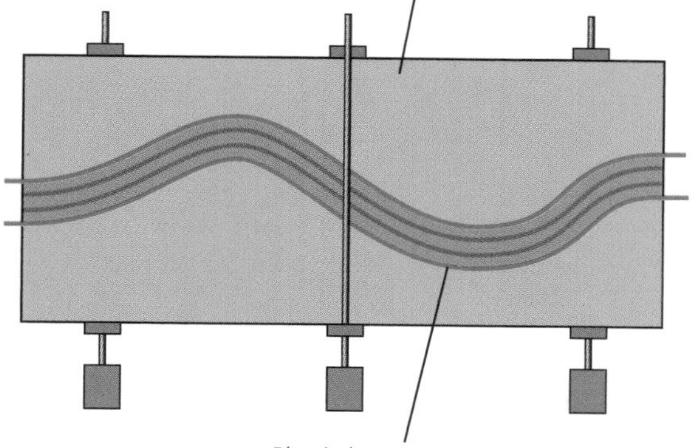

Figure 7.12 **Salad server moulds using simple male and female formers**

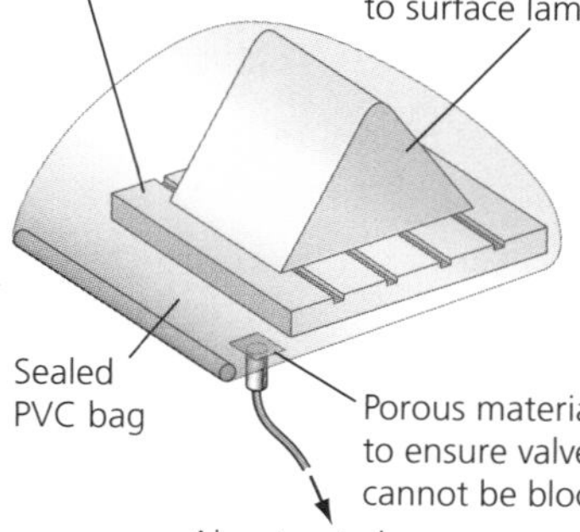

Figure 7.13 **A vacuum press system**

Bending, rolling and forming

Steam bending is quicker than laminating and has little waste. Steam bending combines heat and steam to make strips of wood pliable so they can be shaped over a former.

The wood absorbs the steam in a steam box; it is then bent over a former and clamped until it dries.

Sheet metals can be bent and rolled into shape for prototypes by:

- pressing the sheets between formers
- bending them over an object such as a former
- using a hammer and shaping mallet with a leather sand bag to form curves in small sheet sections.

Acrylic sheets can be heated on a line bender and bent on a former to produce an angled bend when the material cools.

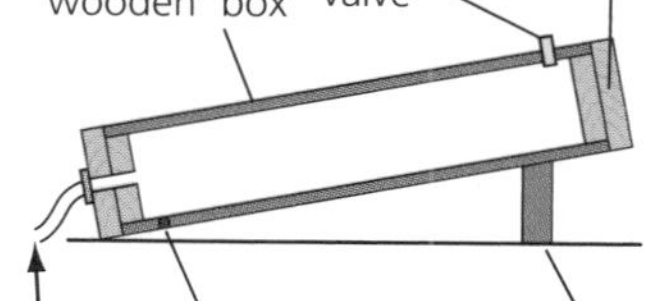

Figure 7.14 **A simple steam chamber for bending wood**

Exam tip

Make sure you know how materials are manufactured for prototypes and how they can be joined together, either with specific joints and/or adhesives and fastenings.

Using digital technology

REVISED

Computer-aided design (CAD) and computer-aided manufacture (CAM) can be utilised for prototype production and there are a variety of options available. CAD/CAM allows models and parts to be made quickly, modelled and even tested prior to full manufacture.

CAM software translates the CAD files into instructions for automated machines that use computer numerical control (CNC).

Table 7.3 Examples of CNC machines

CNC machine	Use
CNC laser cutter	2D machine for cutting and engraving thin sheet materials such as polymer, wood, aluminium
CNC plasma cutter	Similar to a laser cutter but used for electrically conductive materials such as metals; useful for cutting thick sheets
CNC router	2D machine for cutting profiles in timber, polymer and modelling foam. A 3D attachment can be used to rotate an object while cutting to produce a 3D shape
CNC milling machine	Similar to a router but has a greater depth of cut; used for metals and solid timbers
CNC lathe	Used to produce cylindrical shapes in timber, metal or wax
3D printers	Fuses layers of polymer together (most commonly PLA and ABS) to create a 3D object

Ensuring quality and accuracy

REVISED

Jigs, formers, templates and moulds are often used to ensure that parts or components can be made repeatedly, more quickly and without the need for repeated measuring and marking.

- **Jig:** this holds the work and guides a tool, eliminating the need to repeatedly mark out.
- **Former:** a 3D form that allows material to be made to the same given shape.
- **Template:** used to mark out a shape onto material. Can be made from cardboard, MDF or thin aluminium sheet.
- **Mould:** a hollow shape into which a liquid material can be poured so it can set in the shape of the mould.

Key words

Jig: used to hold and position work and/or locate or guide a tool to ensure accuracy and repeatability.

Template: can be drawn around to mark a shape onto material.

Decisions about suitability of materials

REVISED

See Section 5.3 (page 77) for details on how available forms, costs and working properties of materials influence the choice of materials.

Typical mistake

Don't suggest industrial processes for workshop prototypes, for example using injection moulding for a simple polymer handle that could be 3D printed.

Now test yourself

TESTED

1. Name two knock-down (KD) fittings.
2. Give an advantage of using KD fittings over traditional timber joining methods.
3. Suggest a suitable workshop process for making a small jewellery item out of pewter.
4. Give an advantage of using jigs and templates in the manufacture of prototypes.
5. What do the letters CAD, CAM and CNC stand for?

7.3 Using materials and processes to make commercial products

Processes and machinery used in commercial manufacturing

REVISED

Polymer processes

Many household and industrial products are made from polymers. The processes listed in Table 7.4 are used to form polymers into 3D products.

Table 7.4 Polymer processes

<table>
<tr><th>Process</th><th>Key features</th><th>Products</th></tr>
<tr><td>Injection moulding</td><td>
<ul>
<li>Complex 3D shapes can be made.</li>
<li>Fast industrial production method.</li>
<li>High initial tooling cost.</li>
<li>Used for large-scale mass or continuous production.</li>
</ul>
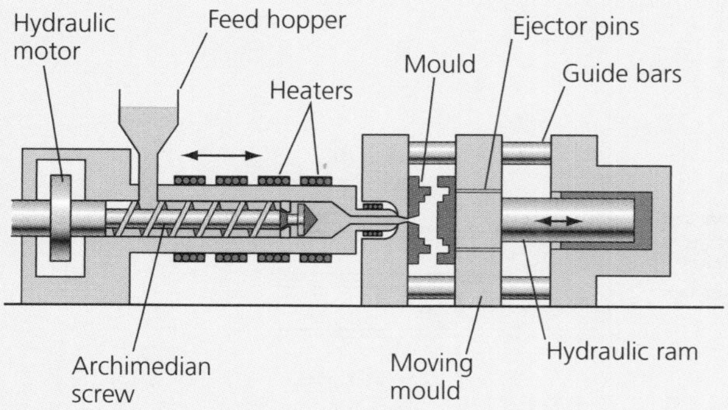

Figure 7.15 An injection moulding machine</td><td>Electrical product casings (televisions, vacuum cleaners, calculators, kettles)</td></tr>
<tr><td>Rotational moulding</td><td>
<ul>
<li>Seamless hollow components with a large wall thickness.</li>
<li>Mould continuously rotated through heating and cooling.</li>
<li>Large-scale batch or mass production.</li>
</ul>
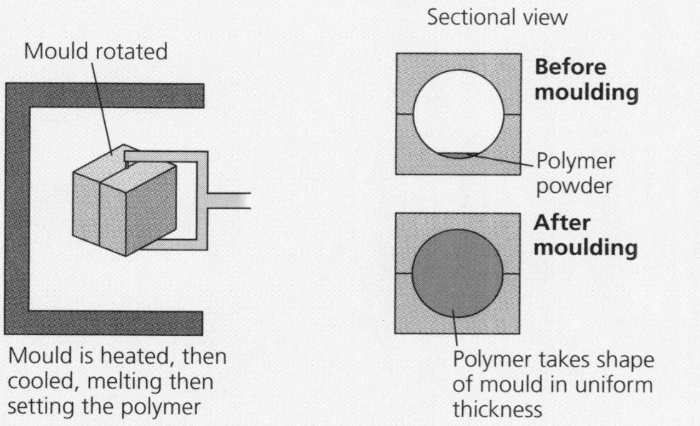

Figure 7.16 Rotational moulding machine and process</td><td>Traffic cones, kayaks, water tanks, kerosene tanks, children's play equipment</td></tr>
</table>

➜

<table>
<tr><th>Process</th><th>Key features</th><th>Products</th></tr>
<tr><td>Compression moulding</td><td>

- Uses a pre-weighed 'slug' of polymer.
- Polymer removed from moulds while still warm.
- Large-scale batch production.

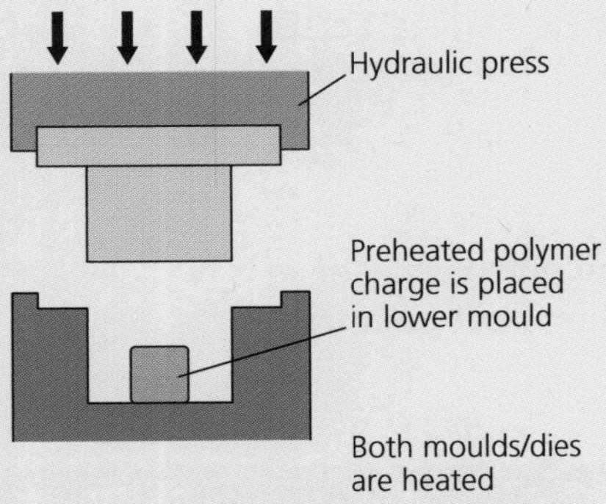

Figure 7.17 The compression moulding process
</td><td>Electrical light fittings, switches, plugs, picnic plates and cups</td></tr>
<tr><td>Extrusion</td><td>

- Like injection moulding except polymer is forced through a die.
- Industrial production method.
- Continuous production.

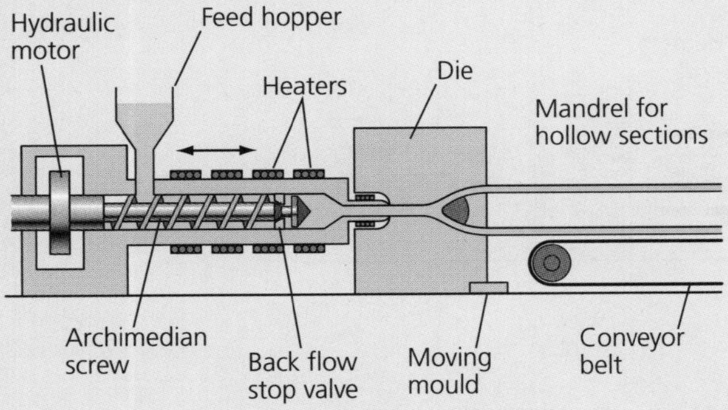

Figure 7.18 The extrusion process
</td><td>Solid rods, tubing, angle sections, curtain track</td></tr>
<tr><td>Blow moulding</td><td>

- Produces hollow thin-walled components.
- High initial tooling cost.
- Used for continuous production.

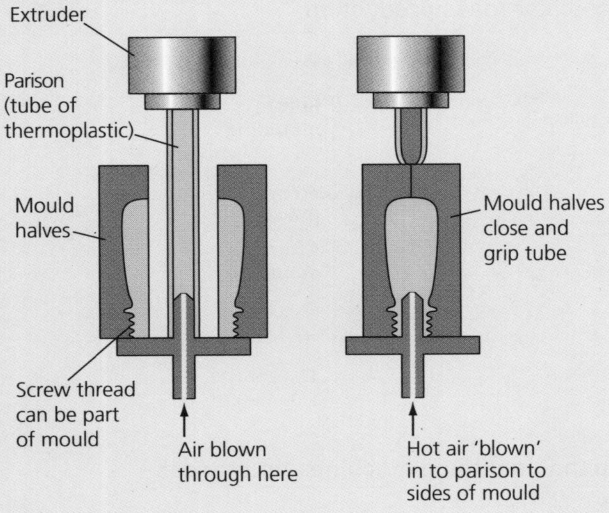

Figure 7.19 The blow moulding process
</td><td>Drink bottles, shampoo bottles, detergent bottles</td></tr>
</table>

Process	Key features	Products
Vacuum forming	• Moulds are relatively easy to make but need a draft angle, air holes and rounded corners. • Not cost effective for one-off manufacture. • Small-scale batch and mass production. 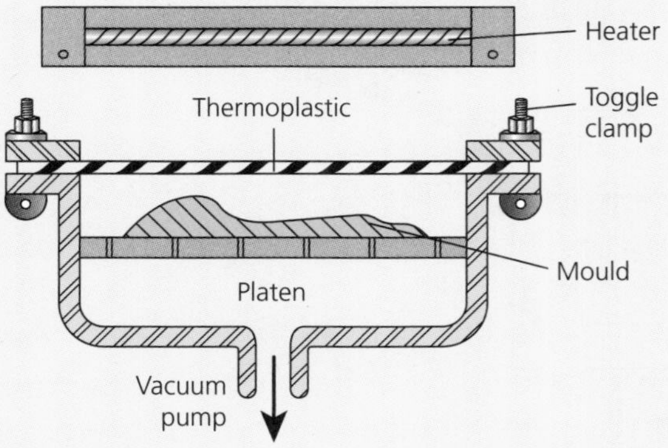 **Figure 7.20** The vacuum forming process	Lightweight trays, box inserts and liners, takeaway coffee cups and yoghurt pots
Thermoforming	• Like vacuum forming, except an additional mould is pressed onto the surface of the polymer sheet at the same time as the vacuum is applied. • Good for fine detail such as moulding in logos. • Slow process, used in industrial production.	Bath, food packaging (fruit punnets, cake boxes, sandwich boxes)

Metal processes

Metals can be shaped into 3D forms using stamping, sand casting and die casting processes.

Table 7.5 Metal processes

Process	Key features	Products
Press forming (stamping)	• Shapes sheet metal into 3D forms. • Often used in conjunction with robots for lifting the sheet into place. • Suitable for mass production or large-scale batch production. 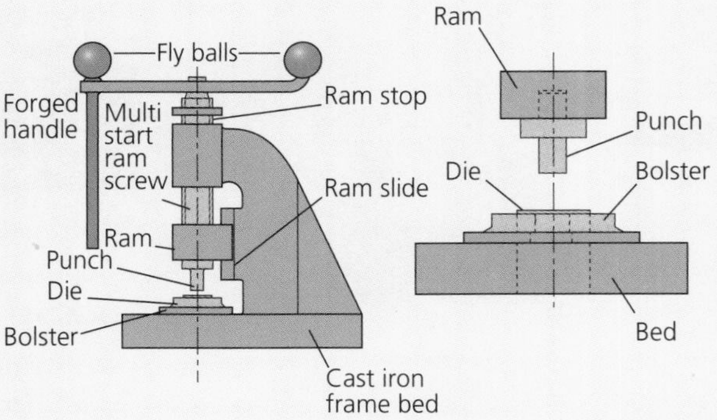 **Figure 7.21** Fly press for stamping or blanking	Metal seats, car body panels, washing machine panels, boxes and containers
Sand casting	• Labour-intensive process. • Not a high-quality surface finish. • Suitable for one-off or small-batch production.	Railway carriage wheels, wood working clamps, vices, motor housings, bollards, drain covers, post boxes

➜

Process	Key features	Products
Gravity die casting	• Lower melt point metals such as aluminium, aluminium alloys and zinc-based alloys. • Relies on gravity to help the metal flow into the mould. • Used for thicker mould sections. • Used for very large-batch and mass production. 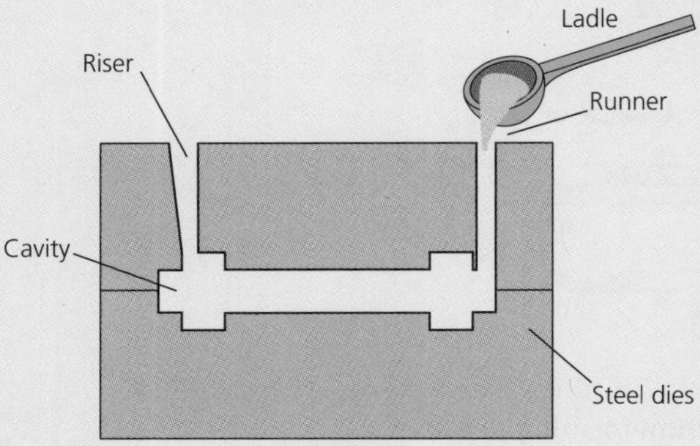 **Figure 7.22** **Gravity die casting**	Alloy wheels, engine components, door knobs and handles
Pressure die casting (hot chamber)	• Lower melt point metals such as aluminium, aluminium alloys and zinc-based alloys. • Molten metal stored in a chamber then a shot of molten metal is forced into the die. • Fast process. • Used for very large-batch and mass production.	Toy cars, collectible figures, decorative door knobs and handles
Pressure die casting (cold chamber)	• Lower melt point metals such as aluminium, aluminium alloys and zinc-based alloys. • Molten metal ladled into the shot chamber and hydraulically pushed into the chamber. • Used for very large-batch and mass production.	Toy cars, collectible figures, decorative door knobs and handles

PROCESS
Permanent mould
Molten metal is forced into a water-cooled metal mould (die) through a system of sprues and runners. The metal solidifies rapidly and the casting is removed with its sprues and runners.

SHAPE
3D solid
Used for complex shapes and thin sections. Cores must be simple and retractable.

MATERIALS
Light alloys
High fluidity requirement means low melting temperature eutectics usually used. Hot chamber method restricted to very low melting temperature alloys (e.g. Mg)

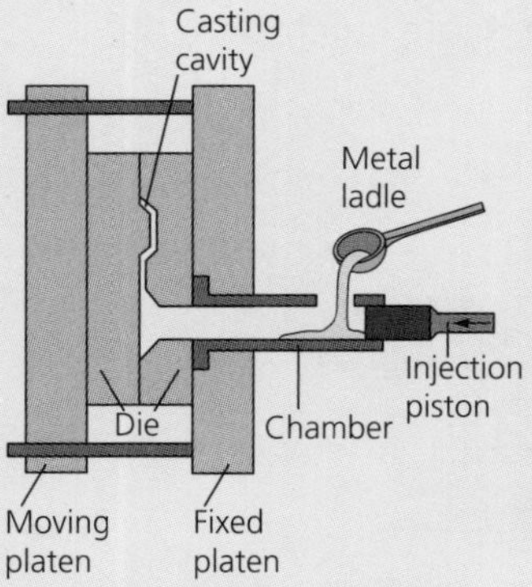

Cold-chamber high pressure die casting. Molten metal is poured into a cold shot chamber. A high pressure plunger forces metal into the single- or multi-die cavity.

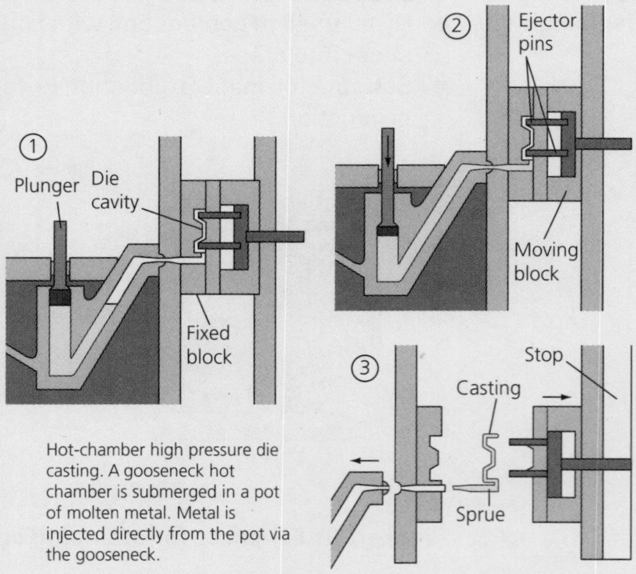

Hot-chamber high pressure die casting. A gooseneck hot chamber is submerged in a pot of molten metal. Metal is injected directly from the pot via the gooseneck.

CYCLE TIME
Solidification time is typically <1s so cycle is controlled by time taken to fill mould and remove casting.

QUALITY
Good surface texture but turbulent mould filling produces high degree of internal porosity.

FLEXIBILITY
Tooling dedicated so limited by machine setting up time.

MATERIALS UTILISATION
Near net shape process but some scrap; in sprues, runners and flash which can be directly recycled.

OPERATING COST
High, since machine and moulds are expensive.

Figure 7.23a **Cold-chamber pressure die casting**

Figure 7.23b **Hot-chamber pressure die casting**

Automated material handling systems

Automated material handling systems use mechanical equipment to move, store and protect materials throughout the production process from manufacture to distribution, use and disposal.

- Mechanical equipment such as fork-lift trucks, pallet trucks, conveyor belts and storage funnels are ideal for industrial contexts where large volumes and/or heavy goods are being moved around an assembly line or factory.
- Efficient movement of materials saves time, and the use of robots and mechanical equipment ensures that manual handling risks are minimised.
- Many factories make the best use of space and employ specific vehicle tracks and overhead conveyor systems to move materials and products around an assembly or production line.

Robotic arms to stack, assemble, join and paint parts

Robots are extremely useful to lift parts, assemble components and carry out repetitive tasks.

- Robots are not subject to manual handling issues or repetitive strain injuries and can work without breaks in hazardous environments to produce the same quality of item repeatedly.
- Robots can be easily programmed to carry out different tasks such as painting or welding and do not require upskilling like a manual workforce.
- Robots still require human intervention for servicing, quality control etc.

Introducing robots to the workplace can have some disadvantages, such as:

- High initial layout costs.
- Software or system breakdowns that stop production and can impact on costs.
- Programming robots is a specialist job (workers may require retraining).
- Some programme languages do not communicate across different software platforms.

Exam tip

Make sure you can give specific examples of products made by each process. You should also know why the process is suited to the product.

Typical mistake

Don't confuse polymer processes with metal processes. Know each process for each material category.

Ensuring consistent accuracy and quality through production

REVISED

Consistency in commercial manufacture plays a huge part in the success of a product. Manufacturers use a range of methods to ensure that each product is the same quality, that joints and connections are in the same place and that processing can be carried out quickly, with repeated accuracy.

- A **jig** holds the work and guides a tool, eliminating the need to repeatedly mark out. For example, a drilling jig for a dowel joint in a shelf would hold the shelf material in place and have guide holes for drilling to occur in the same place on each shelf.
- **Assembly jigs** can also be used to hold a part in place while a process is being carried out, such as a welding jig for a table fame.
- A **template** jig fits over the work and is not always clamped down. They are simple and easy to use and aid accuracy.
- A **fixture** is something that holds the work in a given position while a manufacturing process takes place. Fixtures are always fixed to the machine bed and use set blocks to locate the cutter during the processing.

Key words

Jig: used to hold and position work and/or locate or guide a tool to ensure accuracy and repeatability.

Assembly jigs: can be used to hold a part in place while a process is being carried out.

Template: can be drawn around to mark a shape onto material.

Fixture: holds work in a given position while a manufacturing process takes place. Fixtures are always fixed to the machine bed.

- **Presses** form the material into shape when pressure is applied, such as press forming sheet metals.
- **Formers** are the solid shapes that materials are shaped around, such as the shape needed for press forming or the shape required for a laminated product.
- **Moulds** use a hollow shape into which liquids such as molten metal or polymer resins can be poured to form the solid shape of the mould cavity.

In commercial manufacture it is important that the former or mould used is accurately made in the first instance. Mould making is a specialist job – the final product is only as good as the mould it comes from. Moulds need to be able to withstand repeated use and still provide the same quality outcome, therefore they are often made from materials such as hardened steels or steel alloys.

Key words

Presses: ensure the material is formed to shape when pressure is applied to the material.

Former: used to make sure that parts are formed or bent to the same shape.

Mould: a hollow shape used to pour material into, like a jelly mould.

Optimising the use of materials and production processes (A Level)

REVISED

Cost-effective production

Designers and manufactures want to make successful, well-functioning, quality products but making a profit depends on making the most effective use of materials and resources. Three factors need to be taken into consideration:

1. **Raw materials:**
   - The availability, quality and cost of the materials or components
   - The cost of transporting items to the manufacturing facility
   - The time taken from ordering the materials or components to their arrival for processing.
2. **People:**
   - The availability and cost of a suitably skilled workforce
   - The cost of providing good working conditions (providing welfare facilities, safe working conditions and personal protective equipment, and ensuring any external supplier is not corrupt or exploiting a labour force).
3. **Processing:**
   - The processing options available for manufacture
   - The processing time taken from start of production to end product
   - The use of as few different processes as possible (this may involve redesigning a part)
   - The volume of product produced in a given time frame (is the manufacture automated or labour-intensive?)
   - The cost of the energy required to carry out processing and whether alternative energies can be used
   - The cost of waste disposal and how materials can be used for efficient manufacture (e.g. tessellating parts on a CNC router to reduce waste, reusing sprues from injection moulding so waste and cost is reduced).

Efficient manufacture

Manufacturers can use different methods to help make the manufacture process as efficient as possible but **planning** the whole process is crucial. For example, to reduce lead time, there may be parts of the product that could be made at the same time by different teams such as a wooden dining table could have one group making a frame, the other making the top and the final group working on assembly.

Scheduling tasks for a shift or a production line also keeps products on track and a Gantt chart or similar software can be used to track timings for each task and identify areas for time improvement.

Now test yourself

TESTED

1 Give an example of a product made by the blow moulding process.
2 List the advantages and disadvantages of using robots for manufacture.
3 What is the main purpose of jigs, fixtures, formers and moulds in commercial manufacturing?
4 Give an example of how an assembly jig could be used for manufacture.
5 Define what is meant by the term 'fixture'.

7.4 How manufacturing is organised and managed for different scales of production

Use of different production methods

REVISED

Manufacturing methods are categorised as:

- **high-volume (mass) production**
- **batch production**
- one-off/**bespoke** production.

The decisions about which of these methods to use depends on:

- demand
- type of product
- materials to be used
- premises/equipment available
- workforce size and skill level
- capital and tooling costs
- potential for bulk buying of materials
- potential for using standardised parts in the product range.

Key words

High-volume (mass) production: making large numbers of standardised products in highly mechanised factories.

Batch production: the manufacture of groups of products to increase efficiency and economy.

Bespoke: a product specially made to order for a customer.

One-off/bespoke, batch and high-volume production methods

One-off/bespoke production

One-off or bespoke production is sometimes called job production. It refers to unique, individually designed and manufactured products such as:

- a luxury yacht
- a customised chair for a physically disabled child
- a wedding cake
- a virtuoso player's violin.

Figure 7.24 Hand crafting a bespoke stringed instrument

With this type of production, increased expense, time requirements and more complex processes are often encountered due to:

- individual client consultations and design work
- high levels of making skills required
- lengthy set up for individual manufacturing processes
- fewer economies of scale (e.g. no bulk discount on materials).

Batch production

Batch production is the quality controlled, efficient and cost-effective manufacture of similar products by using simultaneous manufacturing processes. Examples include:

- pottery
- wooden furniture
- high-quality loudspeakers
- jet engines
- electric guitars.

Advantages of batch production include the following:

- The jigs, fixtures and CNC machines used facilitate more accurate and faster production of parts, for example the bodies for electric guitars.
- It offers flexibility for demand-led change of batch size, which might be in the thousands or just a few.
- Fewer skilled workers are required than for bespoke production due to increased automation.
- It offers the potential for special editions, colours and customisation of products such as for cars and clothing.

Figure 7.25 Batch of CNC routed electric guitar bodies

High-volume production

High-volume production is used for manufacturing products that are in constant demand and is often referred to as mass production.

Table 7.6 Mass production methods

Method	Key features	Examples	Advantages and disadvantages
Continuous flow production	• Highly automated. • Raw materials are often processed into finished products in the same factory. • Products can become the materials used in various other applications.	Glass, paper, polymer extrusions, copper wire	• Relatively small workforce needed. • Expensive to set up. • Low level of job satisfaction.
In-line production	• Stages of manufacture are carried out sequentially. • 'Division of labour'. • Conveyors are often used. • A trained workforce is required. • Highly automated.	Cars, appliances, self-assembly furniture, clothing	• Reduced cost compared to batch or bespoke production. • Expensive to set up with high levels of automation.
Fully automated production	• Used for products in high demand. • Dedicated machinery set up for long production runs. • Minimal if any variation in the products.	Screws, staples, paper clips, LEDs	• Low unit costs. • Mainly low skilled workforce. • High capital investment. • Needs effective maintenance system. • Low level of job satisfaction.

Exam tip

If you are asked to explain the different scales of production, try to choose contrasting examples that belong unambiguously in the particular categories. Examples might include:

- One-off/bespoke production: a driftwood chair (the nature of the material being used makes any other scale of production impractical).
- Batch production: a set of cast-iron railings for a bridge refurbishment project (sand casting using a common pattern to ensure that all railings match).
- Mass production: a mass-market car such as a Ford Fiesta, but don't forget to demonstrate, if appropriate to the question wording, your knowledge of the impact of mass customisation.

Key word

Continuous flow production: a highly automated 24/7 production process, usually requiring a small workforce.

Typical mistake

When explaining an appropriate example of mass production, keep focused on key manufacturing points such as the advantages of injection moulding, automated tube bending and integral fittings to produce bulk volumes. Don't be tempted to stray into listing individual design features, which are relevant to the design but not necessarily to the scale of production.

Modular/cell production systems (A Level)

In **modular/cell production systems**, manufacturing cells combine CNC machines, such as lathes, milling machines, drills and grinders, in a group. The cell is programmed to carry out a sequence of operations to provide a flexible manufacturing facility for a wide range of parts such as car engine components.

- Automatic guided vehicles (AGVs) transport materials or parts to and from buffer zones.
- Robots with six axes (directions of movement) load and unload machines.
- Effective production planning is a high priority.

- Rapid tool changes and effective work-piece clamping systems are important features.
- A small team of multi-skilled workers may be involved in running one or more cells.

Just-in-time, Toyota Production System and lean manufacturing

These terms relate to how manufacturing is organised. There are some potentially confusing common elements, but their underpinning principle is to help in the elimination of waste and improvement of quality in production.

Just-in-time manufacture

Just-in-time (JIT) manufacture means that materials or components are delivered only as required for manufacture, in response to orders. It is central to much modern manufacturing and its main features include:

- Good relationships with suppliers, which are pivotal to smooth operation of the system.
- A location with good transport infrastructure for deliveries and to reduce the environmental impact of transporting items.
- No stockpiling of materials or finished products.
- A reduced need for storage or warehousing.
- Computerised stock control and kanban (stock monitoring indicator) systems.
- Good management/employee relationships to ensure continuity of production.

Lean manufacturing

Lean manufacturing concentrates on the following strategies to enhance the JIT approach:

- The reduction of stock and waste (Muda) in all its forms, such as unnecessary **inventory**, motion, defects and processes.
- The use of Six Sigma (see Section 4.3, page 66) to aim to eliminate defects.
- A philosophy of continuous improvement (Kaizen).
- A focus on relationships with customers to improve overall value.
- Employing multi-skilled workers and using versatile, flexible, CNC machinery.

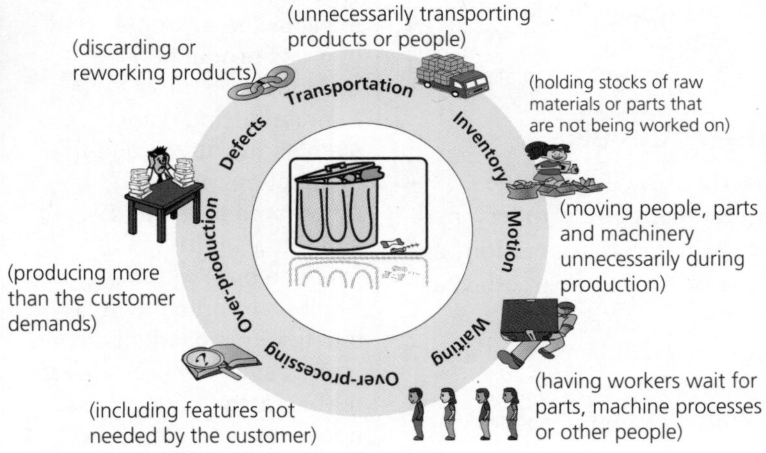

Figure 7.26 The seven types of waste (Muda) targeted in lean manufacturing

Key words

Modular/cell production system: workers, CNC machines, robots and AGVs organised in groups for efficient, flexible manufacturing.

Just-in-time (JIT) manufacture: the manufacture of products as needed, in response to existing orders.

Lean manufacturing: a system that aims to reduce waste and continuously improve in order to add value for customers.

Inventory: a manufacturing company's assets in the form of materials, parts or products.

Toyota Production System

The Toyota Production System (TPS) is regarded as the pioneering lean manufacturing system.

- It encompasses features of both the JIT and lean manufacturing systems.
- The empowerment and training of workers is particularly emphasised.
- Quality is maintained by automatically stopping production if there are problems (Jidoka).

Standardised parts and components (A Level)

- **Standardised components** can be relied upon to fit correctly when adding or replacing elements of a design, such as using a refill in your ball-point pen or punched A4 paper in your ring-binder.
- Screw fasteners are one of the most important examples of standardisation and most of the world now uses a metric International Standards Organisation (ISO) screw thread system.
- Light bulbs and fittings are another example of standardised components.
- Bayonet fittings, for example, are regulated by BS EN 61184, which dictates their dimensions, tolerances and other requirements.

Key word

Standardised components: parts made to a common, interchangeable, standard, such as bolts and light bulbs.

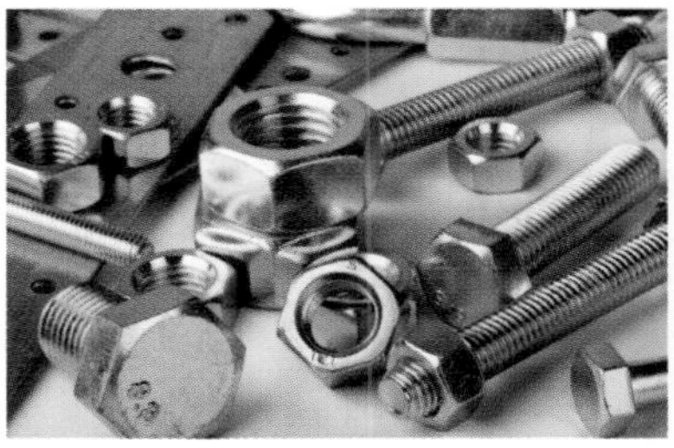

Figure 7.27 Standardised screw threads

Bought-in parts and components (A Level)

Standardisation ensures that bought-in parts and components will integrate seamlessly in a manufacturer's products. These include:

- tyres
- audio connectors
- batteries
- fuses
- printer cartridges
- ball-point pen refills
- memory cards.

The benefits for manufacturers of using bought-in components include:

- The availability of sub-assemblies (e.g. electric motors, hydraulic valves and gearboxes).
- Suppliers make standardised CAD files available for easy integration into CAD designs.
- The components can be bought in bulk, which considerably reduces the unit cost.
- There is no need to have their own expensive and potentially time-consuming manufacturing facility.
- The specialist equipment and expertise of suppliers is not required in their own factory.
- Specialist manufacturers working to specified **tolerances** maintain quality.
- The ISO 9001 accreditation framework can be used to maintain quality standards.

Key word

Tolerance: the acceptable upper and lower limits of accuracy of a measurement.

Fully automated manufacture (A Level)

This is sometimes referred to as 'lights-out manufacturing' due to the lack of human involvement.

Robots are usually heavily involved, working alongside automated machines:

- They most commonly take the form of robot arms, usually with six axes of movement.

- They provide consistent and precise handling of materials and parts.
- They are programmable for a wide range of roles from 'pick and place' to complex welding operations.

Production, planning and control (PPC) and other related computer software systems provide for:

- the organisation of materials and parts as well as manufacturing operations
- maintenance scheduling to keep machines running efficiently and accurately.

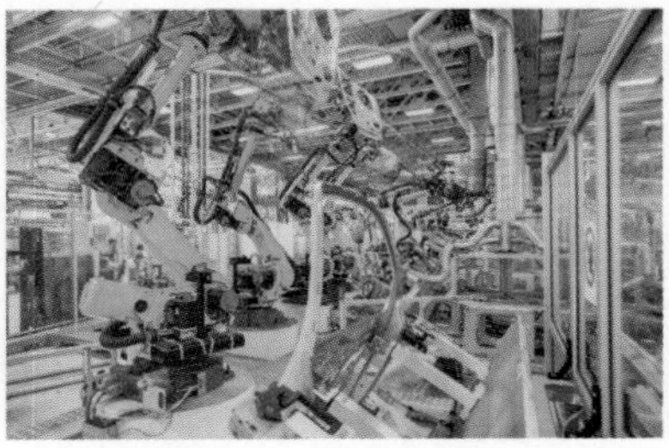

Figure 7.28 Robots in a fully automated car plant

How ICT and digital technologies are changing modern manufacturing (A Level)

REVISED

Computer-aided design (CAD) means using computer software such as SolidWorks to design parts and products, rather than using hand methods to draw designs. It offers:

- a wide range of tools for creating, modifying and saving complex computer models
- fast and potentially global generation and sharing of ideas
- ease of rapid prototyping
- tool paths automatically generated by CAD model for use in computer-aided manufacturing (CAM).

CAM is the use of a wide range of highly productive computer numerically controlled (CNC) machines which offers many advantages:

- Once set up, CNC machines can work with minimum need for intervention.
- Standardised files facilitate the use of global manufacturing facilities.
- Computer-operated inspection and quality-monitoring equipment can be incorporated.
- Robots can serve machines set up in cells to further reduce the need for human input.

Developments such as CAD and CAM help to facilitate a rapid response to changing fashions in products and computer-controlled systems are used in production, distribution and storage (see computer integrated manufacture (CIM) on page 111).

Customised manufacture systems (mass customisation)

CAD and CAM facilitate the **mass customisation** of products such as sports shoes, computers and cars, which are ordered online to enable the incorporation of personal touches and individual specifications without the level of expense normally associated with bespoke products.

Rapid prototyping

For details of rapid prototyping see Section 7.1 (page 90).

Additive and digital manufacture methods

This primarily involves the use of 3D printing, which is mainly used for making iterative models as seen in Section 7.1 (page 90).

Direct digital manufacturing (DDM) uses selective layer sintering (SLS) 3D-printed metals and other resistant materials to facilitate the production of tooling, parts and products from CAD models such as:

Key words

Mass customisation: a manufacturing technique which uses online ordering to combine the flexibility and personalisation of custom-made products with the low unit costs associated with mass production.

Direct digital manufacturing (DDM): a system where parts are produced by machines such as 3D printers directly from CAD files.

- metal and ceramic patterns and moulds
- complex, otherwise 'impossible to manufacture', engineering components using titanium, stainless steel and aluminium
- custom prosthetics, joints, and bone replacements which can be 3D printed in titanium.

Some of these DDM technologies are still in the development stage and simultaneous 3D printing of a combination of materials will be a key element required to facilitate further development.

Stock control, monitoring, purchasing logistics in industry

Some important aspects of this topic are also covered in Section 3.4 (page 52).

Computer integrated manufacture (CIM) is the term often used to describe how computers oversee all the stages of bringing a product to market, from design and manufacture through to distribution. CIM offers many advantages:

- It ensures the efficient integration of materials, parts, processes and products for the optimum flow of high-quality goods.
- Demand can be forecast and optimum suppliers identified.
- It has stock control capabilities which are integral to the smooth running of this highly complex process, such as:
  - The monitoring, costing and ordering of materials or parts (using barcodes, RFID tags, kanbans).
  - Computerised warehouse organisation with automatic guided vehicles (AGVs), forklifts and narrow-aisle stacking robots.
  - Distribution through optimum loading patterns for freight containers and delivery schedules.
  - Electronic point-of-sale (EPOS) systems which record sales of products and automate re-stocking.
  - Organisation of optimum level of buffer stock, if required.

As with all computer systems there are potential drawbacks which need to be considered, such as:

- digital data security issues
- set-up, software and training costs
- the need for back-up systems.

Figure 7.29 SLS 3D-printed titanium components

Key word

Logistics: the detailed organisation of activities such as the transportation of materials, parts and products.

Figure 7.30 Narrow-aisle stacking robot in a computerised warehouse

Now test yourself

TESTED

1. What scale of production would be appropriate for making windows to be fitted in a barn conversion project?
2. Name two examples of standardised components.
3. What is the difference between bespoke and mass customised products?
4. What is the name of the manufacturing system in which 3D printers can be used to make the final product rather than just a model of it?
5. Name three aspects of computer integrated manufacture (CIM) that improve stock control.

7.5 Controlling quality through manufacture (A Level)

Processes to ensure products meet legal requirements and are high quality

REVISED

For products to be successful it is essential that they meet customers' expectations. The following measures are designed to maintain the quality that customers demand.

Quality control

Quality control (QC) is the monitoring, checking and testing of quality assurance tolerance conformity throughout production, specified by the strict guidance documentation of user and stakeholder requirements. Compliance of materials with the manufacturer's specification can be checked by:

- simple visual checks
- chemical analysis of samples (e.g. moisture content or chemical composition)
- colour matching for pigments or paints.

Dimensional accuracy can be checked by:

- digital measuring devices such as micrometers and digital vernier calipers
- dedicated checking equipment such as go/no go gauges
- interval sample testing, using equipment such as profile projectors, conducted in a QC department
- laser measuring sensors or probes linked to computers.

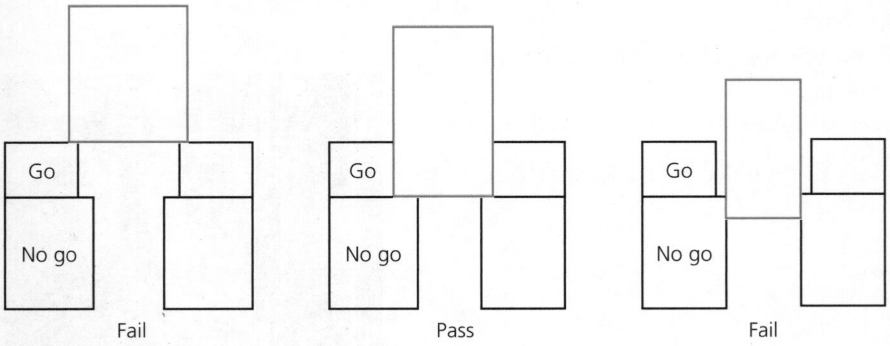

Figure 7.31 How a go/no go gauge works

Checks on additional product features and properties, such as toughness, transparency, flammability and water resistance, can be carried out on appropriate samples using dedicated QC department equipment.

Quality assurance

Quality assurance (QA) involves procedures and policies to ensure products meet quality standards and are 'right first time and every time'. Effective QA procedures reduce the number of QC issues and rejects.

Examples of QA procedures and policies include:

- using materials and components from ISO 9001 Quality Management Standard suppliers
- checking correct temperatures for effective cavity filling in moulding procedures
- rigid machinery and cutter maintenance schedules to maintain tolerances

Key word

Quality control (QC): monitoring, checking and testing procedures used throughout production.

Key word

Quality assurance (QA): procedures and policies which ensure that products meet specification criteria.

Typical mistake

Confusion between quality control (QC) and quality assurance (QA) is very common. Remember that QC is all about specific control and testing measures during manufacture, while QA is the planning of procedures and policies that ensure good-quality products.

- pre-production CAD modelling to check fit and assembly
- finite element analysis (FEA) to analyse the effect of stresses and reduce the possibility of parts fracturing in use
- mould flow analysis (MFA) to predict material flow within moulding machinery
- incorporation of embossed mould identification marks for tracing faults.

Figure 7.32 Glass bottle base showing mould identification number

Total quality management (TQM)

Total quality management (TQM) is a management system designed to remove waste and make products right first time by continuous improvement of the whole manufacturing process.

- All stages of design and manufacture are constantly monitored and evaluated.
- The workforce's views, feedback, teamwork and communication are highly prioritised.

Key word

Total quality management (TQM): a system to improve quality assurance (QA) by harnessing workforce expertise.

British and European standards

British and European standards are documents that set quality, safety and other requirements for a wide range of services and products.

The most important quality standard to guide manufacturers and other organisations is called ISO 9001:

- This quality management system guides organisations in satisfying the requirements of customers and other stakeholders who interact with its products or services.
- Companies who follow this globally recognised standard are at an advantage when seeking contracts.
- ISO 9001 certification is sometimes essential when obtaining contracts from certain organisations.

Additional standards exist for specific products, and designers need to be aware of them, such as the following examples applying to the manufacture of toys.

Table 7.7 Examples of British Standards for toys

Reference no.	Standard	Covers issues such as:
BS EN 71-1	Mechanical and physical properties	Could it break in use?
BS EN 71-2	Flammability	How easily might it catch fire?
BS EN 71-9	Organic chemical compounds	Are any toxic finishes used?
BS EN 14960	Inflatable play equipment	Will it be stable in windy conditions?
BS EN 62115	Electric toys	How secure is the battery access panel?

Some aspects of this topic are also covered in Section 8.1 (page 117).

Exam tip

If a question requires information about how you organised your Non-Exam Assessment (NEA) to ensure a good-quality practical outcome, don't just give a diary-style list of processes. It is essential to include reference to the implementation and organisation of quality control measures, which could be shown in the form of a flowchart as seen in Section 4.1 (page 60).

Now test yourself

TESTED

1 Explain the difference between quality assurance (QA) and quality control (QC).
2 Give two examples of how materials might be checked before use by a manufacturer.
3 Give two QA measures that might be set in place to ensure that an injection-moulding process is carried out successfully.

Exam practice

1 Name and describe **three** contrasting modelling methods that might be used during the development of a car design and how they would be particularly appropriate for communication with different groups of stakeholders.
2 Use notes and diagrams to explain the potential advantages of using a 3D printer rather than a CNC router or milling machine for the manufacture of complex models.
3 Explain how standardised, bought-in components are an essential feature of car design, from the point of view of manufacturers and consumers.
4 Use notes and simple diagrams to explain the term 'modular/cell production' and how the elements involved would be combined to produce a large batch of high-quality steel components which require lathe turning operations followed by milling and then grinding.
5 Explain the advantages of 'just-in-time (JIT)' manufacture over conventional methods, and its potential disadvantages.
6 Give an example of a one-off, bespoke product and explain in detail why it would be more expensive to design and manufacture than an equivalent batch-produced version.
7 Explain, using examples from specific products, why it is important for manufacturers to conform to British and European standards.
8 Name **two** contrasting methods for carrying out quality control (QC) checks for dimensional accuracy. Use examples to explain when they might be used and why they are appropriate.
9 Give an example of where and when a manufacturer would use a jig.
10 Give **two** advantages and **two** disadvantages injection moulding offers a manufacturer.
11 Explain why compression moulding is a suitable process for manufacturing an electrical light fitting.
12 Suggest **two** reasons why a manufacturer might use pressure die casting rather than gravity die casting when manufacturing 100 identical toy soldiers.
13 Name a specific product manufactured by rotational moulding and give **two** reasons why rotational moulding is suitable for the product you have named.
15 Discuss the advantages and disadvantages the use of knock-down (KD) fittings has on the furniture industry.

ONLINE

8 Viability of design solutions

8.1 Assessing whether a design solution meets its stakeholder requirements

Critical evaluation of how a design solution has met its intended requirements

REVISED

Functionality

Designers seek to ensure that any product meets users' expectations. Testing is undertaken to ensure the product:

- meets its intended purpose
- meets regulatory standards
- functions correctly.

During the design process, designers evaluate prototypes and gather feedback from stakeholders. Designers avoid design fixation by considering feedback from all stakeholders while also considering the product's environment of use.

Figure 8.1 Small changes to products can ensure they are usable by all. Tactile paving assists visually impaired pedestrians and warns them of danger ahead

Ease of use and inclusivity of the solution

Usability refers to how easy a product is to use and how clear its functions are. Inclusive design considers how easily a product can be used by everyone without special adaptation.

Market research aims to recreate the environment of use and will include:

- discussion with user groups
- group tests
- small-scale roll outs.

This research determines how the user interacts with the product and aids designers in producing a good **human interface** that allows users to learn through trial and error. Designers aim to simplify interfaces so new users are not daunted by numerous buttons and possible interactions.

Key word

Human interface: the part(s) of a product that the user comes into physical contact with or that provides feedback, such as images or sound.

Testing of users considers:

- common mistakes
- situations where manual operation is difficult
- problems understanding the interface
- how often users cannot proceed.

User needs

The primary user is normally the most important consideration when designing any product. Designers gather a broad range of opinion from a wide variety of potential users to avoid biased opinion. The feedback provided is used throughout the design stages to consider:

- Who will use the product?
- How will they interact with the product?
- What is the product used for?
- What environment is the product used in?
- When and how often will the product be used?
- What other products will interact with the interface?

Testing design solutions

REVISED

Pre-production testing takes place regularly and is shared with stakeholders through mind maps, models, simulations or mock ups.

Sketch models are utilised to allow designers to judge user interaction and gather feedback. These models are often produced quickly and may only be a model of part of the product. Rapid prototyping is often used to produce more complete products to allow for discussion, observation or to gather answers to pre-planned questions.

Figure 8.2 Rapid prototyping allows designs to quickly gain feedback. Here a shoe is manufactured from a 3D CAD file

Multi-disciplinary working is used by designers utilising web or cloud-based software to share and discuss concepts. This enables the collaboration of a range of specialists in areas such as manufacturing, marketing and finance to assess the viability of a design.

When the design reaches the delivery phase after development, the design team undertakes a series of checks and actions. These include:

- testing of the final product by stakeholders
- approval and launch
- setting targets for future developments or the streamlining of processes or costs
- on-going evaluation and feedback to identify possible improvements to future production.

Testing the feasibility of getting a product to market

REVISED

Competing against existing firms with established brand identities is difficult, so designers need to undertake a number of tests to identify and address possible issues that may impact on the potential feasibility of a new product entering a market.

Table 8.1 Testing product feasibility

Method	Type of testing
CAD testing	Visual testing of the product and packaging
User trialling	User testing by consumers and expert testers
Focus group tests	Group feedback and discussion
Clinic tests (similar to focus groups)	Hand-picked groups of a chosen demographic who will often have experience in giving feedback and discussing designs

Consideration of cost

The costing of a product will determine if it is successful. Designers forecast sales and determine a price point to maximise profit and units sold. The costs to consider include:

- materials and components
- design and development
- production and manufacturing

- legal
- marketing
- packaging
- transportation.

Appeal to consumers

Creating a product that appeals to consumers is essential. Designers undertake feasibility studies into the possible branding options of a product to best meet consumer demand. Careful consideration of differing factors is required to generate sales. These will include:

- personal taste
- fashion
- trends
- brand loyalty
- aesthetic appeal
- function.

Figure 8.3 Packaging is not just the materials that allow ease of transport and protection but also the shape and styling of a product

Packaging

Packaging has a big impact on the viability of a design. Packaging refers to the materials that wrap or protect a product and also the shape, style or form of the product. All packaging adds additional cost to the product and impacts on how feasible it is in terms of profit. Considerations for packaging include:

- material costs
- printed areas and colours
- level of protection for the product
- additional functions or requirements such as water resistance
- added value in terms of appeal
- environmental impact.

Typical mistake

Don't focus only on the product itself but remember to consider the additional impacts of packaging, testing, R&D and consumer expectations. This will demonstrate a deeper understanding of the concerns a designer must plan for.

Exam tip

Keep up to date with current issues and product releases. Having a broad understanding of topical examples will enable you to back up your essays with a range of supporting statements.

Relevant standards that need to be met (A Level)

REVISED

Standards are published documents which contain precise information which can be used as a consistent rule, guideline or definition.

British Standards Institute

The British Standards Institute (BSI) is an internationally recognised standards body. It provides standards in five formats:

1. specifications
2. methods
3. guides
4. vocabularies
5. codes of practice.

Standards are continually reviewed and changed as required. Products and services which meet the BSI's standards may be awarded the BSI Kitemark. This mark gives consumers confidence that the products they are purchasing have been tested and meet high standards.

Figure 8.4 Customers will look for quality standards marks on products. Here we see the BSI Kitemark and the CE European Standards symbols

For a company to obtain a Kitemark, it must show that it has considered a number of quality assurance practices in detail. These include:

- manufacturing systems
- tests
- checks
- record keeping
- procedures dealing with identified failings.

Designers often plan to ensure a new product is BSI compliant and may consider:

- durability
- materials
- finish
- fitness for purpose
- ease of disposal
- environmental impact
- product labelling
- energy efficiency.

International Organisation for Standardisation

The International Organisation for Standardisation (ISO) is broadly similar to the BSI and shares many documents and standards. Depending on their geographical location companies may choose to apply to either agency for a quality assurance mark.

Table 8.2 The seven steps required for an ISO standards award

Step	Aspects considered
Design and development planning	Are data-handling and quality checks in place?
Design inputs	Have customer or regulatory requirements been taken into account?
Design and development outputs	Has the documentation, data and assembly instructions needed to manufacture the product been produced? Have the instructions for final use been produced?
Design and development review	Is there documentation to record stakeholders' views and quality reviews?
Design and development verification	Is there documentation to show that regulatory requirements have been met?
Design and development validation	Are there records to show that full testing has taken place?
Control of changes	Is there documentation to cover possible changes and any subsequent knock-on effects?

Now test yourself

TESTED

1. What is the name of the quality assurance mark issued by the BSI?
2. Why are standards for measurements useful in global manufacturing?
3. State four costs for a new product that must be considered by a designer.
4. Explain what 'inclusive design' means.
5. State four ways in which the packaging of a product will have an impact on its viability.

8.2 Assessing whether a design solution meets the criteria of technical specifications

Physical testing

REVISED

Designers will normally analyse a product's viability once a final design has been completed. Pre-production models undergo rigorous testing in their environment of use. These tests will check:

- fitness for purpose
- ease of use
- suitability of materials
- suitability of manufacturing techniques.

Functionality

Tests are carried out to check a product has met its technical specification and user needs. These include:

- destructive physical tests
- non-destructive physical tests
- user trials.

Figure 8.5 Tolerances are checked at various stages. Here a crankshaft is checked; parts found to be outside of tolerance will likely wear more quickly or not work or fit as intended

Accuracy

Errors in manufacture could make a product useless or mean that parts do not fit together during assembly. Defined tolerances and the monitoring of variables are fundamental in ensuring the quality of a product.

Designers and manufacturers use quality control to monitor:

- uniformity of parts
- tolerances
- performance
- differences in materials
- machinery tolerances
- machine sensor accuracy.

A variety of tests are undertaken to ensure the quality of the product including its electronics, bought-in components and component parts. These tests take place at various times and frequencies depending on the product and may include:

- visual checks
- data comparisons
- accuracy of dimensions checks
- weight checks
- quality of finish checks.

Performance

Physical performance tests for a product are based around the technical specification requirements. These tests reproduce the types of damage caused by users and products are stressed to the expected levels they will encounter during use. This type of testing looks at:

- flammability tests
- circuitry tests
- safety checks
- durability analysis
- stress testing.

Manufacturers will use total quality management (TQM) to ensure that both the products and the system manufacturing them are of the required quality level.

Figure 8.6 Flammability tests are important for products such as children's Halloween fancy dress clothing. A number of high-profile cases have been in the news where outfits have caught on fire due to proximity to naked flames

How physical testing systems are integrated into the manufacturing process (A Level)

REVISED

Testing of materials for durability and aftercare

Fabric testing takes into account tolerances of washing machines when considering labelling and washing instructions. They will often determine conservative temperatures to ensure products are not damaged during washing.

Destructive and non-destructive methods

A range of destructive and non-destructive tests are available to judge materials or parts at various stages of the production process.

Table 8.3 Methods of destructive and non-destructive testing

Test	Type of test and method
Tensometer	Tensile test (destructive) A material is placed under tension and how it performs in terms of force/extension until its failure is plotted.
Vickers pyramid hardness test	Hardness test (destructive) A diamond tip is pressed onto a material and the indent is measured.
Izod impact test	Impact test to toughness or brittleness (destructive) A pendulum breaks the material during its swing and the energy taken to do so is measured.
Brinell hardness test	Hardness test (destructive) A hardened standard size steel ball is forced into the material's surface using a pre-set load. The diameter of the indent in the surface is measured.
X-rays	Hidden defects (non-destructive) An X-ray beam passes through the material or part and an image is projected onto a display screen, allowing the observation of tiny details such as hairline cracks within the material.
Ultrasonics	Hidden defects (non-destructive) Sound waves are pulsed into the material and different sounds indicate faults. Determines the ferocity of welds or material defects.
The Shore scleroscope hardness test	Hardness test (non-destructive) A diamond-tipped hammer is used to judge the hardness of large ingots or metal parts that are inconvenient to move or are unsuitable for destructive methods of testing.

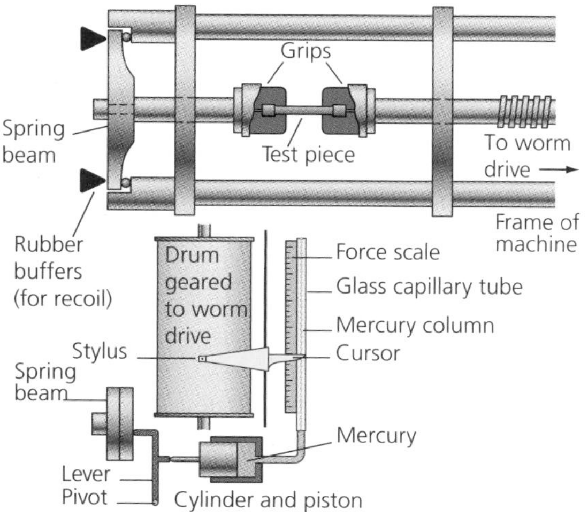

Figure 8.7 Tensometer test rig

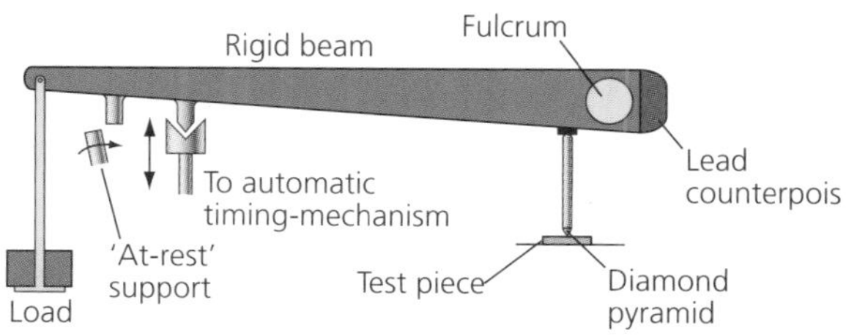

Figure 8.8 Vickers rig

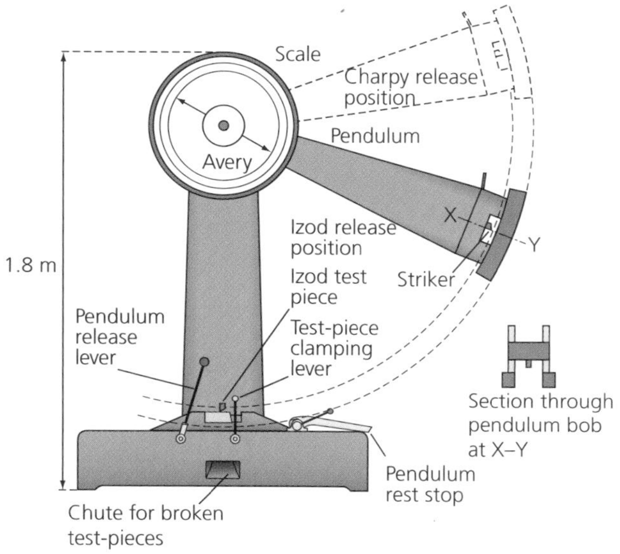

Figure 8.9 Izod rig

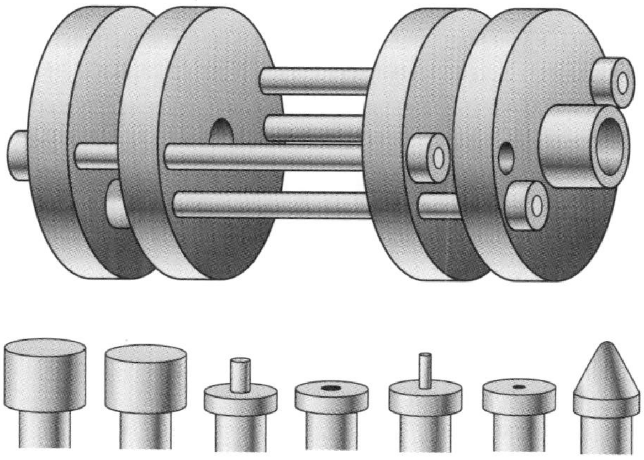

Figure 8.10 Compression cage for carrying out the Brinell test

Testing models and prototypes for performance and fitness for purpose

REVISED

Models and prototypes will be extensively tested to make sure that they perform correctly and can be used for the purpose for which the product is marketed. These tests will aim to highlight any potential issues with the design, materials and manufacturing processes used. Some companies will use this as part of their marketing for the product, for example Ikea has made commercials showing their product testing in action to show the durability of their furniture.

Testing products in use

REVISED

Consumer testing

Consumer testing takes place to check that the final product will meet customer expectations. Consumers are given products to test and questionnaires to fill in looking at every aspect of the product in order to test whether the product matches their needs. The questions will look at aspects such as:

- quality
- functionality
- visual appeal
- issues or problems using the product
- whether the consumers understand how to use the product.

One form of testing is called consumer acceptance. A panel of users is recruited to test the product and will use the product for a period of time before giving their feedback.

Exam tip

Make sure you know a broad range of tests and which materials they are suited to. Products in the exams may include material choices from other specialisms so understanding other areas will aid your ability to consider a wide diversity of components or options.

Virtual testing

Virtual testing can be carried out using CAD software, allowing designers to test different aspects of the product to confirm that they will meet design requirements. CAD software can analyse the effects of using different materials and the effects of the stress caused to the product when a load is applied to it. Designers can see the outcome of the test on screen and adapt the product to meet the required standards.

Now test yourself

TESTED

1. Explain the term 'tolerance'.
2. Explain why a performance test on flammability may be important for children's Halloween fancy dress clothing.
3. State three checks manufacturers will undertake to ensure accuracy during production.
4. State three tests that may be undertaken on samples of new stock to ensure they match existing stock.
5. What are the three ways to test that a product meets the technical specification?

Typical mistake

Don't describe a type of testing which is inappropriate to the product in question due to material, scale of production or stage of development.

8.3 Determining whether design solutions are commercially viable (A Level)

Feasibility studies

REVISED

Designers and manufacturers use various methods to assess the feasibility of a product – whether it is commercially viable – in terms of being able to bring it to market quickly and efficiently, ensure sales and make a profit.

The design solution's impact on user lifestyles

Designers often aim to prove that a new product is viable by showing that it will have a positive impact on a user's lifestyle. The feasibility of an intended product can be hard to prove, however, so designers use a range of historical data including:

- buying data
- demographic information
- results of trials
- previous demand
- the positive impacts of new materials or production processes.

Unexpected negative impacts can be a problem for designers and often only come to light after the product has been rolled out. These may include:

- language barriers
- loyalty to competitor brands
- poor market place traction.

How well a product performs

A product must meet performance standards to be viable. Viability hinges on the product breaking even in terms of profit. Performance may be judged using:

- wearer trials
- user trials
- destructive testing
- focus groups and clinics.

Designers must take care not to over-engineer products, making them overly strong or able to perform above the requirements of their normal expected use. Over-engineering will add significant costs and mean that the expected price point is no longer viable.

Accurate feasibility studies are essential to establish that a product is viable and they take into consideration:

- customer demand and the perceived need for the product
- warranty requirements
- forecast sales
- customer satisfaction.

Technical difficulty of manufacture

Profit and the viability of the final product are often closely linked to the production costs. These costs are determined by the complexity of the design.

Complex designs are often possible but the tooling and manufacturing costs can make them unfeasible. Designers utilise Design for Manufacture (DFM) to ensure designs are easy to manufacture with the aim of reducing costs to improve viability.

Feasibility analysis considers the demand for the product and the scale of production. For example:

- Batch or one-off production is not suited to automated processes.
- Lower-volume products often require a greater input of manual labour.
- The number of human hours required to make the product.
- The investment in new plant or machinery required to make the product at a given scale.

Figure 8.11 Fully equipping a factory with the required plant is likely to require considerable investment. Feasibility studies must plan for these costs to ensure viability

Stock availability of materials and components

The correct materials and resources must be available for a product to be manufactured. Feasibility studies take into account the unit costs associated with obtaining and transporting them.

Stock issues occur when:

- the unit cost fluctuates or is above the expected cost originally planned for
- the supplier of materials is unreliable
- the quantity of available materials is insufficient
- there are long lead times between ordering the materials and delivery
- there is strong demand or competition for the materials or parts
- sustainability issues arise from sourcing the material.

Feasibility studies also take into account supply chains and the risks of outsourcing to suppliers. This approach is often used in complex products like cars which use JIT production.

Typical mistake

Don't assume that the costs affecting a product are only the immediate costs such as material or labour. Show your understanding of how the wider costs affect the viability of a product such as transport, economies of scale, supply chains or production scale.

Costs and profit

For a product to be viable it must break even in terms of profit. Costs of production are often variable and can fluctuate. This means that companies must plan their expected costs to ensure that the product is placed at a price point that will generate sales and ensure profit.

Manufacturers aim to reduce costs by:

- a reduction in the costs of parts or materials from suppliers
- a reduction in waste
- the effective use of total quality management (TQM).

Costs are generally categorised as fixed or variable. Fixed costs are constant regardless of the number of units produced, for example regular monthly payments. Variable costs fluctuate according to the number of units produced and changes in the market. Sometimes there are mixed costs, for example where power is paid for at a fixed monthly cost, but there are possible variables in cost according to the amount used.

Feasibility studies account for the fact that costs will sometimes change from being fixed to variable or vice versa over time.

Table 8.4 Types of costs

Cost	Type
Rent or mortgage	Fixed
Power	Mixed
Insurance	Fixed
Wages	Variable
Miscellaneous	Variable
Machinery	Fixed
Materials	Variable
Tooling	Variable

Timescales involved

Feasibility studies take into account the exact timing of a product launch with the aim of maximising its sales and traction in a market. Bringing a product to market must consider a variety of issues including:

- releasing too late into a market area where a competitor is already aggressively expanding
- seasonal demand
- economic changes
- changes in fashion and trends.

Other time factors impact on the viability of a design. These may be:

- The time the feasibility study itself takes – extended studies could mean the product is beaten to market by a competitor
- Transportation and shipping times – this may be of raw materials but could include consumables that could go off in transit
- The time taken for regulatory checks of certification or to secure intellectual property rights.

Figure 8.12 Ecover aims to maintain a positive brand image to promote its environmentally friendly cleaning products

Promotion, brand awareness and advertising potential

Companies test consumers' opinion of their brand identity and aim to raise brand awareness to confirm it is viable and appropriate. Feasibility studies can clarify that the branding is:

- recognisable
- suited to the product
- pitched correctly to reach the selected demographic
- linked to a positive consumer experience.

Studies into advertising will consider:

- appropriate tactics to use
- levels of demand
- effective marketing strategies
- **customer reach**
- product sales forecasts.

Key word

Customer reach: the number of potential customers a company can reach through a marketing strategy.

Balancing supply and demand

Feasibility analysis is undertaken to ensure that there are the correct levels of supply to meet demand. Supply of a product can change due to numerous factors, including:

- meeting demand as consumers purchase more of the product
- reduced demand as the product goes into decline
- expanding into new territories or markets.

Table 8.5 Balancing supply and demand

Too little supply to meet demand	Too much supply of product
• If demand outstrips supply, consumers may go to other competitors • Unexpected pressure on a company to grow to meet demand can mean problems in securing investment or capital • If the price of products rise, the high costs for consumers can jeopardise future sales or traction in the market	• A saturated market place means that products will need to be sold at a lower price to remain competitive • Products that remain unsold go to waste • Products that have a limited shelf life may expire before being sold

After roll out, companies can track both sales and changing demand using an **electronic point of sale (EPOS)** system. This allows the compilation of historical data and live tracking to monitor fluctuations in supply and demand.

Market analysis of similar products

Analysis is undertaken to determine what products exist in the market before, during and possibly after a product is designed. Studies aim to show how the intended product may be affected by competitor products or whether there is sufficient market share available to make a profit.

Studies will look at:

- competitor products
- sales trends
- promotions
- opportunities.

Analysis of competitor products will allow judgements to be made on:

- copyright law
- materials and manufacturing
- quality
- product problems
- the new product's USP.

Key word

Electronic point of sale (EPOS): a computerised system used in retail shops to record sales and track levels of stock.

Exam tip

Prior to the exam, consider a number of household products and what design decisions were made to ensure they were viable. Aim to consider the impacts of branding, brand loyalty, cost, packaging and the saturation of products in their particular part of the market. Being well practised in identifying issues will mean you can answer exam questions on this topic with a range of well-thought out responses.

Now test yourself

TESTED

1 Give an example of a fixed cost.
2 Why might an economic downturn have an impact on the launch of a product?
3 Manufacturers will often use total quality management (TQM) to reduce costs. State two costs they may aim to reduce.
4 What problems may occur after the roll out of a product if feasibility studies have not been thorough?
5 How might over-engineering a new design affect sales?

Exam practice

1 State **three** considerations designers take into account when observing users to determine how they interact with a new human interface.
2 Manual labour is often used for producing products in lower volumes. State **two** possible impacts this might have on viability.
3 Give **three** reasons why stock availability must be considered when planning the production of a new product.
4 What performance tests would be suitable to confirm that the production of a vehicle steering column met the required standards?
5 State **three** ways a company may benefit from attaining a standards agency mark.
6 State **three** ways in which a company manufacturing and selling products benefits from the electronic point of sale (EPOS) system.
7 Explain the issues surrounding supply and demand that must be considered when bringing a product to market.
8 How might high levels of complexity in terms of production for a product affect its viability?
9 A company is producing a product with an integrated three-pin plug. Give **two** examples of how tolerances will be important and how they might be checked.
10 Explain how the packaging for a cosmetics product might have an impact on its viability.

ONLINE

9 Health and safety

9.1 Ensuring safety in a workshop environment

Safe working practices in the workshop

REVISED

A safe working environment is a right for all employees. Health and safety is everyone's responsibility but employers need to consider ways of minimising risks to keep employees safe and free from harm in the workplace. Employers must ensure procedures are implemented and abide by legislation to keep employees safe and to prevent them being harmed or at risk of illness due to work.

Risk assessment and identifying hazards

Part of the process of keeping people safe is **risk assessment**.

- An employer is required by law to carry out risk assessments and these should be recorded in any establishment where there are five or more employees.
- The risk assessment must consider what might cause harm to people, and if reasonable steps are being taken to prevent that harm.
- Not all risks can be eliminated, but the employer must take all reasonably practicable measures to identify potential **hazards** and minimise the risk (the likelihood or chance that someone may be harmed as a result of being exposed to the hazard).
- Risk assessments must be regularly reviewed by the employer.

Key words

Risk assessment: a statutory process that considers what might cause harm to people and what reasonable steps might be taken to prevent that harm.

Hazard: anything that could cause someone harm.

Control measure: any action carried out in advance that protects against a possible danger or injury.

Table 9.1 An example of a basic risk assessment for a manufacturing process

Process	Drilling holes into wood on a pillar drill
Hazard(s)	• Moving material • Flying particles • Flying chuck • Rotating parts
Potential harm	• Cut risk for the operator and bystander • Particles in the eye of the operator • Entanglement of the operator
Control measures	• Clamp material • Wear safety goggles • Remove chuck before operating machine • Tie back any loose items • Provide training for operators
Review date	• The risk assessment is signed by person assessing the risk. The 6- or 12-month review date is also noted.

Typical mistake

Don't use generic terms to describe potential risks and control measures, for example the person could get hurt so they should be careful in the workshop. State the specific hazard and control measure, for example a person could get a wood particles in their eye and to prevent this they should wear safety goggles.

Exam tip

Make sure you are able to identify hazards and control measures to write a risk assessment for common workshop and industrial practices.

Safe working procedures and equipment

REVISED

Safe working procedures are fundamentally the same for schools, colleges and industry. They aim to keep the person doing the work, as well as those in the vicinity, safe and free from harm.

Safe working covers factors such as:

- **Training:** machinery or equipment should not be operated unless you have been trained in its use.
- **Personal protective equipment (PPE):** must be worn when using machinery.
- **Guards:** should be used on machinery.
- **Work areas:** should be kept neat, clean and free of hazards.
- **Emergency procedures:** all persons must be aware of fire evacuation routes and muster points, emergency phone numbers, the locations of fire extinguishers, emergency stops, first aid kits.
- **Walkways:** should be kept clear and free from trip hazards. Designated walk zones may be used in industry.
- **Illness/accidents:** if a person becomes ill or injured or in the event of an accident, this should be reported to a supervisor/teacher.
- **Job rotation:** so that workers are not at risk of repetitive strain injury (RSI) or injury caused by a lapse in concentration from doing the same task with no variation.
- **Safety signage:** should be posted to warn of potential harm or to mandate the wearing of specific PPE.

Figure 9.1 Examples of mandatory signage from a construction site

Now test yourself

TESTED

1 Explain what is meant by the term 'hazard'.
2 Explain what is meant by the term 'risk assessment'.
3 Give an example of mandatory PPE to be worn on a construction site.
4 Suggest two reasons why a production plant may use designated walkways.
5 Give three examples of safe working practices in a school or college workshop.

9.2 The implications of health and safety legislation on product manufacture (A Level)

Duties of employers and employees

REVISED

Health and safety is designed to protect employees from harm. Employers must comply with specific legislation to protect employees in the manufacturing industry.

The **Health and Safety Executive (HSE)** is a national independent watchdog for work-related health, safety and illness.

- The HSE helps companies and employers to meet health and safety obligations.
- It produces guidance documents and also investigate accidents in the workplace.

Health and Safety at Work Act 1974

The **Health and Safety at Work Act 1974 (HASAWA)** is the main piece of legislation for British health and safety law.

- To comply, all employers must ensure (so far as is reasonably practicable) that all employees and visitors to the workplace are protected in terms of health, safety and welfare.
- Compliance includes assessing risks and adopting appropriate safety measures to provide a safe environment for product manufacture.

Control of Substances Hazardous to Health Regulations 2002

To comply with the **Control of Substances Hazardous to Health (COSHH) Regulations 2002**, employers need to prevent, reduce or control their workers' (and any worker in the vicinity) exposure to substances that may be hazardous or cause ill health.

- Hazardous substances include:
  - paints, varnishes, cleaning agents and adhesives that may be used during work
  - fumes that may be created as a result of processes such as soldering or brazing
  - airborne particles such as wood dust created by sanding timber.

Key words

Health and Safety Executive (HSE): a national independent watchdog for work-related health, safety and illness.

Health and Safety at Work Act 1974 (HASAWA): the main piece of legislation for British health and safety law.

Control of Substances Hazardous to Health Regulations 2002: legislation to prevent, reduce or control people's exposure to hazardous substances in the workplace.

- Hazardous substances will usually show a symbol that meets the classification labelling and packaging (CLP) regulations.
- The CLP hazard pictograms in Figure 9.2 allow easy identification of the hazard as corrosive, flammable, toxic, etc.
- Hazardous product suppliers will supply a safety data sheet with information on safe use, safe storage, ingredients and first aid procedures.

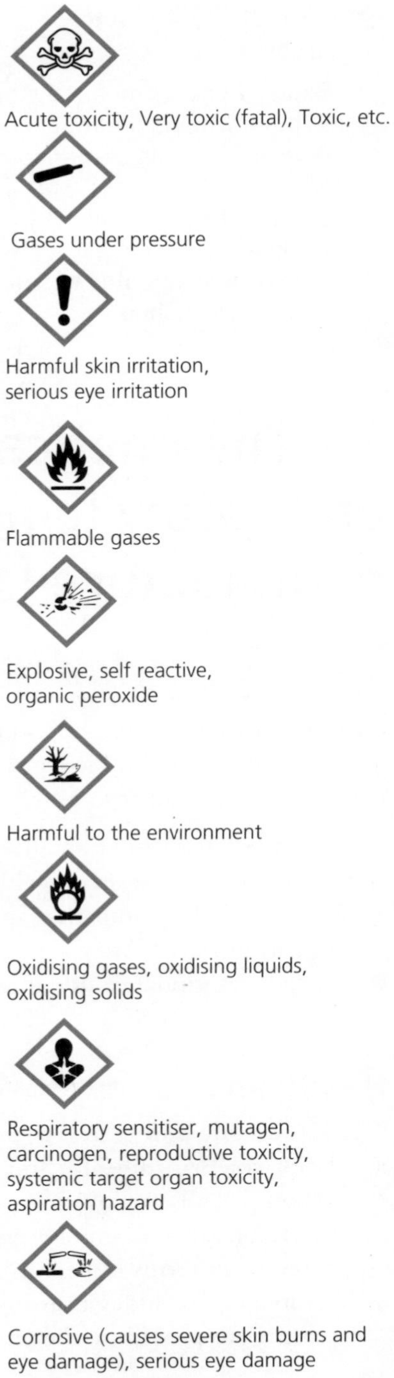

Figure 9.2 CLP hazard pictograms

Personal Protective Equipment at Work Regulations 1992 and 2002

In addition to providing training, carrying out risk assessments and making people aware of procedures such as for evacuation and accidents, keeping people safe in the workplace also involves the provision and use of personal protective equipment (PPE).

Even after risk assessments and control measures have been put in place, some hazards might remain, such as to:

- **Lungs:** from breathing in contaminated air such as wood dust or paint fumes.
- **Eyes:** from flying particles or splashes from solder, acids or corrosive liquids.
- **Skin:** from corrosive liquids.
- **Head, feet or body:** from falling materials.
- **Ears:** from loud noises such as a jack hammer used in construction.

To reduce the risk from the hazard, PPE should be used. The employer also has a duty of care under the Personal Protective Equipment at Work Regulations 1992 and 2002 to provide PPE and ensure people are trained in how to use it properly, for example a safety harness for working at height.

As a guide, employers should:

- choose products which are CE (Conformité Européenne) marked and meet the PPE regulations
- ensure products fit the user
- instruct the user in how to wear and use the PPE
- maintain the PPE to ensure it is in good working order for example, replace scratched safety glasses.

Figure 9.3 Examples of PPE signage

Product labelling and product assurance related to safety

REVISED

Making the product safe to ensure the safety of the potential user is something designers and manufacturers need to consider during the design and manufacture process.

Many products have specific legislation and standards that state requirements that the product must meet. If goods are found to be faulty or do not perform as the manufacturer claims, the consumer can get their money back.

The **Consumer Protection Act (CPA) (1987)** gives consumers rights to expect relevant health and safety information on products and to claim compensation if a defective product causes injury, death or damage.

The **Consumer Rights Act 2015** is designed to safeguard consumers from faulty products by giving consumers certain rights. The act is split into three parts:

- **Part 1:** concerns consumer contracts for goods, digital content and services.
- **Part 2:** concerns unfair terms.
- **Part 3:** concerns other miscellaneous provisions such as letting agencies.

The British Standards Institute

The British Standards Institute (BSI) is a national standards body that works with industry and government to produce a set of standards to assure consumers that products are well-produced, safe and fit for purpose.

- A standard is documented agreed way of doing something, providing assurance of consistently reliable and safe products.
- The BSI Kitemark is a quality mark, used on hundreds of products such as glass, cycle helmets and electric plug casings, and is one of the most recognised symbols of quality and safety in the world.

Toys

Toy manufacturers must comply with the **Toys (Safety) Regulations 2011**, which is part of the **European Toy Safety Directive** as well as **British Standard BS EN 71**.

Toys must:

- be designed and manufactured to comply with the safety requirements during its normal period of use
- have a safety assessment, have instructions for safe use and safety information where appropriate
- show they meet the assessment procedure for the CE marking
- have information identifying the toy and manufacturer on the toy or packaging.

Exam tip

Make sure you know the full name of the specific acts or legislation and can describe their purpose.

Now test yourself

TESTED

1. What is the Health and Safety at Work Act 1974?
2. Suggest two things an employer should do to provide a duty of care under the Personal Protective Equipment at Work Regulations 1992 and 2002.
3. To comply with the COSHH Regulations, hazardous product suppliers must provide information to the consumer. List two items they must supply.
4. State two different hazards a CLP hazard pictogram may show.
5. List two specific pieces of legislation designed to help protect the consumer when buying a product.

Typical mistake

Don't refer to generic standards or legislation – you need to be specific. For example, instead of writing, 'safety standards help prevent people being harmed by a product', a better answer may be 'The British Standards Institute BSI Kitemark on a product shows the consumer the product has passed certain safety tests such as electrical safety for an electric plug'.

Exam practice

1. Suggest **two** ways an employer can comply with the Health and Safety at Work Act 1974.
2. What does the acronym COSHH stand for?
3. State **two** ways in which a manufacturer can comply with the COSHH Regulations.
4. What is the British Standards Institute (BSI)?
5. Give a specific example of a product which would display a CLP hazard pictogram, and state what pictogram it would display.
6. Write up a risk assessment for drilling a hole in a piece of pine using a pillar drill in a school workshop.
7. State **two** specific hazard controls an employer would have to adopt for workers undertaking MIG welding.
8. Give **three** examples of safe working procedures which would be expected in a workplace.
9. What is meant by the term 'control measure'?
10. Suggest **two** ways in which an employer can meet the Personal Protective Equipment at Work Regulations 1992 and 2002.

ONLINE

Success in the examinations

AS Level

REVISED

If you are completing AS Level Product Design:

- you will take **one** written exam worth **90 marks** (this is 50 per cent of your total AS Level mark)
- the exam will last for **one hour 45 minutes**
- you will be tested on **Principles of product design**.

The questions will include:

- a mixture of short and long answer questions
- at least one question that will require you to analyse a product
- at least one question examining your mathematical skills
- questions requiring sketching to show the construction of a product
- two extended answer questions to test your use of terminology and your synoptic knowledge.

A Level

REVISED

If you are completing A Level Product Design you will sit two written exams.

Paper 1 – Principles of product design

- The paper is worth **80 marks** (26.7 per cent of the total A Level).
- The exam will last **1 hour and 30 minutes**.

The questions will include:

- a mixture of short and long answer questions
- at least one question that will require you to analyse a product
- at least one question examining your mathematical skills
- questions requiring sketching to show the construction of a product
- one extended answer question to test your use of terminology and your synoptic knowledge.

Paper 2 – Problem solving in product design

- The paper is worth **70 marks** (23.3 per cent of the total A Level).
- The exam will last **1 hour and 45 minutes**.

The paper will consist of a series of long answer questions. OCR suggest 35 minutes of allocated reading time. This could be completed at the start but it is suggested that you skim-read the resource booklet content and make notes to get a solid overview, and return to sections to undertake more detailed analysis.

You will be required to:

- read and respond to the resource booklet
- use knowledge, skills and understanding you have gained over the course
- demonstrate how you solve problems using critical analysis and evaluation skills to show the suitability of your design solutions.

Types of questions to expect:

- At least one question will require you to utilise mathematical skills.
- Some questions will focus on implications of wider factors of design including cost, sustainability, viability, trends, design thinking and communication.
- There will be two extended essay style questions which will ask you to use and apply knowledge gained throughout the course.

Understanding the resources

Practise the skills below prior to the exam to help you to get the most out of your reading time.

Predicting content

It's a good idea to make predictions by looking at images and headings before you read more detail:

- What do the images show?
- What do the headings and subheadings tell you?
- What topic might the resource be about?
- What do you already know about this topic with specific thought about the environment of use?

Skimming

Skimming involves reading quickly to get the main idea of the text. Reading topic sentences (usually the first and last sentences of a paragraph) can be an effective way of understanding the main idea of each section of the resource booklet.

Scanning

Scanning involves searching for numbers, symbols and long words in a text. This is a useful way of locating answers.

Reading for detail or intensive reading

We use this skill when we need to understand every word in a section of the booklet, for example when answering detailed questions that require you to justify your answers or link your answers to specific data or arguments within the resource booklet.

Command words

You will need to understand the meanings of the different command words that are used to ask questions:

- Analyse: Separate information into components and identify their characteristics. Discuss the pros and cons of a topic or argument and make reasoned comment.
- Annotate: Add to a diagram or image words that describe and/or explain features.
- Apply: Use relevant skills/knowledge/understanding appropriate to context.
- Assess: Offer a reasoned judgement supported by relevant facts.
- Calculate: Generate a numerical answer, with workings shown.
- Compare: Identify similarities and differences.
- Contrast: Identify differences.
- Define: Give the meaning of.
- Describe: Give a detailed account of.

- Discuss: Look at the advantages and disadvantages.
- Draw/sketch: Produce a rough drawing in pencil or pen.
- Evaluate: Give an opinion by exploring the good and bad points.
- Explain: To give account of the purposes or reasons.
- Give: Supply.
- Identify: Recognise, list, name or otherwise characterise.
- Illustrate: Show by explaining and giving examples.
- Interpret: Translate information into recognisable form. Explain the meaning of something.
- Justify: Present a reasoned case for actions or decisions made.
- Name: To provide appropriate word(s) or term(s).
- Outline: Concentrate on the main points of the topic or item.
- Recommend: Suggest/put forward as being appropriate, with reasons why.
- Select: Carefully choose as being the most suitable for a task or purpose.
- State: Express in precise terms, express in unequivocal terms.
- Summarise: Give the main points of an idea or argument. Leave out unnecessary details.

Your response

You will be asked to communicate your technical understanding of design opportunities. It is likely that you will be asked to repurpose a product or determine construction options for it. It is important to understand that you are not being asked to offer new ideas or design concepts.

You should:

- Demonstrate your understanding of manufacturing techniques
- Show a breadth of material knowledge and understanding
- Critically analyse your suggestions and justify how they meet the requirements
- Carefully consider the environment of use for the product
- Produce drawings that are detailed and annotated, well drawn and clear

When answering extended answer questions, you should use appropriate technical terms, including materials, manufacturing techniques and subject-specific terminology. The questions will normally use one of the following key words:

- **Analyse** will require you to separate information and identify characteristics. You should aim to produce clear arguments that show the pros and cons of a topic area.
- **Assess** questions will require you to make a justified or reasoned judgement based on facts relevant to the topic area.
- **Discuss** questions will require you to evidence the advantages and disadvantages of the subject matter.
- **Evaluate** answers will demonstrate your opinion of the good and bad points in comparison with each other.

Sample examination questions

Paper 1

Sample question

The diagram below shows a low-carbon steel bracket.

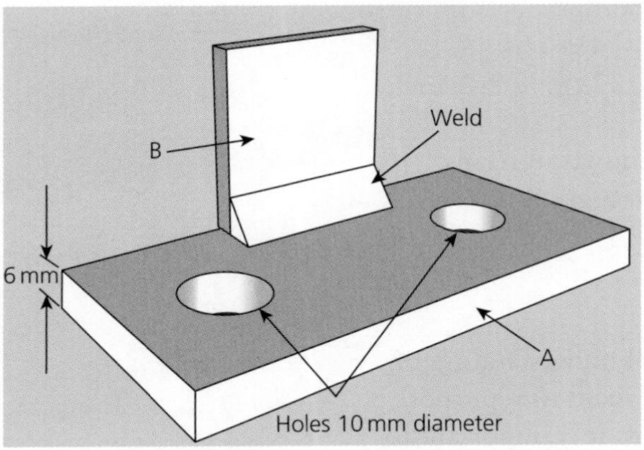

A manufacturer is producing 100 identical brackets.

a State **two** different manufacturing aids and explain how each could improve the efficiency of the manufacturing process. [4 marks]

b Calculate the total volume of waste material resulting from the drilling of all the holes for this batch of components. Give your answer to the nearest cubic mm. [3 marks]

Candidate response

a A jig would be used to help with drilling the holes. It would consist of a device with two hardened guide bushes to resist wear from the drill. The bushes would be in exactly the right place for the holes required and the jig would slot positively on to part A before to ensure that the operative could drill the holes accurately without needing to do any marking out.

A fixture would be required to ensure that part B is welded in exactly the right position. This consists of a simple clamping device that positively engages both pieces and locks them in place. A simple cam or lever-operated locking mechanism would be preferable to a threaded clamp as it would be quicker to operate and would further improve efficiency. The time and expense of manufacturing both the jig and fixture would be repaid by the greater efficiency of manufacture and the reduced likelihood of defects adversely affecting the quality of the batch.

b The volume of each hole is $\pi r^2 \times$ thickness and there are 200 holes $= \pi \times 25 \times 6 \times 200 = 94{,}200\ \text{mm}^3$

Assessment comment

a This is an excellent response that covers everything that is required. Each of the following points is worthy of credit:
- jig for drilling holes
- hardened guide bushes/wear resistance
- accurate positioning of bushes
- positive location
- no need for marking out
- fixture/welding in correct position using positively engaging clamping device
- cam or lever-operated locking mechanism
- advantage over screw clamp.

b The candidate has correctly calculated the volume of material involved and has shown the working, so is awarded the full 3 marks.

Paper 2

Sample question

A range of existing products are used by shoppers to carry shopping home.

A supermarket chain has identified an opportunity to launch a new system to be used by shoppers to reduce long term plastic use. The manufacturer wants to address the problems associated with single-use plastic bags or the limited use of reusable plastic bags.

A wide range of stakeholders and users will have different needs and requirements of the new product being considered.

Critically examine the challenge a designer of the new shopping system will face when considering the needs of all stakeholders and users.

Supermarket Chain Aims To Gain Business Through Going Plastic Free

A large supermarket chain is aiming to gain a larger market share by removing all plastic packaging from their own brand goods and by encouraging shoppers to choose reusable items to transport products home. The chain is planning on trialling a new system across ten flagship stores nationwide to reduce its estimated output of 80,000 tonnes of annual plastic waste. The grocery market was worth £179.1 billion last year.

Research was undertaken by WRAP (Waste & Resources Action Programme) to understand consumer bag usage and attitudes in England*. The observational study looked at in-store usage of bags and containers. Among the findings were:

- Regardless of business size, around 70 per cent of all bags or containers used to pack purchased items were new single-use carrier bags.
- Reused bags and containers made up 26 per cent of all bags or containers used.
- 66 per cent of observed grocery transactions resulted in the use of new single-use carrier bags compared to 42 per cent of consumers stating that they 'always' or 'usually' take single-use carrier bags from the till when doing their main food shopping.
- Consumers did not actively plan to bring their own bags or containers on their shopping trips. The use of new single-use carrier bags was often due to consumers not having their own bags to hand.
- Store interventions were also a factor in new single-use carrier bag usage. Packing by store staff was more likely to result in the use of new single-use carrier bags.

Data shows that the supermarket chain has an average footfall of 23,500 customers in its identified trial stores per week. Shoppers can purchase reusable shopping bags at a cost of 15–25p each and over 50 million have been sold in the UK alone.

Reusable bags require more energy to produce than common plastic shopping bags. One reusable bag requires the same amount of energy as an estimated 28 traditional plastic shopping bags or eight paper bags. If used once per week, four or five reusable bags will replace 520 plastic bags a year. A study commissioned by the United Kingdom Environment Agency in 2005 found that the average cotton bag is used only 51 times before being thrown away. In some cases, reusable bags need to be used over 100 times before they are better for the environment than single-use plastic bags.

Customer surveys show that shoppers are willing to buy into a system that removes bags entirely, providing that a deposit or cost to them is no more than £15. Items would need to be reusable and easy to return if need be. The survey also showed that consumers were significantly less likely to use a system if they perceived it to be unclean or have a previous user's rubbish in it.

**Source: WRAP, 2014, London, Carrier bags usage and attitudes: Consumer research in England, Prepared by Brook Lyndhurst.*

Candidate response

The primary stakeholder for the system to be a success is the consumer. The use of single-use bags is common amongst shoppers with only 26 per cent of consumers using reused bags or containers. It is clear from the evidence that the supermarket chain may struggle to implement the scheme due to the limited uptake of readily available normal reusable bags. Customer surveys imply that they are willing to buy into the scheme, spending up to £15 for the system. It can be argued that consumers who buy into the system will likely use it as they have invested in it. The scheme may need significant investment to raise consumer awareness which will need to be considered in feasibility studies of the new system.

If the product is to be successful, the designer will need to consider how shop assistants influence single bag use versus the new system. Many supermarkets offer packing and it was shown in the survey data that this meant more single-use bags were used. Shop assistants will need training to aid both the implementation of the system and to cut down on the number of bags used whilst still meeting consumer needs. Discounts, loyalty schemes or a free trial of the system may help uptake of the scheme.

Bags are often seen as the easy option, with 70 per cent of sales resulting in the use of a new one. Changing consumer culture will be a challenge. Streamlining of sign up to the new scheme, and the deposits required to ensure the scheme can run without losing money for the supermarket, will all need to be considered. With many consumers moving to click and collect or delivery this could easily be built into this aspect with the drivers simply delivering one system and picking up the last one. This would also allow cleaning of the product by the supermarket which would address a major concern raised in the survey.

The scheme will need a suitable number of users to be feasible for both the supermarket and the manufacturer. The trial scheme had a footfall of 23,500 customers in a week. This is a large customer base and converting only a small number of these customers to the new scheme would have a significant impact. If the new scheme can encourage the removal of at least as much plastic as the annual use of reusable bags, it will aid the removal of 520 bags per customer per year. If just 2350 (10 per cent of weekly consumer footfall using reusable bags) signed up then there could be an annual reduction of 1,222,000 bags used in this single store. This would go a long way towards meeting the goal of 80,000 tonnes of annual waste.

Assessment comment

The student refers to the resource booklet regularly and then makes use of their product design knowledge and understanding to augment and flesh out answers into clear arguments. Note the references to challenges and various stakeholders.

Glossary

Additive manufacture: involves joining or building up material such as the creation of models in a FDM 3D printer.

Additive printing: a manufacturing process joining materials from 3D model data.

Aesthetics: aspects relating to the visual appeal of products.

Anodising: coating (usually aluminium) with a protective oxidised layer by electrolysis.

Anthropometrics: scientific measurements of the human body applied to the design and construction of products.

Assembly jigs: can be used to hold a part in place while a process is being carried out.

Batch production: the manufacture of groups of products to increase efficiency and economy.

Bespoke: a product specially made to order for a customer.

Biological nutrients: organic non-toxic materials that can safely re-enter ecosystems.

Carbon footprint: the total amount of carbon dioxide released into the atmosphere as a result of the activities of an individual, a community or an organisation.

CFRP: carbon fibre reinforced plastic.

Cloud computing/storage: web-based hosting of computer files/applications for access in multiple locations.

Collaboration: working as a team, rather than individually, to achieve a goal.

Composite material: a material comprised of two or more different materials, resulting in a material with enhanced properties.

Compressed boards: made from chips, strands or particles of timber glued together under a compressive force.

Computational fluid dynamics (CFD): 3D CAD simulation tool for fluid or gas flows in or around a product.

Computer-aided engineering (CAE): the simulation and analysis of product and component performance using computer software.

Continuous flow production: a highly automated 24/7 production process, usually requiring a small workforce.

Control measure: any action carried out in advance that protects against a possible danger or injury.

Control of Substances Hazardous to Health Regulations 2002: legislation to prevent, reduce or control people's exposure to hazardous substances in the workplace.

Copyright: gives rights to creators of original ideas, information or intellectual works.

Critical path analysis (CPA): analysis of the stages in a project to ensure time-efficient completion.

Culture: the social behaviour of different societies influenced by their customs and ideas.

Customer reach: the number of potential customers a company can reach through a marketing strategy.

Cycle time: the time taken to complete a manufacturing process.

Demographic: a particular sector of the population. This may relate to age, education level, spending power, geographical location etc.

Design for Disassembly (DFD): a strategy that considers the future need to disassemble a product for it to be repaired, refurbished or recycled.

Design rights: gives rights to the designer or creator of a design (does not cover 2D work).

Direct digital manufacturing (DDM): a system where parts are produced by machines such as 3D printers directly from CAD files.

Eco-materials: often called environmentally friendly materials, those materials that enhance the environmental improvement throughout the whole lifecycle.

Ecological footprint: the impact on the environment and natural resources.

Electronic point of sale (EPOS): a computerised system used in retail shops to record sales and track levels of stock.

Electroplating: involves the coating of an object with a thin layer of metal by using electricity.

Emerging technologies: new technologies that are currently being developed.

Enterprise: a new business venture or project.

Ergonomics: the promotion of optimum design usability and efficiency through the study of how people interact with products and their working environment.

Exploded view: a drawing, usually in isometric projection, showing the relative position of parts for assembly.

Fairtrade: involves better prices, decent working conditions, local sustainability and fair terms of trade for farmers and workers in the developing world.

Fast fashion: a term explaining a quick transition from catwalk to high-street stores to capture current trends.

Feasibility analysis: a consideration of how possible and realistic it is to proceed with a project.

Ferrous: metals that contain iron.

Finite element analysis (FEA): software which analyses the stress in elements of a CAD design.

Fixture: holds work in a given position while a manufacturing process takes place. Fixtures are always fixed to the machine bed.

Flowchart: a diagrammatic representation of a process using standardised symbols.

Former: used to make sure that parts are formed or bent to the same shape.

Functional performance: how the product works or functions.

Galvanising: a process in which steel is coated with zinc.

Gantt chart: a graphical method (bar chart) of showing the time allocation for organising the stages of a manufacturing process.

Generative design: the production of large numbers of alternative design possibilities using biomimicry-related techniques.

GRP: glass-reinforced plastic.

Hardwoods: timber from a broad leaf deciduous tree. Usually slow growing.

Hazard: anything that could cause someone harm.

Health and Safety at Work Act 1974: the main piece of legislation for British health and safety law.

Health and Safety Executive (HSE): a national independent watchdog for work-related health, safety and illness.

High-volume (mass) production: making large numbers of standardised products in highly mechanised factories.

Human factors: the study of how humans behave physically and psychologically in relation to a product.

Human interface: the part(s) of a product that the user comes into physical contact with or that provides feedback, such as images or sound.

Hydrophobic: highly water repellent.

Iconic design: usually a highly innovative design regarded as an inspirational benchmark to other designers.

Inbound marketing: market research used to establish whether a gap in the market exists.

Inclusive design: designing products for ease of use by consumers with the maximum possible range of abilities, without the need for adaptations.

Intellectual property: rights covering all types of intangible, non-physical products.

Invention: a completely new device, machine or system that didn't previously exist.

Inventory: a manufacturing company's assets in the form of materials, parts or products.

Isometric drawing: a pictorial drawing method showing horizontal lines sloping at 30° to horizontal.

Iterative design: is a cyclic approach to creating optimum designs by incorporating feedback from on-going, evaluative testing processes.

Jig: used to hold and position work and/or locate or guide a tool to ensure accuracy and repeatability.

Just-in-time (JIT) manufacture: the manufacture of products as needed, in response to existing orders.

Knock-down (KD) fittings: allow products to be assembled and disassembled many times, without weakening the joint.

Laminated boards: layers glued together in a well-organised structure with a synthetic resin that sets rapidly under heat and pressure.

Lean manufacturing: a system that aims to reduce waste and continuously improve in order to add value for customers.

Lifecycle assessment (LCA): analyses and evaluates the economic impact of a product through all the stages of a product's life, from the initial extraction of raw materials through to final disposal or recycling (not to be confused with the product lifecycle).

Logistics: the detailed organisation of activities such as the transportation of materials, parts and products.

Low temperature casting: used for metals such as pewter which melt at low temperatures and can be poured into a variety of mould material.

Market penetration: increasing the market share of an existing product, or promoting a new product by using a variety of marketing and advertising strategies.

Marketing mix: the best blend of marketing methods used to engage the intended target market.

Mass customisation: a manufacturing technique which uses online ordering to combine the flexibility and personalisation of custom-made products with the low unit costs associated with mass production.

Mathematical modelling: the use of simulation software to model the effect of changes in designs prior to manufacture.

Mechanical properties: properties associated with how a product reacts to an external force.

Metal alloy: a metal made of two or more metals, or combining two or more elements, one of which must be a metal.

Microcontroller: an electronic device that can be programmed to carry out specific tasks.

Modelling: preliminary stages of designing, using a range of 2D and 3D techniques to explore potential design iterations.

Modern materials: materials that are developed through the invention of new or improved processes.

Modular/cell production system: workers, CNC machines, robots and AGVs organised in groups for efficient, flexible manufacturing.

Mould: a hollow shape used to pour material into, like a jelly mould.

Non-ferrous: metals that do not contain iron.

Oleophobic: highly oil resistant.

Outbound marketing: marketing that raises awareness and allows the customer to 'find' the product.

Participatory design: a design process that requires the involvement of all stakeholders and users.

Patent: gives rights to technical and functional aspects of a product or invention.

Percentile: a specific statistical percentage range, often used to define appropriate anthropometric data for design purposes.

Perspective drawing: a 3D drawing method that adds realism by the use of receding size for more distant elements.

Physical properties: properties associated with actual make-up or structure of the material.

Planned obsolescence: the process of designing a product to go out of fashion or no longer function after a specific time period.

Presses: ensure the material is formed to shape when pressure is applied to the material.

Price point: the chosen price for a product to retail at.

Price skimming: a company sets its prices high when launching a product to quickly recover initial expenditures associated with production and advertising. The aim is to achieve a profit quickly.

Pricing strategy: how companies price their products to take account of production, labour and advertising costs as well as incorporating a profit margin.

Product lifecycle: the marketing lifecycle from the introduction through to decline of a product.

Project management: the organisation of teamwork to satisfactorily achieve a particular objective.

Prototype: a functioning or non-functioning pre-production design evaluation model.

Quality assurance (QA): procedures and policies which ensure that products meet specification criteria.

Quality control (QC): monitoring, checking and testing procedures used throughout production.

Rapid prototyping: the use of machines such as 3D printers to produce realistic 3D models from CAD files.

Registered design: give rights to appearance of a product.

Reinforcing: adding to, or altering the form of, a material or component to strengthen it or reduce its chances of wear.

Risk assessment: a statutory process that considers what might cause harm to people and what reasonable steps might be taken to prevent that harm.

Sacrificial parts: weaker parts of a product designed to fail first in order to protect more significant parts.

Sand casting: a metal-casting process that uses sand as the mould material.

Schematic diagrams: these show the layout of components such as an electronic circuit with transistors and resistors.

Scrum: this strategy makes use of workforce teams using iterative design methods to respond quickly to issues in product design and manufacture.

Shape-shifting materials: materials that change their shape in response to a physical stimulus such as an electric voltage or current, a change in temperature or the presence of a magnetic field.

Six Sigma: this system aims to reduce manufacturing defects to the minimum possible level.

Sketch models: models made quickly using compliant materials in order to visualise ideas early on in the design process.

Smart material: material whose physical properties change in response to an input or change in the environment, such as electricity, pressure, temperature or light.

Social footprint: the impact on society of cultural and ethical issues.

Social media marketing (SMM): a form of internet marketing that utilises social networking websites as a marketing tool.

Softwoods: timber from coniferous trees. Generally, faster growing.

Stakeholders: the stakeholders of a product are all those come into contact with it, have some sort of interest or 'stake' in it, or are affected by it in some way.

Standardised components: parts made to a common, interchangeable, standard, such as bolts and light bulbs.

Stiffening: reducing flexibility in materials or structures.

Stresses: a range of factors that may cause a material, or product to fail.

Structural integrity: the ability of a product or system to hold together when under load.

Subtractive manufacture: methods, such as machining or carving, which involve material removal.

Systems thinking: concentrating on component interactions and connections, and their role within the overall system.

Tablet: a mobile touchscreen computer. Note that graphics tablets are used mainly as input devices for design software.

Technical nutrients: man-made materials (e.g. polymers and alloys) for repeated use.

Template: can be drawn around to mark a shape onto material.

Thermopolymers: deform whenever heated and can be remoulded many times. This makes them suitable for recycling.

Thermosetting polymers: once these polymers have been shaped and hardened, they cannot be reshaped or softened by heating.

Throwaway society: the collective mind-set of consumers to dispose of products rather than repair them.

Tolerance: the acceptable upper and lower limits of accuracy of a measurement.

Total quality management (TQM): a system to improve quality assurance (QA) by harnessing workforce expertise.

Trademark: used by a company to identify and distinguish its products or brand.

Triangulation: adding cross-members to increase the rigidity of a framework.

Usability of a product: how easily a product can be used, particularly with reference to understanding how it functions.

User interface design or **user interface engineering:** a 'human-centred' design approach with a main focus on the effectiveness of the user interface for interaction with products, particularly electronic devices such as computers and appliances.

Viscosity: (of a liquid) a measure of its resistance to an object moving through it.

Working drawings: detailed orthographic views supplemented by enough information to facilitate manufacture.

Picture credits

Fig.1.1 © Arthur Didyk/stock.adobe.com; Fig.1.3 © Stefan Auth/ImageBROKER/Alamy Stock Photo; Fig.1.6 © Syda Productions/stock.adobe.com; Fig.2.1 © Varts/stock.adobe.com; Fig.2.2 © Teamjackson/stock.adobe.com; Fig.2.3 © Funkyfood London - Paul Williams/Alamy Stock Photo; Fig.2.4 © Ian Dagnall/Alamy Stock Photo; Fig.2.5 © Hackenberg-Photo-Cologne/Alamy Stock Photo; Fig.2.6 © Dotan/stock.adobe.com; Fig.2.7 © Andrey Armyagov/stock.adobe.com; Fig.2.8 © Ktsdesign/stock.adobe.com; Fig.2.9 © Branislav Zivkovic/stock.adobe.com; Fig.2.10 © Goldpix/stock.adobe.com; Fig.2.11 © Goodluz/stock.adobe.com; Fig.2.12 © Practical Action/Anna de la Vega; Fig.2.13 © Andrew Mayovskyy/Alamy Stock Photo; Fig.2.14 © Ukartpics/Alamy Stock Photo; Fig.2.15 © Al/stock.adobe.com; Fig.2.16 © Andreacrisante/YAY Media AS/Alamy Stock Photo; Fig.3.1 © Overcrew/stock.adobe.com; Fig.3.2 © Mrmrsmarcha1/stock.adobe.com; Fig.3.3 © Petovarga/123RF; Fig.3.4 © INSAGO/Shutterstock.com; Fig.3.5 © PhotoProRo/Shutterstock.com; Fig.3.6 © DRN Studio/Shutterstock.com; Fig.3.8 © Designua/Shutterstock.com; Fig.3.9 © Paul prescott/Shutterstock.com; Fig.3.10 © Ctvvelve/stock.adobe.com; Fig.3.11 © Oilly.Ar/Shutterstock.com; Fig.3.12 © i viewfinder/Shutterstock.com; Fig.3.13 © THATREE/stock.adobe.com; Fig.4.6 © Mathew Alexander/Shutterstock.com; Fig.4.8 © Fernando Batista/stock.adobe.com; Fig.5.1 © Ivan Kurmyshov/stock.adobe.com; Fig.5.2 © Svetamart/stock.adobe.com; Fig.5.3 © PhotographyByMK/stock.adobe.com; Fig.5.5 © Sergey0506/stock.adobe.com; Fig.5.6 © StudioAraminta/stock.adobe.com; Fig.5.7 © Robert lerich/stock.adobe.com; Fig.5.8 © Akulamatiau/stock.adobe.com; Fig.5.9 © James Dale/123RF; Fig.5.10 © ThamKC/stock.adobe.com; Fig.5.12 © Aapsky/stock.adobe.com; Fig.5.13 © Bakicirkin/stock.adobe.com; Figs.6.3 & 6.4 Chris Walker; Fig.6.5 © Onairjiw/stock.adobe.com; Fig.6.6 © Kennymac - Fotolia.com; Fig.6.8 © Will Thomas/stock.adobe.com; Fig.6.9 © Gudellaphoto/stock.adobe.com; Figs.7.1 & 7.2 Chris Walker; Fig.7.3 © Kirill4mula - stock.adobe.com; Fig.7.24 © FreeProd/stock.adobe.com; Fig.7.25 © Arief Priyono/Alamy Stock Photo; Fig.7.27 © Coprid/stock.adobe.com; Fig.7.28 © Nataliya Hora/stock.adobe.com; Fig.7.29 © Mari1408/stock.adobe.com; Fig.7.30 © Tatty/stock.adobe.com; Fig.7.32 Julia Morrison; Fig.8.1 © Slowcentury/stock.adobe.com; Fig.8.2 © Denis Ronin/Shutterstock.com; Fig.8.3 © Vlad Kochelaevskiy/stock.adobe.com; Fig.8.4 top KITEMARK and the Kitemark device are reproduced with kind permission of The British Standards Institution. They are registered trademarks in the United Kingdom and in certain other countries; Fig 8.4 bottom © European Union 2019; Fig.8.5 © Richard McDowell/Alamy Stock Photo; Fig.8.6 © Gennadiy Poznyakov/stock.adobe.com; Fig.8.11 © Nd3000/stock.adobe.com; Fig.8.12 © DANIEL KARMANN/dpa picture alliance/Alamy Stock Photo; Fig.9.1 © Johndwilliams/stock.adobe.com; Fig.9.3 © Barry Barnes/stock.adobe.com

SIMPLY RED
HOME

PIANO VOCAL GUITAR

Published 2003

Griffin House 161 Hammersmith Road London W6 8BS England

Music arranged and engraved by Artemis Music Ltd
Art direction & design by Peacock. www.peacockdesign.com

Photography by Rick Guest and Gusto/Hugh Turvey
except band photograph by Andy Earl
Pages 34 & 56 photography by Gusto/Hugh Turvey

CW00495465

HOME

What's worth nothing else but love? Take a walk down any street now. Every one of us in our own little world, looking for a heart with whom to beat now.

What's worth nothing else but love? I'm prepared to take the heat now. What's worth more than anything else at all to keep you firmly on your feet now?

So fake cool image should be over, 'cause I long for a feeling of home. Real life, depicted in song. A loving memory. After long, home is a place where I yearn to belong.

Where the land meets the sea, she'll be smiling so sweetly now. I hope that she'll be here much longer than I will. My heart loves her with every beat now.

So fake cool image should be over, 'cause I long for a feeling of home. Real life, depicted in song. A loving memory. After long, home is a place where I yearn to belong.

FAKE

Watching love drifting away, and I feel like I'm someone else. The hurting is rough. Long are the days. And you have hurt me enough.

You're scared to be loved, you know that's your way. Your youth has made you too tough. You're hurting for love in so many ways. The truth has hurt you enough.

I read a book, and it's your face. Fake... it's your face now. Still my love for you was no mistake. Fake... I will always love you. Fake.

Hoping for love day after day, and it's always someone else. The hurting is rough. Long are the days. And you have hurt me enough.

You're burning your hair on your cigarette, oh baby. Turning your nose up at the clothes your girlfriend wears. I don't care.

Always, always, always I will love you.

SUNRISE

As I look into your eyes I see the sunrise. The light behind your face helps me realise.

Will we sleep and sometimes love until the moon shines? Maybe the next time I'll be yours and maybe you'll be mine.

I don't know if it's even in your mind at all. It could be me, at this moment in time. Is it in your mind at all? It should be me, it could be me. Forever.

Wandering through life will love come home to you, and the love you want forever will they be true to you?

Will we sleep and sometimes love until the moon shines? Maybe the next time I'll be yours and maybe you'll be mine.

Easy, ready, willing, over time. Where does it stop where do you dare me to draw the line? You've got the body now you want my soul. Don't even think about it say no go.

YOU MAKE ME FEEL BRAND NEW

My love, I'll never find the words, my love. To tell you how I feel, my love. Mere words could not explain. Precious love. You held my life within your hands. Created everything I am. Taught me how to live again.

Only you, cared when I needed a friend. Believed in me through thick and thin. This song is for you, filled with gratitude and love.

God bless you. You make me feel brand new. For God blessed me with you. You make me feel brand new. I sing this song 'cause you, make me feel brand new.

My love, whenever I was insecure, you built me up and made me sure. You gave my pride back to me. Precious friend, with you I'll always have a friend. You're someone who I can depend to walk a path that never ends.

Without you, my life has no meaning or rhyme. Like notes to a song out of time. How can I repay you for having faith in me?

HOME LOAN BLUES

Just a man, good and sometimes bad. But striving to do the best that I can. Help a hand when the one close by you falls. Understanding can do the rest and that ain't all.

Hope I can please you but the truth isn't easy to say. The more that you're spending the more it'll get in your way. I say it to please you to forget what you have done, so pray. I got the blues from the debt of the people today.

You can have it all but you've got to pay. You can have it all don't pay me today.

Wotcha man as the bills around you grow. Providing you take a loan to pay for them all. Help a hand when the one close by you falls. Depending if the fool keeps spending it all.

You can have it all but you've got to pay. (You can have it), credit cards, mortgage, home loans for your holiday.

POSITIVELY 4TH STREET

You got a lotta nerve to say you are my friend. When I was down you just stood there grinning.

You got a lotta nerve to say you gotta helping hand to lend. You just want to be on the side that's winning.

You say I let you down, you know it's not like that. If you're so hurt, why then don't you show it?

You say you lost your faith, but that's not where it's at. You had no faith to lose, and you know it.

I know the reason that you talk behind my back. I used to be among the crowd you're in with.

Do you take me for such a fool to think I'd make contact with the one who tries to hide what he don't know to begin with?

LOST WEEKEND

You see me on the street, you always act surprised. You say, "How are you?" "Good luck", but you don't mean it.

When you know as well as me, you'd rather see me paralyzed. Why don't you just come out once and scream it?

No, I do not feel that good when I see the heartbreaks you embrace. If I was a master thief, perhaps I'd rob them.

And now I know you're dissatisfied with your position and your place. Don't you understand it's not my problem?

I wish that for just one time, you could stand inside my shoes and just for that one moment I could be you.

Yes, I wish that for just one time you could stand inside my shoes, you'd know what a drag it is to see you.

(Sunshine in my soul, sunshine in my soul).

My lost weekend, been more now than a year. Oh I hoped not. 'Cause since you put me down, my world merely spins around. Did you play me for your fool? Oh honey, I know you didn't mean to.

'Cause you tremble with a problem. You carry the weight of pain from the past.

The sunshine in my soul is here to tell you, that pain doesn't have to last. The love that's in my heart is here to pray that pain will go away. Feel it honey, blowin' away.

My lost weekend, more now than a year. Oh and it goes on. 'Cause since you let me down, my world merely spins around. Did you play me for your fool? Oh honey I know you didn't mean to.

'Cause you're pent up with a problem, you carry the weight of pain from the past. The sunshine in my soul is here to tell you, that pain doesn't have to last. The love that's in my heart is here to pray that pain will go away.

The sunshine in my soul is here to tell you, that pain doesn't have to last. The love that's in my heart is here to say that pain will go away.

Watch that pain go away. Feel it honey, blowin' away. My lost weekend.

MONEY IN MY POCKET (PLAN B MIX)

Money in my pocket but I just can't get no love. Money in my pocket but I just can't get no love. I'm praying for a girl to be my own.

Soon you said she coming but I don't believe a word she say. 'Cause she run away and left me one rainy day. She made me had in mind that her love would never die. And now I'm alone, so alone, so alone, yeah, yeah.

Money in my pocket but I just can't get no love. Money in my pocket but I just can't get no love.

The love I had in mind, was very, very hard to find.

It's hard for a man to live without a woman. And a woman needs a man to cling to. You'll see what love can do, after making me feel blue. Ain't that a shame, whoa baby, ain't that a shame, to make me feel blue.

I've got money in my pocket.

SOMETHING FOR YOU

Anyone would cry over you, too bad if they do. But baby I could try if you want me to, to help you let yourself go.

Any man would die for you, but they're mad if they do. But baby let me get closer to you, so I can let you know. I got something for you, the joy of letting you know what you have done for me.

Loving you has smiled on the face of a lonely man. Loving you has pride in the place of our home again. Loving you has smiled on the face of a lonely man. Loving you has pride in the place of our home again.

Smile on the face of a lonely man. Pride in the place of our home again.

Smile on the face. Pride in the place.

When I get tired I'm gonna try, let you wonder why, any man would die.

IT'S YOU

Loving you just goes on, on and on, on and on, and on.

Growing with you is pleasure for two, raising my spirits, hoping for you, and I do.

And being with you I see a side of my life, a chance to grow, in a way that I never knew. 'Cause baby it's you, honey, it's you.

Find a movie where there's no one, on and on, just having fun, on our own.

Twenty-two different shows on, don't care which one, just as long as we're having fun, on and on and on.

'Cause being with you I see a change in my life, a chance to grow, in a way that I never knew.

'Cause baby it's you, you you you, you you you, it's you, honey it's you. Baby it's you,you you you, you you you, you you you, honey it's you.

HOME (REPRISE)

Fake cool image should be over, 'cause I long for a feeling of home. Real life, depicted in song. A loving memory. After long, home is a place where I yearn to belong.

HOME

Words by Hucknall
Music by Hucknall, Steven Lewinson and Pete Lewinson

F
G
Am
look-ing for a heart with whom to beat now. What's worth
G
Dm7
G
no-thing else but love? I'm pre-pared to take the heat now.
Am
Em
F
3
What's worth more than a-ny-thing else at all to keep you firm-ly on your
G
Fmaj9
Cadd9
feet now? So fake cool im-age should be ov - er, 'cause I

F
Cmaj9
Dm7
long for a feel - ing of home: real life
G11
Cmaj9
Fmaj9
de - pict - ed in song, a lov - ing mem - 'ry.
Fmaj7
Em7
Dm7
Af - - - - ter long, home is a place where I
C
Em/B
Am
Em
yearn to be - long. Where the

Am
G
Dm7
land meets the sea, she'll be smil - ing so
G
Am
Em
sweet - ly now. I hope that she'll be here much long - er than I will.
F
G
Fmaj9
My heart loves her with ev - 'ry beat now. So fake cool im-age should be ov -
Cadd9
F
Cmaj9
- er, 'cause I long for a feel - ing of home:

Dm7 G11 Cmaj9
real life de-pict-ed in song, a lov-ing
Fmaj9 Fmaj7 Em7
2º only
mem-'ry. Af - - - ter long,
2º only
Dm7
1. C
2. C
home is a place where I yearn to be-long. yearn to be-long.
Fmaj7 Em7 Dm7 C
Repeat ad lib. to fade
Fake cool im-age should be ov - er, home is a place where I yearn to be-long.

FAKE

Words by Hucknall
Music by Hucknall, Mark Jaimes, Gota Yashiki, Ian Kirkham, Steven Lewinson, Dee Johnson, John Johnson, Kenji Suzuki, Sarah Brown, Chris De Margary and Kevin Robinson

B♭
Dm
like I'm some-one else.
The hurt-ing is rough.
Long are the days,
E♭
F11
B♭
Dm
and you have hurt me e-nough.
You're scared to be
E♭
F11
loved. You know that's your way,
and your youth has made you too
B♭
Dm
E♭
F11
tough. You're hurt-ing for love
in so ma-ny ways.

B♭
A♭maj7
The truth has hurt you e - nough.
(I read a book, and it's your face,
E♭
B♭
Dm
the Fake.
Still my love for you was no mis - take,
A♭maj9
E♭
Fake.)
B♭
Dm
E♭
F11
Hop - ing for love day af - ter day, and it's al -

Bb
Dm
- ways some-one else.
The hurt-ing is rough,
and long
Eb
F11
Gm7
3
are the days,
and you have hurt me e - nough.
(You're burn-ing your
Ab
Bb
Bb/A
hair) on your ci - gar - ette,
ooh ba - by.
Gm7
Ab
F11
(Turn-ing your nose up) at the clothes your girl - friend wears.

B♭
A♭maj7
(I read a book and it's your face,
E♭
B♭
Dm
the Fake.)
Still my love for you was no mis - take,
A♭maj9
1.
E♭
Fake.
I read a
2.
E♭
B♭
A♭

Eb7
Ab
To Coda
Bb
Ab
Eb
Ab
D.%. al Coda
(no repeat)
Coda
Bb
Ab
Eb
Ab
Vocal ad libs.
1, 2.
3.
Bb

SUNRISE

Words and Music by Hucknall, Daryl Hall, John Oates and Sara Allen

Will we sleep and some - times love un - - til the
Will we sleep and some - times love un - - til the
moon shines. May - be the next time I'll be yours and may - be
moon shines. May - be the next time I'll be yours and may - be
you'll be mine. (Sun - - rise.) I don't know if it's ev - en in your
you'll be mine. (You'll be mine.) I don't know if it's ev - en in your
A♭add9
Cm7
Gm7
Cm7
mind at all. (Could be me.) At this
mind at all. (Could be me.) At this

𝄋𝄋
Fm7 B♭ A♭add9 Cm7 Gm7
mo - ment in time, is it in your mind at all?
mo - ment in time, love's in - de - scri - ba - ble.
(Should be
Cm Gm7 Fm9 Gm7
1.
Fm9
To Coda ⊕
me, it could be me.)
'Cause it could be you're mine for ev - er,
for ev - er.
8va
2.
Cm7 F Cm7
ev - er.
(Ea - sy, rea - dy, will - ing, ov - er time.
Where does it stop, where do you

A♭ B♭ Cm7 F
dare me to draw the line? You've got the bo - dy, now you want my soul.
Cm7 A♭ B♭ Fm9
Don't ev - en think a - bout it, say no go!) Yeah!
8va
D.%. al Coda
(Sun - rise) I don't know if it's ev - en in your
(8va)
Coda
Fm9 Fm7 B♭
D.%%. to fade
- ev - er. (Sun - rise) At this mo - ment in time, is it in your

YOU MAKE ME FEEL BRAND NEW

Words and Music by Thomas Bell and Linda Creed

F9sus4
F7
Fm/B♭
B♭
A♭m7
D♭7
ex - plain.
Pre - cious
back to me.
Pre - cious
G♭
C♭m/G♭
G♭
love, you held my life with - in your hands, cre -
friend, with you I'll al - ways have a friend. You're
C♭m/G♭
G♭
C♭m/G♭
- a - ted ev - 'ry - thing I am, taught me how to live a -
some - one whom I can de - pend to walk a path that some - times
G♭
B♭m7
- gain. On - ly you
wends. With - out you,

E♭m7
B♭m7
E♭m7
cared when I need - ed a friend, be - lieved in me through thick and thin.
life has no mean - ing or rhyme, like notes to a song out of time.
A♭m9
C♭maj7
G♭/B♭
A♭m7
G♭/B♭
C♭maj7
This song is for you, filled with gra - ti - tude and love.
How can I re - pay you for hav - ing faith in me?
D♭7sus4
D♭7
A♭m7
D♭
C♭maj7
God bless you,
God it's you,
A♭m9
B♭m7
E♭m7
A♭m7
D♭
you make me feel brand new, for God blessed me with
you make me feel brand new, for God blessed me with

C♭maj7 A♭m9 B♭m7
you. You make me feel brand new. I
you. You make me feel brand new. I
To Coda
E♭m7 A♭m7 D♭ C♭maj7 B♭m7 A♭m7 C♭/D♭
sing this song 'cause you make me feel brand
sing this song for
G♭ C♭m/G♭ C♭ G♭
D.%. al Coda
new. 2. My love,
Coda
Repeat ad lib. to fade
C♭maj7 A♭m9 B♭m7 E♭m7 A♭m7 D♭
you, You're mak-ing me feel so brand new.

HOME LOAN BLUES

Words by Hucknall
Music by Hucknall, Mark Jaimes, Gota Yashiki, Steven Lewinson, Ian Kirkham and Kenji Suzuki

Cm7
F9
Just a man, good and some - times bad; but
2° Instrumental
Cm7
F9
G7aug(♯9)
N.C.
striv - ing to do the best that I can.
Cm7
F9
Help a hand when the one close by you falls. Un-der-
Cm7
F9
G7aug
- stand - ing can do the rest, and that ain't all.

Cm7
F9
Both times
Hope I can please- you, but the truth is-n't ea-sy to say. The
Cm7
Am7(♭5)
A♭maj7
G7aug
more that you're spend-ing, the more it-'ll get in your way. I
Cm7
F9
say it to please- you, to for-get what you have done, so pray:
Cm7
B♭m7
A♭6
N.C.
G7aug(♯9)
To Coda
I got the blues from the debt of the peo-ple to-day.

Cm7
F9
You can have it all, but you've got to pay.
Cm7
F9
G7aug(♯9)
N.C.
You can have it all, don't pay me to-day.
Cm7
F9
Watch a man, as the bills a-round you grow, pro-
Cm7
F9
G7aug(♯9)
N.C.
-vi-ded you take a loan to pay for them all.

Cm7
F9
Help a hand when the one close by you falls, de-
Cm7
F9
G7aug(♯9)
N.C.
-pend-ing if the fool keeps spend-ing it all.
Cm7
F9
You can have it all, but you've got to pay:
Cm7
F9
G7aug(♯9)
N.C.
D.%. al Coda
cre-dit cards, mort-gage, home loans for your ho-li-day.

Coda
Cm7
F9
You can have it all, but you've got to pay.
Cm7
F9
You can have it all, don't pay me to - day.
Cm7
F9
You can have it all, but you've got to pay.
2º rit.
Cm7
F9
N.C.
G7aug(♯9)
Cm9
Cre-dit cards, mort-gage, home loans for your ho-li - day.

POSITIVELY 4TH STREET

Words and Music by Bob Dylan

Bm
E
When I was down, you just stood there grin - ning.
A
Bm
D
A
2. You got a lot of nerve to say you got a help-ing hand to lend.
Bm
E
You just want to be on the side that's win - ning.
𝄋
A
Bm
D
A
3. You say I let you down, you know it's not like that. If
(Verses 4-8 and 9-12 see block lyric)

Bm
E
you're so hurt
why then don't you
show it?
A
Bm
D
A
Bm
E
To Coda
D.S. al Coda
Coda
A

Verse 4:
You say you lost your faith
But that's not where it's at.
You had no faith to lose
And you know it.

Verse 5:
I know the reason
That you talk behind my back.
I used to be among the crowd
You're in with.

Verse 6:
Do you take me for such a fool
To think I'd make contact
With the one who tries to hide
What he don't know to begin with?

Verse 7:
You see me on the street
You always act surprised.
You say "How are you?" "Good luck."
But you don't mean it.

Verse 8:
When you know as well as me
You'd rather see me paralysed.
Why don't you just come out once
And scream it!

Instrumental

Verse 9:
No, I do not feel that good
When I see the heartbreaks you embrace.
If I was a master thief
Perhaps I'd rob them.

Verse 10:
And now I know you're dissatisfied
With your position and your place.
Don't you understand
It's not my problem?

Verse 11:
I wish that for just one time
You could stand inside my shoes
And just for that one moment
I could be you.

Verse 12:
Yes, I wish that for just one time
You could stand inside my shoes.
You'd know what a drag it is
To see you.

LOST WEEKEND

Words and Music by Hucknall

Emaj9
Amaj7
Emaj9
lost week - end, been
lost week - end, more
Amaj7
Emaj9
Amaj7
more now than a year. Oh, I hoped not,
now than a year. Oh, and it goes on,
B11
Emaj9
'cause since you put me down
'cause since you let me down
Amaj7
Emaj9
my world mere - ly spins a - round.
my world mere - ly spins a - round.

Amaj7
Emaj9
Did you play me for your fool?
Did you play me for your fool?
Amaj7
Emaj9
Oh honey, I know you didn't mean to.
Oh honey, I know you didn't mean to.
Amaj7
F♯m7
C♯m7
'Cause you tremble with a problem. You
'Cause you're pent up with a problem. You
(Instrumental on 𝄋)
F♯m7
B11
C♯m7
carry the weight of pain from the past.
carry the weight of pain from the past.
The

F♯m7 G♯m Amaj7 Bsus4/2 C♯11
sun - shine in my soul is here to tell you that pain
Amaj7 Emaj9 A A6 E
does - n't have to last. The
F♯m7 G♯m Amaj7 Bsus4/2 C♯11 Amaj7 Emaj9
To Coda
love that's in my heart is here to pray that pain will go a - way.
1.
A A6 E Amaj7 Emaj9 Amaj7 Emaj9
(Sun - shine in my soul.)
Ad lib. vocal

2.
D.%. al Coda
Amaj7
Emaj9
A
A6
E
(Sun-shine in my soul.)
My
Coda
(Vocal ad libs.)
(Sun - shine in my soul.)
(Sun-shine in my soul.)
(Vocal ad libs.)
(Sun - shine in my soul.)
My lost week - end.

MONEY IN MY POCKET (PLAN B MIX)

Words and Music by Dennis Brown and Joe Gibbs

Em D A7 Am D11
Mon-ey in my pock-et, but I just can't get no love.
Em D A7 Am D11
Mon-ey in my pock-et, but I just can't get no love. I'm
Em D A7 Am D11
pray - - ing for a girl to be my own.
Em D A7 Am D11
Soon she said she'd call me but I don't be-lieve a word she say,

Em
D
A7
'cause she ran a-way and a left a-me one rain - - y day.
Am
D11
Em
D
She made me have in mind that to
A7
Am
D11
Em
love would nev - er die. And a-now I'm a-lone,
D
A7
Am
D11
so a - lone, so a -

Em D A7 Am D11
-lone, yeah.
Em D A7 Am D11
Mon-ey in my pock-et, but I just can't get no love.
Em D A7 Am D11
Mon-ey in my pock-et, but I just can't get no love.
1.
2.
Am D11 Em D
The love I had in mind was a-

A7 Am D11 Em
- ve - ry, ve - ry hard to find. It's hard for a man
D A7 Am D11
to live with - out a wo - man, yeah. And
Em D A7
a wo - man needs a man to cling to.
Am D11 Em D
You'll see what love can do af - ter

A7
Am
D11
Em
3
mak - - - ing me feel blue. Ain't that a shame,
D
A7
Am
D11
woh ba - by. Ain't that a
Em
D
A7
Am
D11
shame to make me feel blue?
Repeat ad lib. to fade
Em
D
A7
Am
D11
Mon - ey in my pock - et, but I just can't get no love.

SOMETHING FOR YOU

Words by Hucknall
Music by Hucknall and Joe Sample

F♯5
C♯5
F♯m7
D9
- by I could try if you want me to,
to help you let your-self go.
me get clo - ser to you
so I can let you know.
1.
C♯5
F♯5
C♯5
F♯m7
Guitar
8vb
8vb
2.
C♯m7
G♯m7
I got some-thing for you,
the
C♯m7
G♯m
A13
joy of let-ting you know what you have done for me.
Lov-ing

D/A
A
G/A
D/A
A
you has smiled on the face of a lone - ly man.
D/A
A
G/A
D/A
Lov-ing you has pride in the place of our home
A
1.
2.
G♯sus4
a - gain.
Lov - ing
C♯m9
G♯m9
C♯m9
G♯m9
Smile on the face of a lone - ly man.

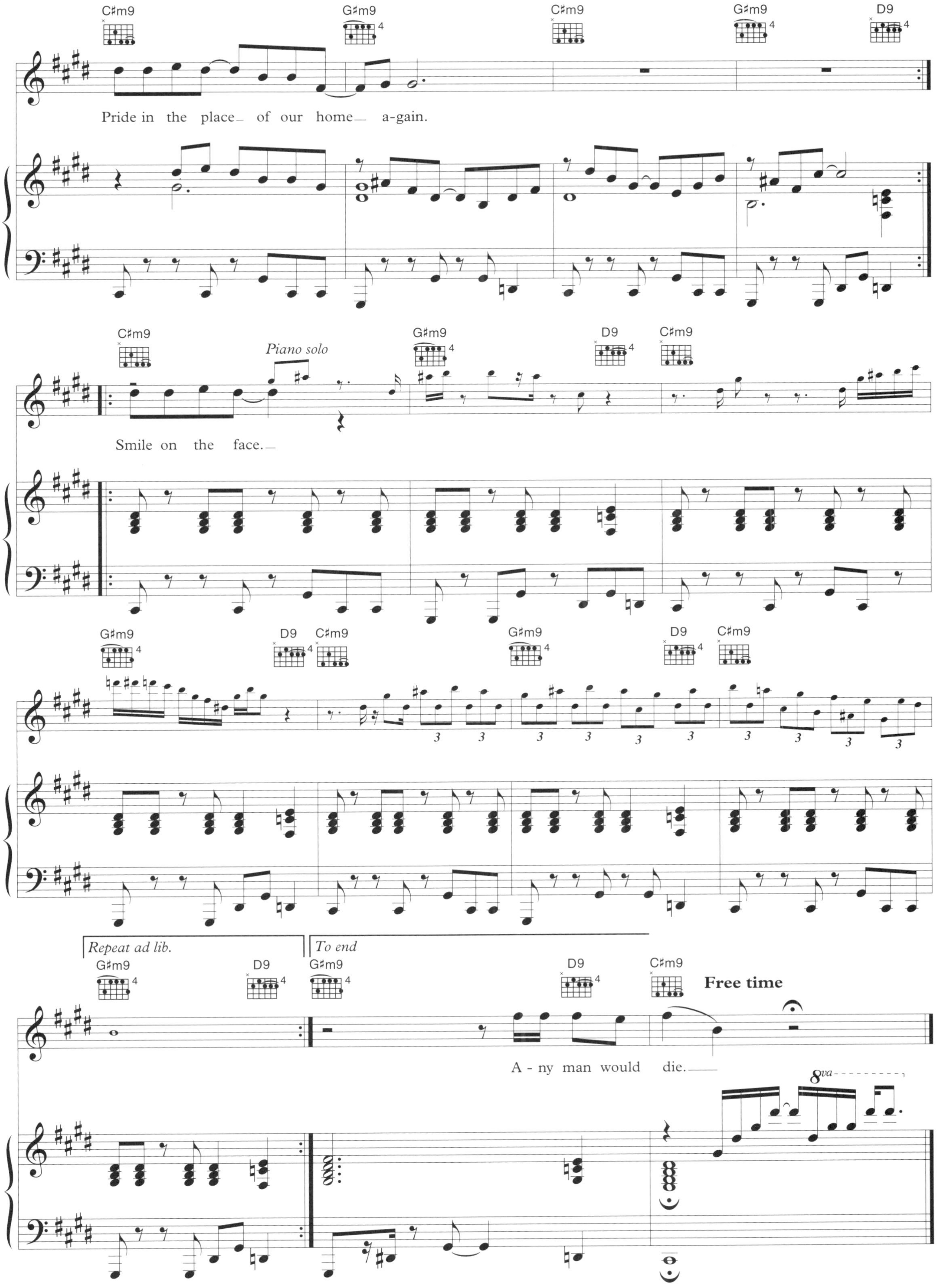
C♯m9
G♯m9
C♯m9
G♯m9
D9
Pride in the place of our home again.
C♯m9
Piano solo
G♯m9
D9
C♯m9
Smile on the face.
G♯m9
D9
C♯m9
G♯m9
D9
C♯m9
Repeat ad lib.
G♯m9
D9
To end
G♯m9
D9
C♯m9
Free time
A-ny man would die.
8va

IT'S YOU

Words and Music by Hucknall

Fm7 add11
Gm7
Fm7
Gm7
B♭11
E♭
Fm7
Gm7
Fm7
Grow - ing with you is plea - sure for two,
Twen - ty - two diff - 'rent shows on. Don't care which one,
Gm7
B♭11
A♭7/B♭
rais - ing my spi - rits, hop - ing for you; and I
just as long as we're hav - ing fun, on and on
E♭maj9
A♭maj7
do. And be - ing with
and on. 'Cause be - ing with

B♭m7
Cm7
you, I see a side of my life, a
you, I see a change in my life, a
D♭
E♭11
To Coda
chance to grow in a way that I never
chance to grow in a way that I never
A♭maj9
E♭11
A♭maj9
knew, 'cause baby it's you.
E♭11
A♭maj9
D♭maj9
D.%. al Coda
Honey, it's you.

Coda
A♭maj9
E♭11
A♭maj9
knew, 'cause ba - by it's you.
E♭11
A♭maj9
E♭11
You, you, you; you, you, you. It's you; hon - ey, it's
A♭maj9
E♭11
A♭maj9
you. Ba - by, it's you.
E♭11
A♭maj9
E♭11
rit.
N.C.
A♭maj7
You, you, you; you, you, you, you, you, you; hon - ey, it's you.

HOME (REPRISE)

Words and Music by Hucknall

Fmaj7
Em7
mem - 'ry. Af - - - - ter long,
Am add9
F
home is a place where I yearn to be - long.
Cmaj7
Fmaj7
Oh,
Cmaj7
Fmaj7
rit.
Cmaj7
home.